THE ULTIMATE SURVIVAL GUIDE

THE ULTIMATE SURVIVAL GUIDE

General Editor: Chris McNab

amber BOOKS

Published by
Amber Books Ltd
74–77 White Lion Street
London
N1 9PF
United Kingdom
www.amberbooks.co.uk
Appstore: itunes.com/apps/amberbooksltd
Facebook: www.facebook.com/amberbooks
Twitter: @amberbooks

ISBN: 978-1-78274-142-8

Project Editor: Michael Spilling
Design: Colin Hawes
Illustrations: Tony Randell (© Amber Books Ltd)

Printed in China

Picture Credits:
Browning: 168; FEMA: 7; Photos.com: 112;
U.S. Army: 8, 256; U.S. Marine Corps: 70, 214;
U.S. Navy: 326

DISCLAIMER

This book is for information purposes only. Readers should be aware of the legal position
in their country of residence before practicing any of the techniques described in this
book. Neither the author or the publisher can accept responsibility for any loss, injury, or
damage caused as a result of the use of the techniques described in this book, nor for any
prosecutions or proceedings brought or instigated against any person or body that may
result from using these techniques.

Contents

Introduction

Researchers who have studied the behaviour of people in disaster situations have noted several different types of response. Many people seem to lapse into denial that the situation is happening at all.

For example, when the ferry ship *Herald of Free Enterprise* sank off Zeebrugge, Belguim, on 6 March 1987, killing 193 people, survivors reported that there were some people still chatting as if everything was OK when the ship was at a 45-degree list. For many, the extremity and fundamental strangeness of a disaster results in a kind of withdrawal, a rejection of the idea that anything is wrong at all.

Crisis response

There are other types of responses. Some people dissolve into hysterical fear and panic, while others – perhaps the majority – partially overcome their fear to make attempts to survive, however faltering and ineffective. Yet another group observed by the researchers were utterly focused on survival from the very first seconds of the disaster. They later remembered having almost tunnel vision, focusing on nothing but the strategies by which they and their families could stay alive.

Needless to say, the researchers concluded which group were more likely to survive a disaster situation – those who were very proactive in their responses. Those who dissolved into denial or panic were far more likely to be on the fatality lists. It would be disrespectful, of course,

to push this point too far. When dozens, hundreds or even thousands of people die in disasters, the dead will include both the brave and the fearful, regardless of their efforts to survive. However, your chances of surviving a disaster are significantly improved by facing reality squarely and acting with an emphatic decision to survive.

Survival techniques

Of course, deciding to survive is only part of the equation. You also need the knowledge of techniques and tactics that are proven to aid survival.

Such is the purpose of this book. Through dozens of different survival situations, it shows key techniques for staying alive in even the most adverse of circumstances, whether that involves building a shelter, hunting a deer, fighting off attackers, escaping from imprisonment or treating a serious injury.

Some cautions are warranted for those learning survival techniques. Don't just rely on book knowledge – instead, get professional training from survival experts, and take time to practice your new-found skills in realistic settings. The word 'realistic' is key. If you train repeatedly in high-pressure scenarios, the chances are that you will not succumb to mental paralysis when you are faced with a

genuine threat. Yet note that the experts never think they are invulnerable – nature and circumstances can still overcome you if they are powerful enough.

Preparation is key

For this reason remember that the best survival skill is not to put yourself in a dangerous situation (or at least one that you can't control) in the first place. Also remember that certain survival techniques may well need adapting and even rejecting entirely based on your specific circumstances. Don't simply perform a technique because you have learnt it, but instead ensure that it is the logical choice for the situation you face. The chances of actually confronting life or death situations

Above: American military personnel help with search and rescue efforts along the coast of Mississippi following the devastation wrought by Hurricane Katrina in 2005.

are, thankfully, relatively rare for most of us. Hereby lies the problem. In the developed world, our lives are generally sheltered, wrapped in the protective shell of civilization and modern amenities.

If this shell crumbles, whether because of natural or social disaster, we are then reminded that we are physical, vulnerable creatures. In survival situations, the focus is therefore on the most elemental goals – avoiding injury, finding enough to eat and drink, staying warm, getting to safety. By embracing the reality around you, you are more likely to survive it.

Preparing to survive

Survival begins in many ways with preparation. Just reading a book and imagining how you would perform in an emergency are not sufficient. Instead, you should learn the core techniques by practising them in the wilderness. Furthermore, you need to be fit.

Survival fitness is about building your strength and stamina, and adopting healthy lifestyle choices. The tougher and more resilient your body, the better able it will be to withstand the shocks of the sudden descent into a survival situation.

For this reason, time spent in the gym, or distance running, or doing any kind of sport for that matter, could ultimately make the difference between life and death in the wilderness.

A soldier conducts a rope-traverse exercise. Soldiers are purposely trained to develop mental fitness alongside physical fitness, hence they become natural survivors.

Stress and mental breakdown

Stress is the biggest inhibitor of clear thinking. An involuntary response to threat, stress prepares your body for danger. While stress can save your life, it also makes it harder to think rationally.

Stress overload

While small amounts of stress can be good, too much stress can cause a sensory overload, where judgment and the ability to act quickly are impaired. It is therefore vital to have effective stress-management strategies, both on an immediate and a prolonged basis.

Dealing with stress

When stressed, you adopt a defensive position, breathing gets shallow and your eyes unfocus. Purposefully adopting the physical opposites of these traits can limit the negative effects of stress. Take on a confident and assured body posture, breathe calmly and deeply, raise your chin and make focused eye contact.

Physical effects of stress

- Increased heart rate or chest pain
- Dizziness and sweating
- Nausea or indigestion
- Diarrhoea or constipation
- Nervous habits, such as pacing or talking much more than usual
- Being prone to illness or pain
- Eating too much or not enough
- Sleeping too much or not enough

Mental effects of stress

- Focusing on the negative
- Irrational behaviour
- Increased temper or irritability
- Memory and concentration problems
- Impaired judgment
- Inability to relax or switch off
- Neglecting or refusing responsibilities
- Feelings of depression and isolation

Combat stress

Feeling unable to cope in certain situations is one of the many symptoms of combat stress, often accompanied by anger, depression and confusion. Being aware of the symptoms can make combat stress reaction (CSR) easier to spot in both yourself and others.

Maintaining control

Training your mind to prepare for and deal with stress can minimize its negative effects. Just as physical training makes your body stronger, mental training makes your brain stronger.

Being in control

Operating complex combat technologies requires advanced training as well as powerful mental composure. In times of stress, vocalizing your next move can help you maintain concentration, such as saying out loud: 'I now need to check the radar for hostile aircraft.'

Mental focus

All professional armies look for certain core attributes. The US Army, for example, expects recruits to have the following qualities: mental preparedness, physical fitness and readiness. In a nutshell, being physically and mentally able to cope with stress and perform at optimal levels is essential no matter what the situation.

Resiliency

Resiliency is the ability to stay mentally strong in the face of repeated hardship and trauma. It is a key personality trait expected in military officers, who often have to make split-second decisions that could affect the lives of those under their command. Develop resilience by keeping focused on completing one or two manageable goals at a time, and seeing them through to completion.

Time management

Checklists can save you time and energy, as well as allowing you to focus your thoughts. Rank tasks in order of importance, only ticking them off when you have nothing more to do on that task. Focus your attentions on fulfilling the most important tasks and delegate others if you can.

Sharing experiences

Talking through difficult situations or fears can help you to put them in perspective. While this is often easier in civilian life than in military life, sharing experiences can reduce the negative effects of stress on both the individual and the unit. Whatever your situation, remember you are not alone and it is likely that many others are sharing your fears.

Making decisions

The saying 'doing something is better than doing nothing' is well known. Quick decision-making is vital for elite forces members, where you may have split seconds to form a plan, then act on it.

Readiness

These soldiers know they could be attacked at any moment. Note how each soldier is assigned a specific sphere of observation, meaning they do not have too much to handle. A state of readiness is essential, as if one team member is not prepared, there could be adverse consequences for the entire group.

Pressure testing

Stress-testing can take many forms. One technique used by US military research groups involved soldiers being asked to complete life assurance forms while aboard a plane apparently about to crash land. Such training is thought to reduce combat stress reaction.

Decisions in action

This map of a tank commander negotiating his way through obstacles highlights the importance of decision-making, earned by a combination of military training and experience. While planning is important, the need to be adaptable and think quickly can be vital.

Rule-of-three thinking

If you find yourself wracked by indecision about your best course of action in a survival situation, use the 'rule-of-three' decision-making process as taught to the US Marines. When faced with a problem, think of three different solutions. Any fewer than three and you do not have enough options, and any more than three and you have too many alternatives. Honestly assess the positives and negatives of each option, then, without dwelling obsessively on detail, choose what seems the best solution. Importantly, stick with your choice once it is made. US Marine officers are taught that the biggest danger in extreme circumstances is not making the wrong decision, but making no decision at all. Do not worry too much if there are still problems in your plan; you can negotiate these as you go along. Rule-of-three thinking has the advantage of giving a structure to your thinking processes in extreme circumstances. Additionally, being the first to take action often means your chances of winning are much greater.

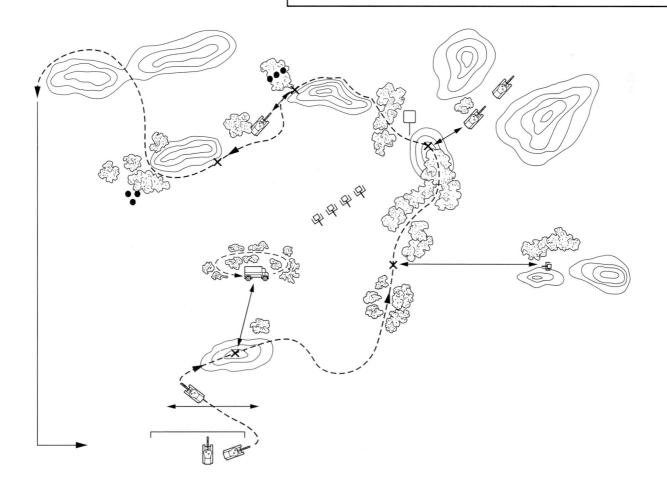

Preparing to survive

Acting under pressure

In high-pressure situations, there is rarely enough time to formulate the perfect plan. The US Marine Corps advocates the 70 per cent solution in such situations, a plan that on balance is highly likely to succeed but which can be enacted now, with improvisational adjustments made as the plan unfolds.

Training realism

Here a military recruit undergoes minefield clearance as part of his training. The task requires cool decision-making under intense conditions. Such tests are often conducted with added stressors, such as nearby explosions, constant shouted instructions – which are often contradictory – and harsh penalties for mistakes. Realistic training better prepares recruits for the streses of battle.

Taking ownership

Once you have made your decision as leader, you need to be clear and concise about what is to be done. The essence of the plan means that people need to know the end outcome and what their role is, but they can figure out the details themselves. Empowering your team means that while you are leading them, they are also managing their own area of expertise. Leading by persuasion, not force, enables people to take ownership of their choices and actions.

Panic response

Humans are programmed to respond instinctively to threat. This instinct to flee from a dangerous situation, even when you have been ordered to move forwards into it, is made worse by prolonged exposure to stress. Dealing effectively with panic and overcoming the natural human instinct to run and save yourself can make all the difference in team situations, where each individual relies on their comrades.

Visualization and hypnosis

Positive mental imagery is a powerful tool in overcoming barriers to success. In stressful situations, the brain searches for similar memories to direct its response and take action.

Brain spheres

The human brain controls involuntary and voluntary physical processes, as well as being a complex tool that enables people to perform great feats of bravery and resilience in times of severe stress. The cerebrum controls thought processes and emotions, and stores memory and personality.

Brain

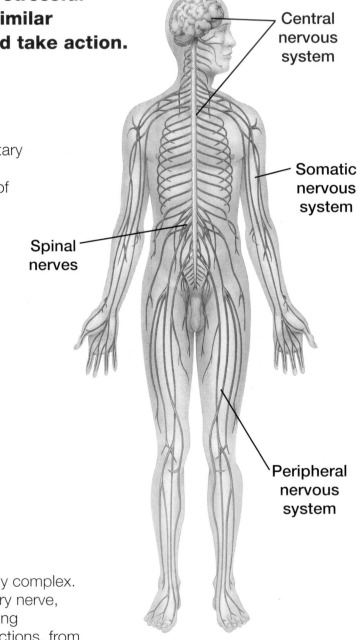

Central nervous system

Somatic nervous system

Spinal nerves

Peripheral nervous system

Nervous system

The body's nervous system is extremely complex. It links the brain and spinal cord to every nerve, muscle and organ in the body, controlling unconscious processes and bodily functions, from breathing to digestion. Every movement you make involves mind and body working as one.

Visualization techniques

Relax your body, then picture yourself in a problematic situation but performing calmly and confidently. See yourself achieving the goals you desire, and imagine how you feel in doing so. Aim to visualize the scene with as much detail as possible, including sights, sounds, colours, smells and sensations of touch. If imagined strongly enough, the brain will not be able to tell the difference between the imagined 'file' and a real one. Furthermore, the imagined picture will provide a model for your physical actions.

Positive visualization

Studies have shown that mentally visualizing (imagining) certain situations, and how you would act in them, can contribute to a successful outcome in the real world. This is the mental equivalent of a rehearsal.

If you suffer from a fear of heights, for example, but know that you will have to go up in a helicopter or climb high mountains during your military training, imagine yourself sitting in the open door of a flying helicopter, feeling stable, composed and enthralled at the view beneath you. You can add some realism by mimicking the physical motions, as if you were acting in reality. For example, if you are planning to ski or snowboard in an area that you know to be dangerous, you can imagine the action you would take if an avalanche began to

develop. Imagine heading at the correct angle towards the edge of the moving slab of snow, maintaining the momentum and entering into an area of stable snow safely.

For example, if you are entering a skiing competition, you can put your ski boots on and stand in your room, then imagine going down the hill, making similar movements with your arms and legs as you go on your imaginary journey downhill. Try to visualize the sights, sounds and smells around you when skiing.

Imagine dealing successfully with all the difficult turns, jumps and obstacles. Imagine crossing the finishing line in front of a cheering crowd. You can use similar techniques to imagine what you would do in an emergency, such as getting off a capsizing boat or ship.

Self-hypnosis

Self-hypnosis involves settling into a relaxed, alert state by concentrating on breathing and softening the muscles. The soldier then takes himself calmly through whatever situation he is concerned about, a process that also helps him to cope with similar situations encountered in everyday life. If you suffer from a fear of drowning, for example, imagine yourself aboard a speedboat or floating in water, feeling composed and safe.

Managing stress

The following technique is useful for controlling stress:

- Either sit or stand in a relaxed position.
- Breathe in slowly through your nose up to a count of five.
- Exhale slowly through your mouth up to a count of eight.
- As you breathe, let your abdomen expand fully so that the breath goes down deep into your lungs.
- Repeat sequence, relaxing your body and mind as you do. Build up to at least 10 minutes daily.

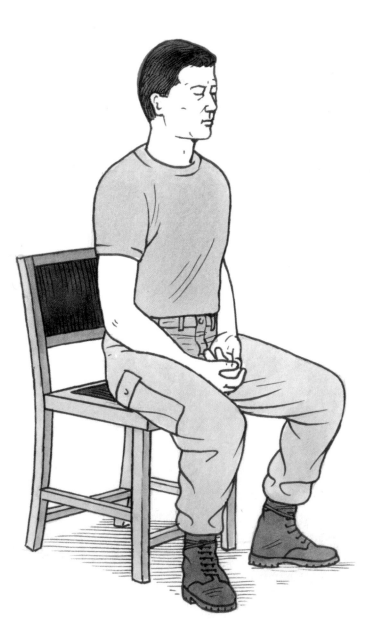

Mindfulness

Using meditation exercises such as 'mindfulness' – an intense focus on your own breathing and well-being – can prepare soldiers for the stress of deployment as well as dealing with post traumatic stress disorder (PTSD) and depression after being in combat. Soldiers are likely to experience relatively severe stress at some point in their service; it is how they react to and move on from this stress that often defines their ability to function as soldiers.

Assertiveness

The more you develop and use these mental tools, the more emotionally resilient you will become. This will increase your confidence, a vital tool in both military and civilian life. Most military leaders appear naturally assured, which is essential for inspiring trust in those who follow them. Even if you are nervous, maintain control over your body and speech, moving calmy and purposefully. Issue any instructions slowly, using commanding language.

Mental toughness

Military life is a profession like no other, with the very real prospect of experiencing the violence and chaos of combat. Soldiers need mental toughness, self-discipline and a warrior spirit.

Dealing with the threat of violence

The most profound distinction between civilian and military life is the presence of violence – often on a scale or intensity that is unimaginable to anyone who has not lived through a war itself. Combat presents sights, sounds and sensations of unique force that can powerfully affect the human psyche.

Survival instinct

Combat is an intense experience both psychologically and physically. Here (to the right) a soldier acts fast, using any available resource in order to survive the blast of a nearby artillery explosion. Exposure to prolonged shellfire has historically been the leading cause of PTSD, even among elite troops.

Training to win

Combining physical and mental trials such as route marches requires you to 'compartmentalize' the discomforts of heavy packs and equipment and focus on the task in hand. It may sound 'new age', but believing you can succeed can make all the difference to your training.

Team support

Being able to depend on team members when in danger is vital for the completion of successful missions. Each team member will contribute a speciality and the team's efficiency depends on each soldier mastering their particular skill. Such shared experiences promote unity.

Disciplined downtime

Disciplining yourself to make the best of every opportunity is something that soldiers quickly learn. For example, taking advantage of downtime to grab a brief, refreshing sleep can compensate for sleep deprivation. Filling free time with activity makes you less likely to dwell on negative events.

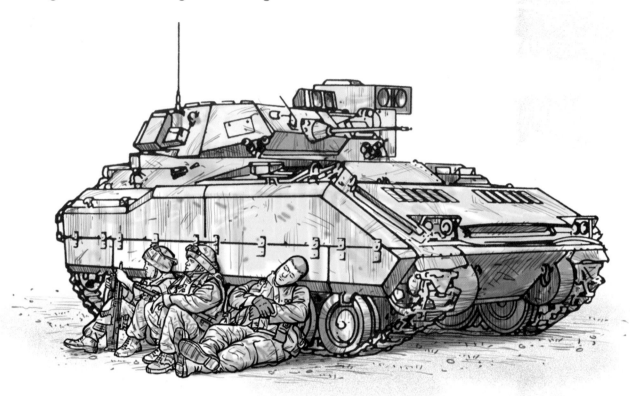

Targeting sleep – night raids

Here night-time artillery fire is used to hit the enemy during his most vulnerable hours. As World War II demonstrated, continual shellfire can be an excellent tool for disorientating and weakening even the most resilient enemy over a matter of days. The effects of sleep deprivation include memory loss, slowed reaction time and mental sluggishness.

Under pressure

These US soldiers have a matter of seconds to ascertain whether a situation is about to become deadly. They must make behavioural and tactical decisions, within the set rules of engagement, about whether it is justifiable to open fire on the vehicle.

Courage through action

Courage is often found not through willpower, but through simple action. Here, a soldier forces himself to stand up – literally raising his head above the parapet – to throw a grenade, breaking his mental paralysis. The rule that doing something is better than doing nothing can save lives.

Physiological effects of fear

Body control The soldier can lose control of his bladder or bowels. Physical shaking – a natural response to fear – can interfere with fine motor control over limbs; this in turn can have serious implications if the soldier's survival depends on successfully operating a complex and sensitive piece of weaponry or equipment.

Vision Under extreme fear a soldier can lose much of his peripheral vision and depth perception; the brain creates a 'tunnel vision' effect that means it is only possible to focus on the most immediate threat. This limited range of vision means that the soldier may be unaware of emerging dangers.

Hearing Fear can make hearing seem muted or distant, resulting in difficulty in comprehending orders or radio communications. In some instances your hearing might appear to shut down altogether. Problems with hearing are often exacerbated by the noise effects of gunfire and explosions.

Thinking Fear drains blood away from the frontal, rational parts of the brain, making reasoned thought difficult. It can also have the effect of slowing down the perception of time.

Tents and equipment

Just like special forces soldiers, be very strict with what you carry into the wilderness. Consider two things above all: climate and terrain, and what emergencies could occur.

Horseshoe pack

Wrap up all the items for carrying in a large sheet (preferably of waterproof material) and tie off the ends, then use further cords to divide the pack into thirds to stop the contents from sliding around. Finally, sling the pack over one shoulder and tie the two ends at the opposite hip.

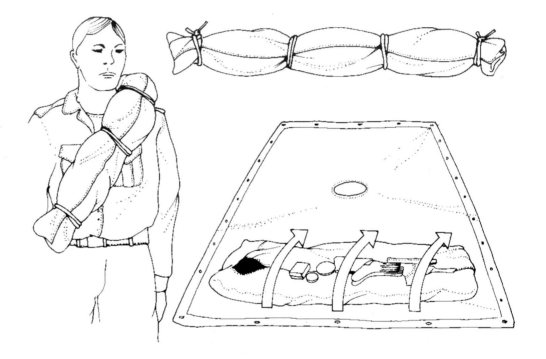

Choosing a sleeping bag

- Know your filler. Sleeping bags are generally filled with either natural down or synthetic filler such as PolarGuard 3D, Lite Loft, Hollofil or Quallofil. Down is more compact and lighter in terms of its warmth-to-weight ratio, but the synthetic materials have greater resistance to wet conditions.
- Choose a sleeping bag that has a three-season warmth rating for your particular part of the world, unless you expect conditions to become very cold, in which case choose a bag with a severe winter rating.
- Choose bags that are made by either offset double layer construction or advanced shingle construction; both avoid the cold spots that can be produced by long stitch lines.
- Buy a sleeping bag with an attached hood, to wrap around the back of your head for extra thermal protection.
- In terms of size, buy a bag with about 20–25cm (8–10in) of extra space below your feet – this can be used as a useful storage space.

Tunnel tent

Often split into sleeping and living sections, tunnel tents are useful for longer trips, especially in temperate climates. They are not at their best in strong winds, but many modern tents include UV treatments to protect you from penetrating sunlight, offering comfort and extra living space or bedrooms.

Geodesic tent

The British Army's own pop-up tent is a geodesic design. These tents offer greater stability in high winds. Look for a tent with poles linked together with shock-cords for quick and easy construction. Single-sheet tents are the lightest, but be sure to choose one made of a breathable material such as Gore-Tex.

Dome tent

For short-term backpacking and hiking purposes the tent should rarely exceed two-person capacity, making dome tents a viable option. Look for tents that have strong polyester flysheets, with a heavier polyurethane-coated nylon groundsheet and glass-reinforced plastic (GRP), fibreglass or aircraft aluminium poles. These will be relatively sturdy, but still light.

Military packs

Military-style packs are purposely designed for hard use as well as long-term comfort. Army surplus shops will have a wide variety of items for sale, but check for any damage before you buy, and ensure that equipment fits you properly. Your pack needs to carry your shelter, sleeping bag, food and cooking supplies; ideally, everything you need to survive in the wild. Look for side pockets, extendable flaps, double stitching and seals.

Bergen pack

Shoulder pack

Belt pouch

Webbing system

Packing a backpack

When filling your pack, work on the simple principle that the items needed most regularly – such as food and wet-weather clothing – go at the top and in side pouches, while items needed less frequently go at the bottom. Edges or corners of hard objects must be kept towards the centre of the pack so that they do not rub against your back. Be realistic about what you pack, keeping the load to under one-quarter of your weight.

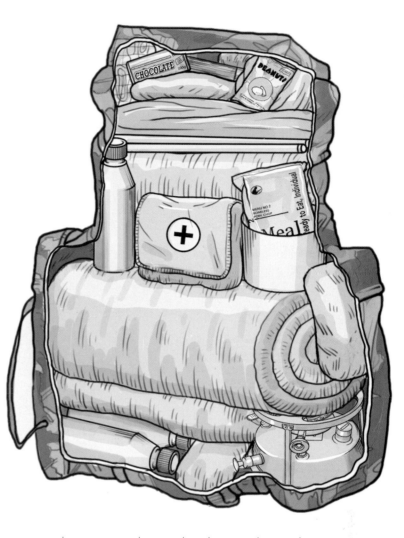

Improvised sleeping bags

If you find yourself without a sleeping bag, you will need to make alternative arrangements. Even in temparate climates, cover as much of your body as possible to prevent the loss of body heat. Ensure that your hands, feet and head are covered and, ideally, that there is a layer between your body and the ground beneath you.

Useful survival kit

Your survival kit can be the last resort in an emergency situation. For this reason, to avoid it being lost or stolen, tuck it away safely in a buttoned or zipped jacket or trouser pocket.

Ration kit

Emergency rations can be weighted towards carbohydrates because carbohydrates require less water for digestion, especially when compared to proteins. Carbohydrates, such as biscuits, chocolate and sweets, are quickly absorbed into the blood stream as sugar.

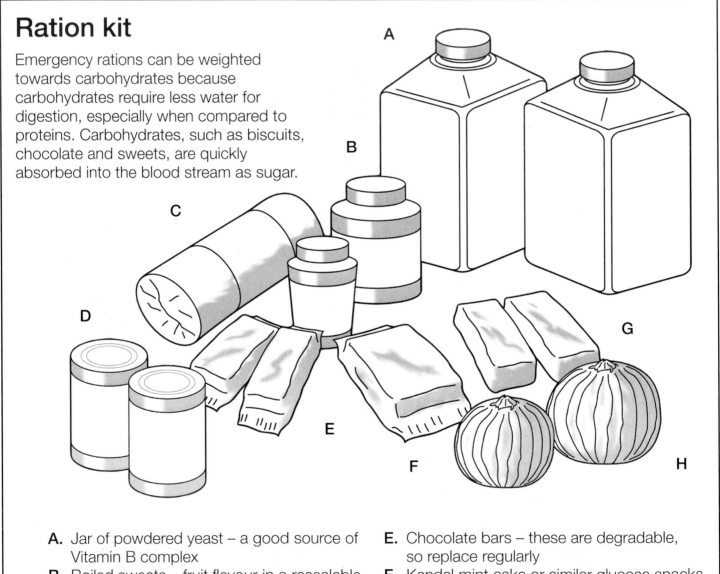

A. Jar of powdered yeast – a good source of Vitamin B complex
B. Boiled sweets – fruit flavour in a resealable tin, with glucose powder
C. Ginger biscuits – ginger in any form helps to ward off seasickness
D. Canned fruit

E. Chocolate bars – these are degradable, so replace regularly
F. Kendal mint cake or similar glucose snacks
G. Muesli bars – these are degradable, so replace regularly
H. Onions – the most vitamin-rich vegetable, but degradable, so replace regularly

Survival tin

Almost all soldiers in modern armies carry survival tins on operations. Regularly check the contents of your survival tin for signs of deterioration. Prevent damage from shaking by packing the contents with cotton balls or cotton wool, which can also be used for making fire or cleaning wounds. Coat any metal objects in a thin film of grease to protect them against rust.

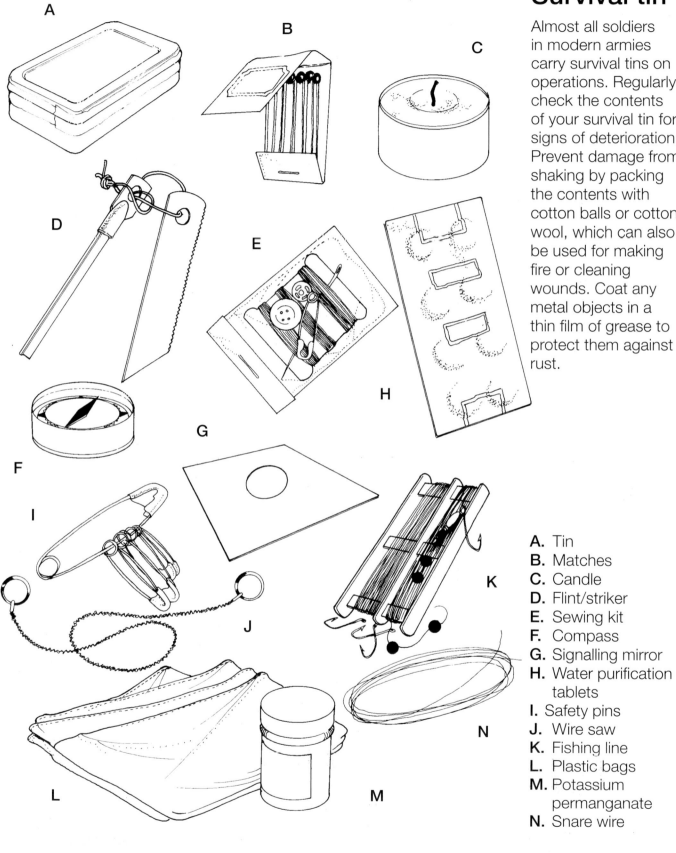

A. Tin
B. Matches
C. Candle
D. Flint/striker
E. Sewing kit
F. Compass
G. Signalling mirror
H. Water purification tablets
I. Safety pins
J. Wire saw
K. Fishing line
L. Plastic bags
M. Potassium permanganate
N. Snare wire

Survival telephone

Many soldiers often carry satellite and mobile phones to supplement their military-issue comms. Satellite phones differ from mobiles in that they have greater coverage from orbiting satellites, the best models being configured to work reliably in any environment on Earth.

Compass

Depending on your situation, a compass could be a key piece of equipment. Learning to use a compass correctly will greatly increase your chances of surviving in a crisis.

Insect repellent

On tropical ops, insect repellent is an essential precaution for soldiers, particularly against mosquitoes and ticks. The US Center for Disease Control recommends repellents with the following chemical composition, based on the length of time between applications:

- 1–2 hours
  <10 per cent DEET
  <10 per cent picaridin
- 2–4 hours
  ~15 per cent DEET
  ~15 per cent picaridin/KBR 3023
  ~30 per cent oil of lemon eucalyptus/PMD
- 5–8 hours
  ~20 per cent–50 per cent DEET*

*This composition is also best used in areas where both ticks and mosquitoes are prevalent.

Mess pack and contents

Being able to keep clean and well-fed makes any camping or survival expedition much more tolerable. Note the moveable handle on the mess tin, designed for use over a camp fire but able to be packed conveniently away after use. Ensure that contents, such as razors or soap, are stored in separate plastic bags to avoid mess or food spoilage.

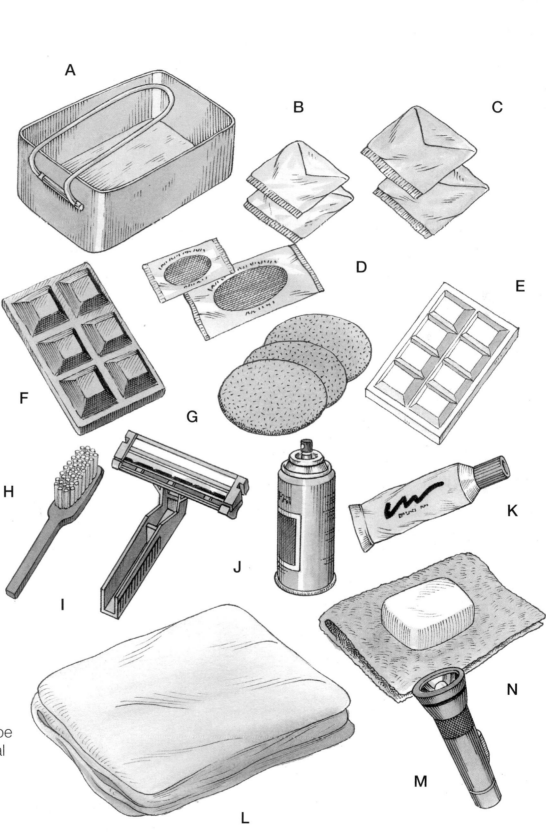

A. Mess tin
B. Tea and coffee pouches
C. Milk and sugar pouches
D. Rice cakes
E. Chocolate
F. Chocolate candy
G. Biscuits
H. Half-toothbrush
I. Half-razor
J. Mini shaving foam
K. Mini toothpaste tube
L. Fluorescent survival bag
M. Small flashlight
N. Soap and flannel (washcloth)

Knives and tools

Knives and axes are vital survival kit, used for everything from skinning animals to making shelters. Many versions are available to buy, but in emergencies, cutting tools can be improvised.

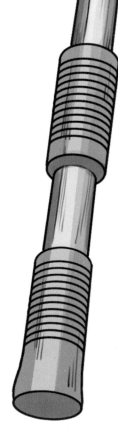

Survival axe

This survival axe features a folding haft, which enables you to store the axe conveniently in a small pouch. Axes are excellent tools for shelter or raft building and for collecting firewood, speeding up the process of gathering materials. Keep the blade clean and sharp – sharpen the axe using a proper steel or a whetstone.

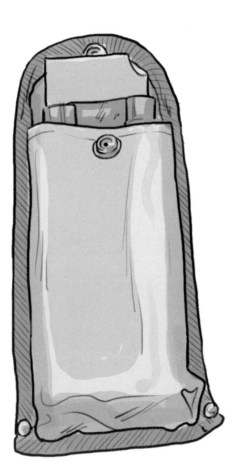

Survival knife

Survival knives can be obtained from military surplus stores. The best is one that has a single blade sharpened on one side only, with a broad opposite edge and wooden handle securely fitted with rivets. Good versions include, in the handle, a button compass, flint and striker and fishing line/weights, plus features on the blade such as a saw edge.

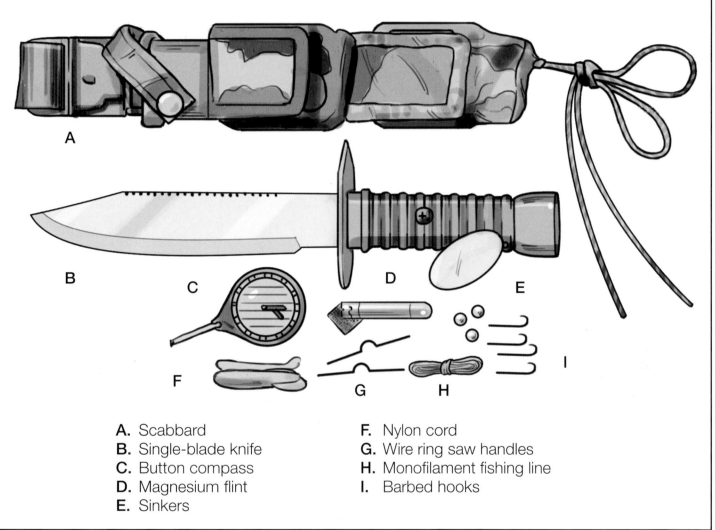

A. Scabbard
B. Single-blade knife
C. Button compass
D. Magnesium flint
E. Sinkers

F. Nylon cord
G. Wire ring saw handles
H. Monofilament fishing line
I. Barbed hooks

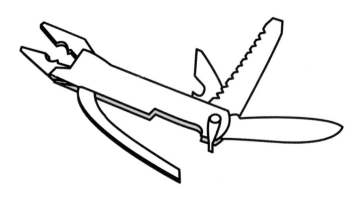

Multitools

Small, lightweight and immensly practical, multitools are essential survival tools. The blades consist of knives, tweezers, mini saws, nail files, folding scissors, toothpick, pliers, etc. Versions specifically for hunting or fishing are also available.

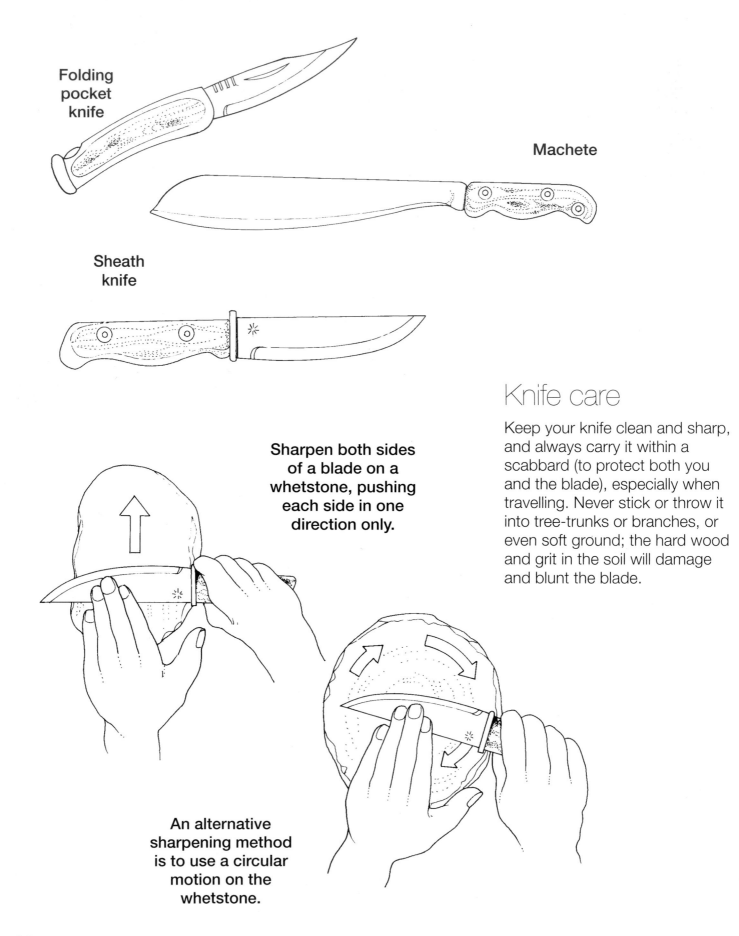

Folding pocket knife

Machete

Sheath knife

Sharpen both sides of a blade on a whetstone, pushing each side in one direction only.

An alternative sharpening method is to use a circular motion on the whetstone.

Knife care

Keep your knife clean and sharp, and always carry it within a scabbard (to protect both you and the blade), especially when travelling. Never stick or throw it into tree-trunks or branches, or even soft ground; the hard wood and grit in the soil will damage and blunt the blade.

Wire saw

This military-style wire saw is often used by special forces as a compact and convenient way of carrying a tool that can cut through wood, plastic and bone, and packs into a convenient canvas pouch.

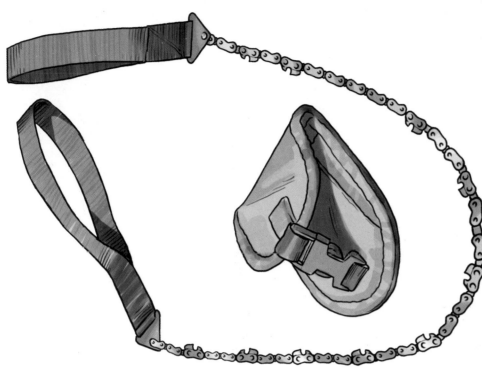

Survival 'pan'

A simple military-style mess tin can be tied to a fork twig to create an elementary form of frying pan. Such utensils may seem crude, but they can reduce the risk of campfire burns.

Layer principle

The fundamental principle of survival clothing is layering, working on the thinking that several light layers provide better insulation than a few heavy layers, also allowing for easy temperature control.

Layering principle

The layering principle offers you the best way of controlling and preserving body heat. The British Army CS95 uniform, for example, consists of seven different items, ranging from a breathable, thermal vest base layer to an outer Gore-Tex jacket.

| Base layer (thermal) | Second layer | Fleece layer | Weatherproof layer |

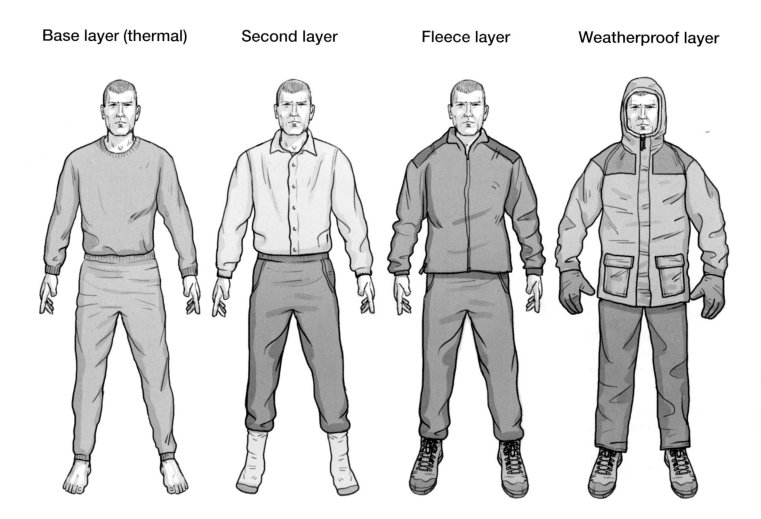

Thermal gloves

Waterproof jacket

Waterproof leggings

Waterproof clothing

In the wilderness, waterproofing is critical, as even the warmest fleece or woollen clothing will lose much of its insulation when it becomes wet. In a survival situation, wet clothes increase your chances of hypothermia. It can also be very difficult to dry clothes when on the move. Note that here there is nowhere for driving wind or rain to enter the clothing, with a full hood, velcro at the wrists and no gaps at areas where layers meet. Ensure that waterproof clothing fits over bulky layers.

Maintaining clothing

Soldiers are taught in basic training to take responsibility for their clothing, knowing that it will lose its protective properties if it is allowed to fall into disrepair:

- Keep it clean. Dirt reduces both waterproofing and heat retention, so if your clothing becomes dirty, clean off the dirt with a non-abrasive method, such as wiping down with a damp cloth.
- Keep it repaired. Sew up any tears in clothing as soon as you get the opportunity, before the tear has a chance to widen.
- Keep it dry. Dry your clothing out at every opportunity, either by hanging it up in the open air or by suspending it near – but not over – an open fire. Never crumple up wet clothing and leave it in a pouch or backpack – it will develop mildew and may begin to rot.

Protecting the extremities

For severe weather conditions, you have to make sure that every part of your body is protected. The nose, ears and fingers are especially susceptible to frostbite.

Gloves

There are many woollen and ski gloves available, but in severely cold climates mittens provide better insulation for your hands. Wearing a pair of thin thermal gloves under your mittens allows you to use your fingers when you need to, but make sure the mittens are attached to the jacket by a cord or they can easily be lost. Look for gloves that cover your wrists without a gap.

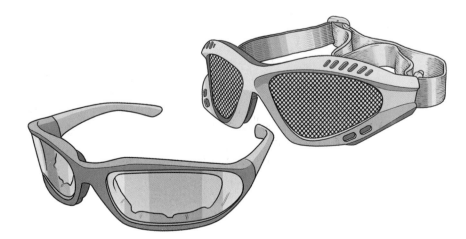

Eye protection

Do not underestimate the danger of sun reflection off snow. Snow blindness can cause pink or reddish vision, pain, watering eyes and eventual loss of vision. Protect your eyes with UV googles, preferably ones with wrap-around protection on the sides so that no glare can reach the eye.

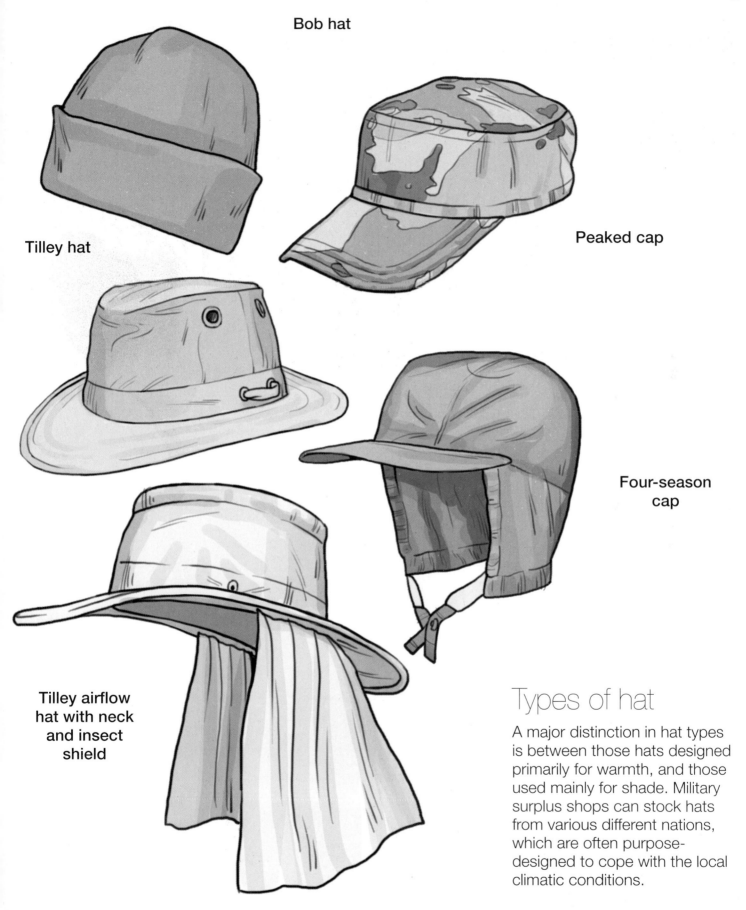

Bob hat

Peaked cap

Tilley hat

Four-season cap

Tilley airflow hat with neck and insect shield

Types of hat

A major distinction in hat types is between those hats designed primarily for warmth, and those used mainly for shade. Military surplus shops can stock hats from various different nations, which are often purpose-designed to cope with the local climatic conditions.

Walking equipment

It is worth taking time to select the right equipment so that you are comfortable and safe. Choose waterproof hiking boots that support your ankles and which are designed specifically for your intended type of activity (the more intense the activity, the stiffer and more durable the sole). Walking poles and ice axes are essential for mountain expeditions. Look for a waterproof and rugged rucksack to protect your gear, ideally with integral raincover and side compression straps.

Treating exposure

Exposure victims need to be wrapped up warm; expose the minimal amount of bare skin to the elements. Remember that heat can be lost through the ground as well as the air, so ensure that the casualties rest on a insulating layer between them and the ground, such as pine branches.

Footwear

Any walking or climbing boots should have adequate traction on the soles. The more jagged the sole, the better the traction it supplies. If you want boots for all terrain, these might be smoother under foot. Such boots can be adapted by adding ice cleats. These consist of a rubber harness that pulls on over your boot, with metal studs, coils or spikes under the sole, allowing safe walking on ice or snow. The more uneven the surface, the more traction you will need.

Maintaining footwear

Obey the following procedures to keep boots in optimum condition:
- Apply boot wax or polishes to keep the uppers supple and waterproof.
- Before putting boots on, check them for signs of damage such as severely worn treads, cracked soles, broken seals or stitching, cracked leather and broken fastening hooks.
- To dry wet boots, stuff them with newspaper if available, and dry them in a warm, airy place. You can place them near a fire to assist drying, but not too close. Too much direct heat will bake and crack the leather.
- Always carry at least two spare pairs of laces. To preserve laces in cold weather, rub silicone or wax into them. It will prevent them from freezing if they become wet.
- Remember to break new boots in before wearing them on an expedition.

Knowing your environment

We can all take safety for granted, especially on familiar ground. Staying alert is key, as is being mindful of escape routes and safety measures no matter where you are in the world.

Personal safety

Unfortunately, women travelling alone are more likely to be attacked than men. Minimize the threat by being aware of your surroundings. Stand close to a wall so no one can move up behind you unseen. Stay away from anyone loitering, especially near exits, and avoid isolating yourself in dark corners or streets. Hold on to belongings securely, wearing handbag straps across the body.

Awareness when travelling

Try to sit near an exit on a subway or train. Should any aggresive or intoxicated individuals enter your carriage, casually exit the train at the next stop and get into another carriage. While crowded carriages make it easier for perpetrators to hide, try to avoid empty carriages, where you might be the only target if anyone does enter it with violence in mind.

Precautions against crime

Try not to display valuables on public transport, especially expensive electronic devices, as you will become a magnet for muggers. When carrying a laptop, use the shoulder strap worn diagonally across the body. If you have to work on transport, give yourself enough time before your stop to stow all equipment away safely.

Aircraft exits

On an air flight, pay attention to where the nearest exit is. In an emergency, however, do not make a move for the exit while the aircraft is still in motion. Wait until it has come to a complete stop.

Preparing to survive

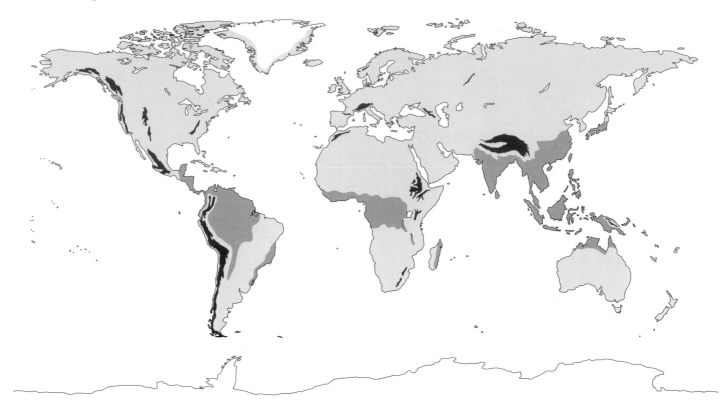

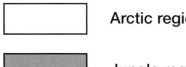 **Arctic regions**

 Jungle regions

 Mountainous regions

Hostile environments of the world

Natural regions of the world are separated into nine types: polar, tundra, coniferous forest, deciduous forest, scrubland, rainforest, grassland, desert and mountainous. The main determinant of food types in these regions is climate and the availability of fresh water. Familiarize yourself with climate and terrain before embarking on a trip.

Travelling as a group

If travelling with children, modify your route planning accordingly. Small children may have prodigious short-term energy, but can easily succumb to fatigue over several hours of exertion. Set a realistic objective which is based on the capabilities of the weakest, not the strongest, member of the group. Activities can be built up in duration gradually.

Travelling alone

Unless you know the territory and local people extremely well, never travel alone. Western travellers are clear targets for criminals, their backpack usually advertising valuable contents.

Using an embassy

If you find yourself in trouble in a foreign country, make contact with your nearest embassy or consulate. Although the embassies of different nations have different procedures and powers, it is good to have a prior understanding of their capabilities and limits. Embassy staff can:

- Issue passports and other documents, and tell you how to transfer money
- Facilitate medical treatment by liaising with your insurance provider
- Provide advice on local doctors, lawyers and interpreters
- Advise you on local cultural and safety issues
- Inform next of kin if you are in trouble and advise them on procedures
- Visit you if you have been arrested or put in prison
- Arrange rescue attempts if you are in life-threatening danger

However, embassies are usually unable to:
- Get you out of prison, interfere in local court proceedings or give legal advice
- Investigate crimes
- Pay any sort of bill for you, including legal, medical or transportation bills
- Provide you with travel details
- Issue you with in-country work permits or visas
- Find you work.

Most crucially, remember you are subject to the laws of the country you are visiting. Employees at your embassy are unable to influence the legal process. It is a good idea to have the telephone number and address of the embassy before you leave home, as this information might be harder to find in an emergency situation. Above all, avoid putting yourself in a dangerous situation.

Stocking your car

Having a car fit for purpose means that you have a head start in the case of a major emergency. Keep a full tank of gas, as well as supplies for nourishment and comfort in the trunk of your car.

Tyre snow chains

Learn how to fit tyre snow chains before an emergency occurs, as the process of doing so is fiddly even under good conditions. After installing your snow chains, drive about 100m (328ft) then stop and inspect them – tighten the chains further if necessary. Ensure that your tyres (including the spare) are in good condition and inflated to the correct pressure.

Snowbound

If you are stuck in your car during a blizzard, stay with the vehicle. Keep a window open a crack for air, stay warm by moving your limbs to keep the blood flowing, start the car engine once every hour and use the heater for 10 minutes to keep the vehicle functioning. Keep the exhaust pipe clear so that fumes can escape.

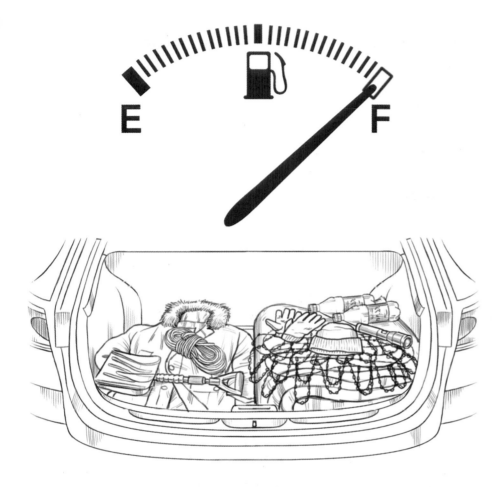

Fuel supplies

In an emergency or evacuation situation, the last thing you will want to do is stop for gas. The stations may also be closed or unable to pump gas. Keep a full tank of gas as much as possible and store cans of spare fuel in a secure location, never using these for non-emergencies.

Car trunk

You should always keep the following items in your car in storm or blizzard conditions: bottled water, blankets, winter coat, gloves, hat, shovel, rope, tyre chains and a flashlight. Just as you do with you home survival supplies, check perishable items for expiration dates.

Emergency kit

A good vehicle emergency kit should include the following items, plus anything else suitable for the terrain you might need to cover:

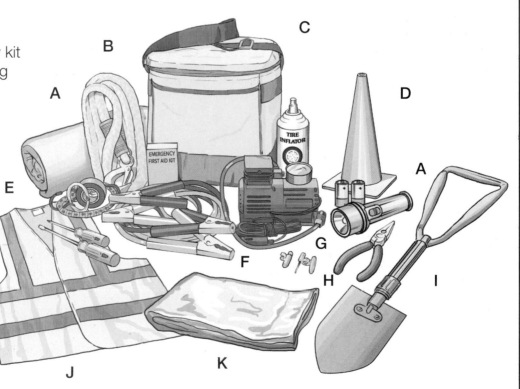

A. Blanket
B. Ropes or bungees
C. Tyre inflation systems
D. Warning cone
E. Maintenance tools
F. Jump leads
G. Flashlight
H. Pliers
I. Shovel
J. HIgh-visibility gear
K. Survival blanket

Route planning

Route planning is an essential element of your preparation. Never head off into the wilderness without a clear idea of where you are going, how you will get there and how long it will take.

Pre-trip planning

Always read about and research a travel destination thoroughly before setting out on your trip. Look into culture, customs and politics as much as flora, fauna and geography, and only use up-to-date, official sources for information. Check visa requirements before you leave, and conduct research into any areas prone to criminality or violence.

Researching land patterns

Research the direction of major land masses in your destination. Knowing that a mountain range runs, say, north-south will give you a constant navigational reference in easy view. Be honest about your capabilities and fitness levels.

ROUTE PLAN

Date: Time: Starting point reference:

Weather forecast:

Members of party:

Description:

To (grid reference)	Description (ot target)	Direction	Distance	Time (for distance)	Height gain	Time (for height)	Total time	Description (of route and terrain)	Possible alternative route	Escape route

Finishing point reference: Estimated pick-up time:

Description: Estimated phone-in time:

Route card

Fill out a route card before every journey into the wilderness and leave it with a responsible person. If the area you will be travelling through is particularly remote, consult with local ranger/mountain rescue officers while planning out your route so that they can highlight pitfalls or overlooked dangers before you set off. Note the weather forecast log. Severe weather conditions should mean you cancel your trip. At the least, build in extra time for completion and dress appropriately.

Planning routes

Make sure that your route planning phase takes into account all the features which are likely to slow your progress, such as dense woodland, river crossings and hilly or mountainous regions, as well as your fitness levels. Build in extra time to safely reach your destination and ensure that each person has enough food and water for the journey.

Country research

Cultural research is just as important as environmental research. During foreign travel, showing disrespect towards or ignorance of the local customs can land you in serious trouble.

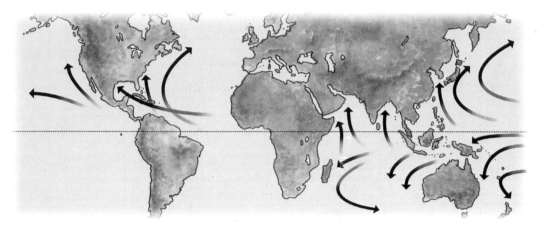

Tropical cyclone paths

When planning a journey abroad, take into account the times and routes of tropical storms, which usually move in from warm seas. In the northern hemisphere, the hurricane season lasts from July to October, while in the southern hemisphere it runs from November to April. Take special care if you are travelling by boat.

Monsoon areas

Monsoon areas can turn a trip to paradise into a journey through hell if a traveller is caught unexpectedly. If travelling into wilderness areas, do so outside of the monsoon seasons. Check with a tourist office for the months and duration of monsoon weather.

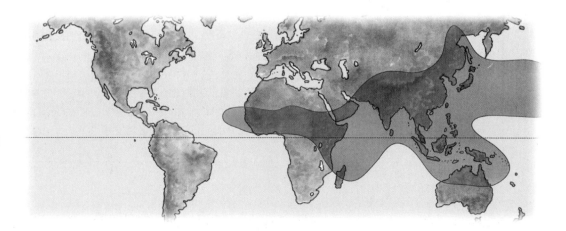

Hearts and minds

Today's soldiers are trained in humanitarian skills, social care and even as de facto political ambassadors. The most important skill for soldiers on peacekeeping is that they are socially flexible and able to identify with people from any cultural or religious background. Building the trust of the local community is a critical goal for peacekeepers.

War zones

If you are apprehended by military personnel, remember to stay calm and show total compliance. Keep your hands visible at all times. Officers need to take firm control when emotions are still running high, and should give clear procedural instructions to every soldier in the unit. In such a situation, try to remember how you would be suspicious of prisoners if you were in the soldier. Try to build a working relationship with key personnel, particularly NCOs.

Health check

A health check is an inventory of your physical state, and it ranges from measuring your heart rate to analyzing how much you eat and drink and how sedentary or active you currently are.

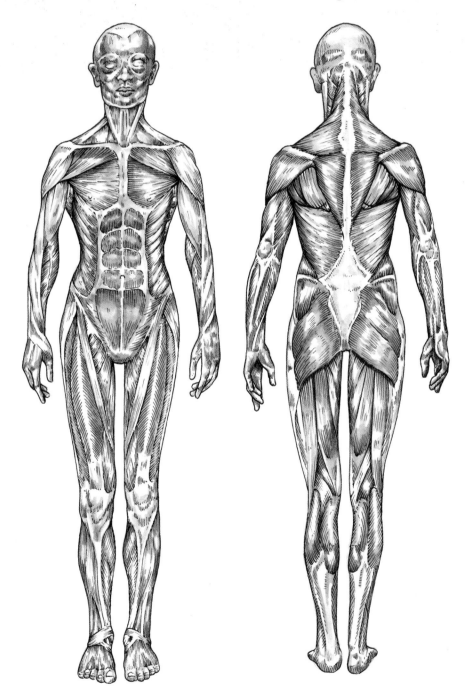

Muscle health

Regular muscle training improves posture and provides an excellent platform for sports and activities. A range of aerobic and strength training and calisthenics will build muscle tone, strength, stamina and speed, enabling you to perform at your physical and mental peak. Identify the key muscle groups in your body, dividing them into the following groups: neck and shoulders; chest, back (upper and lower); arms; abdominals; thighs and buttocks; lower legs. These regions can then be consciously developed through weight training.

Sources of sugar

Chocolate is an excellent source of almost instant energy and is often provided in military Meals, Ready to Eat (MREs). Don't overconsume confectionery, however, as this can in fact lead to a greater sense of fatigue as the sugar rush floods your blood stream, then quickly wears off.

Stimulants, drugs and alcohol

The less you use drugs, chemical stimulants and alcohol, the sharper your mental and physical performance will be over time. It is important not to use these substances as crutches for alleviating stress or worry, as they are likely to make symptoms gradually worse.

Developing aerobic fitness

A healthy fitness regime, involving regular running and exercise, will have numerous positive effects on the body, including stronger bones, muscles and joints, more energy and greater resistance.

Swimming

Swimming is an excellent all-round cardiovascular exercise. It has an extra benefit due to the fact that the body is supported and protected by the water, reducing strain on muscles and the skeleton. It also boosts upper body strength and lung capacity.

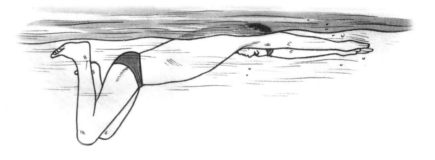

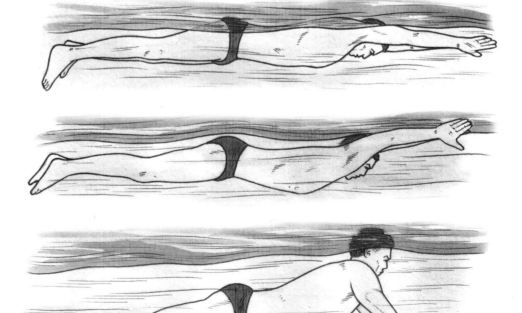

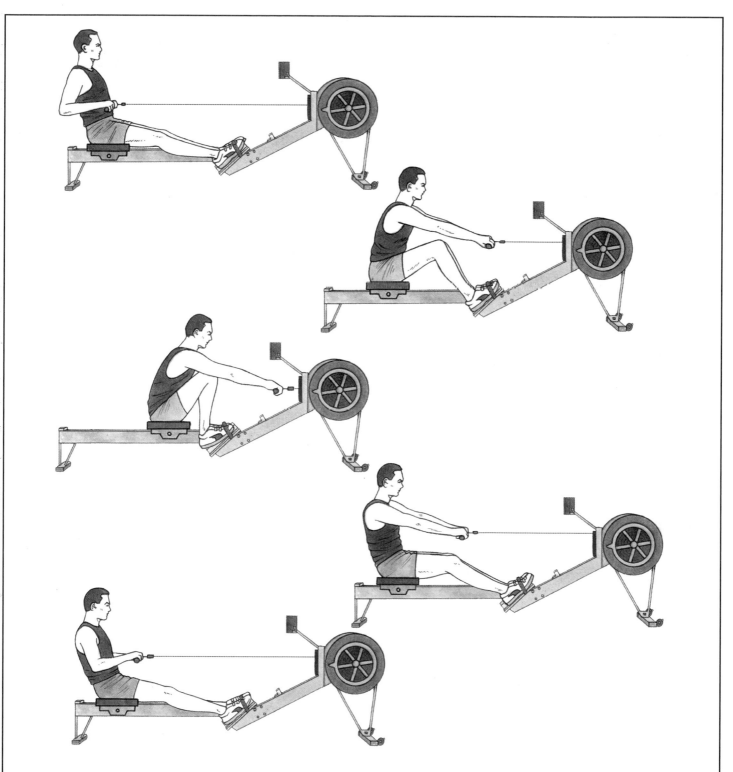

Aerobic training

Aerobic exercise such as rowing is performed at a moderate level of intensity over an extended period of time. This will improve your whole-body endurance and fitness, as the exercise simultaneously works 70 per cent of the body. Avoid strain by not allowing knees or elbows to lock.

Running

Running is the classic base of both your physical and mental preparation, as it will boost both physical strength and mental acuity. A correct running posture involves a relatively straight back, torso slightly tilted forward, and arms running as if on rails to the sides of the body (never crossing in front of the body). This position ensures the trunk of the body remains stable, supported by the core.

Energy use

Exercise should be done in conjunction with healthy diet and nutrition. As the amount of exercise you do increases, so should your amount of calories, unless your initial goal is to lose weight. The table below gives a useful guideline on calories burned during each hour of physical activity.

Energy Use		
One hour of activity	**Calories burned based on weight of 73 kg (160 lb)**	**Calories burned based on weight of 91 kg (200 lb)**
Aerobics (high impact)	530	665
Backpacking	510	635
Basketball	585	730
Boxing	630	725
Canoeing (moderate)	280	350
Circuit training	560	740
Cycling (on flat)	440	520
Football	565	710
Hiking	435	545
Marching	450	530
Martial arts	700	815
Rappelling	560	650
Rock climbing	750	860
Rope jumping	860	1075
Rowing	435	545
Running (8km/h; 5mph)	600	750
Skiing (downhill)	315	390
Stair treadmill	650	815
Swimming (laps, moderate)	520	640
Volleyball	290	365
Walking (5.6km/h; 3.5mph)	300	375
Weight training	365	455

Weight training

Weight training is all about strengthening groups of muscles for optimum performance. Done in conjunction with aerobic training, it can develop muscles and increase power.

Tricep lifts

The triceps muscle is on the back of the upper arm. With one knee resting on a stool, support your weight with one hand and lean forwards. Then, raise the weight in your other hand by straightening your arm. Dumb-bells are excellent hand-held free weights and come in a variety of sizes. Press-ups are another way of working and toning the triceps muscles.

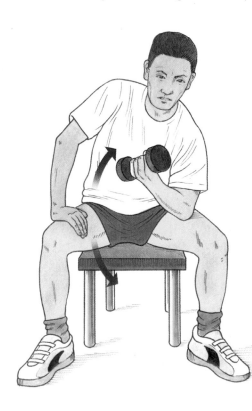

Bicep curls

Sitting on a stool, rest your elbow on your knee. Lift the weight in your opposite hand in towards your body. Aim to do 20 repetitions ('reps'), building up the number of reps and the weight of the dumb-bells as you build up your strength. Never start or finish weight training without proper warm-up and cool-down stretches.

Bench presses

The bench press develops the chest muscles. Lower the weighted bar to a position in line with the centre of your chest, inhaling as you do so. Exhale as you push out, pushing your arms to their fullest extension. A training partner should be ready to take the weight from you if, towards the end of a rep, you reach the point of muscle failure.

Strength training

Your body responds to the physical requirements placed upon it. If there are few or no requirements, it takes a matter of weeks to return to the unfit state. Regular strength training with weights at least two days every week is an important part of your fitness regime in addition to any aerobic training. Your strength training session should include 8–12 different exercises which target all major muscle groups.

Lateral curls

This exercise will work your shoulder muscles. Loosley grasping a dumb-bell in each hand (or a can of food if you have no dumb-bells) raise your arms until they are horizontal, then lower again. Repeat 20 times until you build up your strength.

Leg extensions

Sit comfortably on the bench with your feet under the padded bar. Grip the sides of the bench firmly, and straighten your legs slowly until they are locked. Lower slowly back to the starting position.

Seated pull-downs

Sit down, and reach up to grip the bar. Pull the bar down behind the neck, then allow it to rise under control. Keep the back straight. Note that the bar across the knees prevents them from automatically raising up when you perform the activity.

Seated dumb-bell presses

Sit on a stool or at one end of a bench with a dumb-bell in each hand. Hold the dumb-bell at shoulder height, with palms facing forward. Pushing elbows out at the sides, extend both arms upwards until at full stretch. Hold briefly before lowering to the start position. Repeat 20 times.

Upright rows

Stand with your feet shoulder-width apart, holding the barbell at arm's length down in front of the body. Keeping the bar close to the body, lift it smoothly upwards to just below the chin. Repeat 20 times.

Bench presses

Lie flat on a bench and grasp the bar with hands slightly wider apart than the width of the shoulders. With a straight back, lift the bar off the rack, and hold it straight overhead with the arms fully locked. Now, lower the bar slowly until it just touches the chest. Press it back up to the start position.

Stretches

Before you do any physical exercise, make sure you go through a regular warm-up routine. Pre-exercise stretches enable the muscles to go through a greater range of movement and therefore perform more efficiently.

Hamstring stretch

Ths is a vital stretch for a variety of sports, including running, and it also helps reduce the danger of lower back stiffness. Lie on your back with one leg straight. Bend the knee of the other leg and bring it towards the hip. While the knee is bent, grasp the hamstring of the raised leg. Straighten the leg until you feel a stretch in the hamstring.

Groin stretch

This stretch is especially important for sports and activities that require stretching and reaching with the legs. Sit on the floor with the soles of your feet pressed together in front of you. Bring them as close to your body as you can, then push your knees out and down using your elbows. Maintain and repeat the stretch.

Shoulder stretch

There are a number of shoulder stretches designed to relax this vital part of the upper body. Stand straight with your feet spaced slightly wider than the width of your shoulders. Keep your knees soft and unlocked. Place your right arm horizontally across your chest and use your left forearm to pull the right arm closer to your chest until you feel the stretch in the shoulder. Hold the stretch for several seconds, then repeat for the other arm.

Iliotibial stretches

Stand sideways to the wall with your left hip closest to the wall. Support yourself by holding the wall with your left arm. Cross your left leg in front of your right leg. Move your hip across your body to the right, until you feel a stretch. Repeat the exercise for the other leg, crossing your right leg in front of your left and moving your hips to the left.

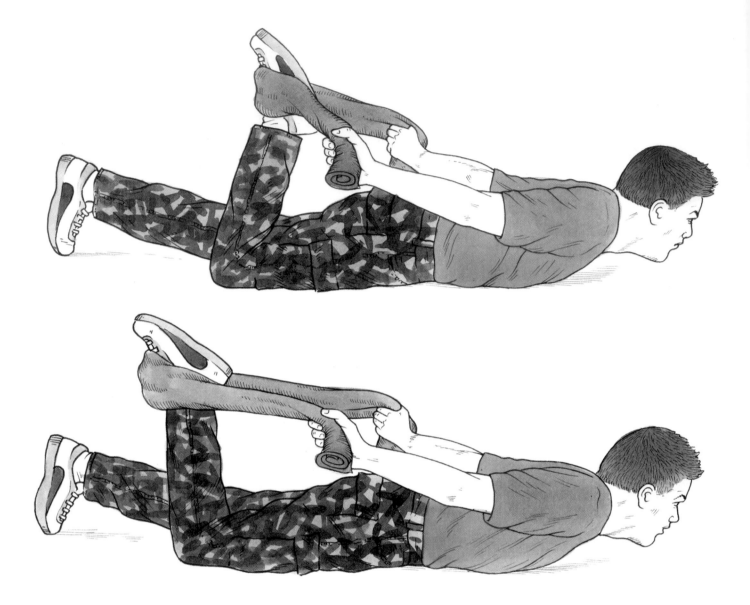

Quadriceps stretch

This stretch will help you to warm up and improve elasticity in the thigh area before taking exercise. Lie on your front, holding a towel or something similar that you can loop around one foot. Push your foot against the towel until you feel the stretch in the quadriceps. Repeat the stretch on each leg.

Gluteal stretch

Like the groin stretch, this exercise is important for sports and activities that involve stretching and reaching. Lie on the floor with your feet flat against a wall and knees bent at right angles. Take your right ankle and cross it in front of your left knee, stretching the gluteal muscles. To increase the stretch, lower the right ankle down your bent leg towards your groin. Repeat on both sides.

Running training programme

Running training programmes are almost infinitely variable, depending on your fitness level, age, size, weight, interests, the kind of distances you are interested in, and so on. This example would suit someone with an average-to-good level of fitness, who is training to run 10 km (6 miles).

Week	Date	Mon	Tue	Wed	Thu	Fri	Sat	Sun
1	6–12 July	Rest/cross training	Easy Run – Distance 3.2 km (2 miles)	Rest/cross training	Tempo Run – Distance 8 km (5 miles)	Rest/cross training	Rest/cross training	Long Run – Distance 9.7 km (6 miles)
2	13–19 July	Rest/cross training	Easy Run – Distance 3.2 km (2 miles)	Rest/cross training	Speedwork – Distance 8 km (5 miles)	Rest/cross training	Rest/cross training	Long Run – Distance 9.7 km (6 miles)
3	20–26 July	Rest/cross training	Easy Run – Distance 3.2 km (2 miles)	Rest/cross training	Tempo Run – Distance 8 km (5 miles)	Rest/cross training	Rest/cross training	Long Run – Distance 11.3 km (7 miles)
4	27 July- 2 Aug	Rest/cross training	Easy Run – Distance 3.2 km (2 miles)	Rest/cross training	Easy Run – Distance 4.8 km (3 miles)	Rest/cross training	Rest/cross training	Easy Run – Distance 6.4 km (4 miles)
5	3–9 Aug	Rest/cross training	Easy Run – Distance 3.2 km (2 miles)	Rest/cross training	Tempo Run – Distance 9.7 km (6 miles)	Rest/cross training	Rest/cross training	Long Run – Distance 11.3 km (7 miles)
6	10–16 Aug	Rest/cross training	Easy Run – Distance 3.2 km (2 miles)	Rest/cross training	Speedwork – Distance 8 km (5 miles)	Rest/cross training	Rest/cross training	Long Run – Distance 12.8 km (8 miles)

Nutrition

In terms of what we eat, carbohydrates generally make up most of our diet. However, it is essential for sustained good health that there are enough proteins, fats and micronutrients in our diet.

Pocket foods

If you are combining healthy nutrition with an increased fitness regime, look for sources of energy such as those shown here. Sweets, grains, nuts, dried fruit, etc. are high in both simple and complex carbohyrdrates, which are essential for optimum mental performance during prolonged training.

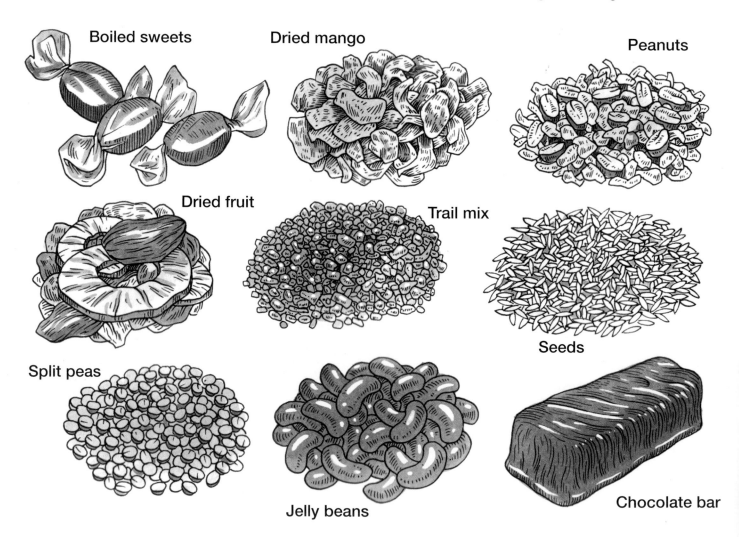

Boiled sweets

Dried mango

Peanuts

Dried fruit

Trail mix

Seeds

Split peas

Jelly beans

Chocolate bar

Varied diet

A well-planned diet will improve your health and sense of wellbeing. It will enhance both physical and mental functions. You should aim for a balance of protein, carbohydrates, vitamin-rich foods such as fruit and vegetables, and some unsaturated fats. The more you vary the fruit and vegetables you eat, the more vitamins and minerals (micronutrients) you will naturally injest. Supplements are readily available, but most professionals agree that the best way to get enough micronutrients is through diet.

Balanced diet

The US government recommends the following amounts of food from each category a day, based on the percentage of total daily calories. By following this guide, you will consistently perform at your best physical and mental abilities, while enabling you to remain in peak health, even when embarking on a new, challenging fitness regime.

Fat – 36%

Carbohydrates – 51%

Trans fat – no more than 1%

Saturated fat – no more than 10%

Protein – 13%

Survival on home ground

We feel safe in our homes, protected by solid walls and all the comforts of modern living. Yet disasters, natural and social, have befallen even the most developed regions of the world, hence survival preparations need to be in place.

The investment in home-ground survival can be as little as having a few extra supplies stored properly in a basement. Alternatively, you could opt for a sophisticated emergency response system, including a dedicated survival bunker.

However extensive your preparations, make sure your whole family is involved, so everyone knows how to respond should the worst occur. From earthquakes to flooding, natural disasters hold fewer terrors if you are ready to meet them.

The devastating effects of a tsunami. Some natural disasters can be predicted, while others strike with horrifying suddeness, devastating the lives of thousands.

Emergency equipment

Every family should put together a basic survival kit that will meet their basic survival needs for a minimum of three days should a disaster occur. This should include food, water and medication.

Keeping warm

Once the heating fails, shared body heat remains an effective way to stay warm. In addition to blankets and duvets, effective insulators include space blankets, sheets of newspaper or anything that traps air. Also control any draughts with improvised draught excluders, as seen running along the door.

Emergency Home Kit

A basic home emergency kit will provide you with the means to survive for several days without resupply. It should include: three days' worth of tinned food (plus can opener) and bottled water; matches; flashlight with batteries; radio; first aid kit; and thick gloves and boots. Remember to include enough food and water for each member of the family.

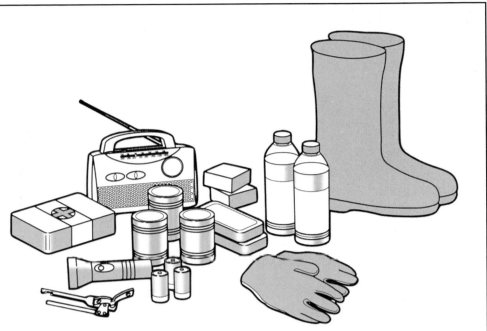

Survival essentials

The items below should form part of any good survival stockpile. If any of the items are perishable, or vulnerable to rodents or insects, store them in strong, sealable plastic containers. Also check the expiry dates of goods, including of 'hard' goods such as

batteries and chem lights, and replace in timely fashion. Containers should be labelled for easy access. Note that it is very useful to include a stock of currency. It is possible that you won't be able to use bank cards for some time, even if you can get to a cashpoint.

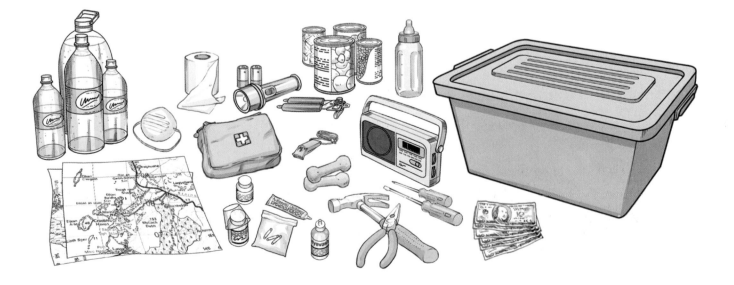

Home survival supplies

As well as the short-term basics such as food and water, equip your home with anything you might need in terms of power, warmth, communication, health and well-being.

Survival safety

Even for the simplest trip out of the home – whether you are travelling by foot or by car – make sure that you pack essential kit such as a map and compass, flashlight, including a spare battery and bulb, a whistle, knife, rations and survival bag/ tin. If necessary, these items can come in useful even if you are staying in the home.

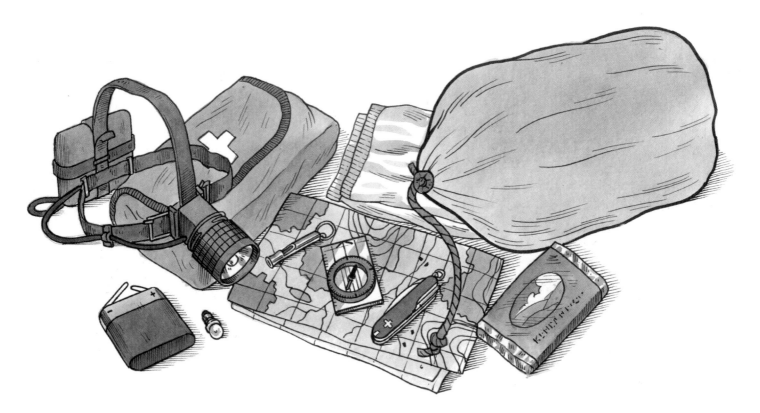

First aid equipment

A good first aid kit should include sticking plasters (adhesive bandages), elastic or crepe bandages, cotton wool, padded dressings, medical tape, scissors, tweezers, antiseptic, iodine, thermometer, flashlight, sunblock, insect repellent and a supply of any prescription medicines needed.

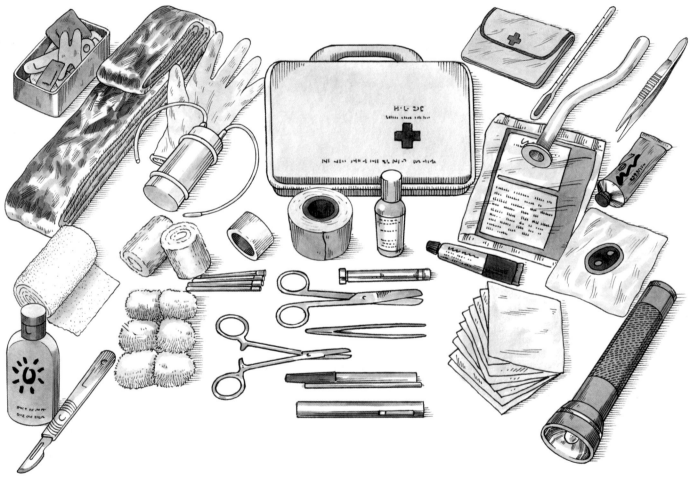

Kits and equipment

Your home should contain stocks of all emergency items. If you need to leave your home, having these items already packed saves you time as well as providing the reassurance of knowing that you have everything you may need.
Add to your peace of mind by ensuring that all supplies are regularly checked for use by dates, and replaced if necessary.

Stockpiling food and water

The best investment you can make for a survival crisis is to build up a well-managed stockpile of food and water. Once built up, you need to monitor, protect and replenish stores regularly.

Storage containers

Any foods not already in pest-resistant packaging should be transferred to plastic or glass containers. The containers should have an air-tight seal to prolong life. Pack them right to the top to reduce the air content inside. See-through containers such as these make it much easier to identify stores of food.

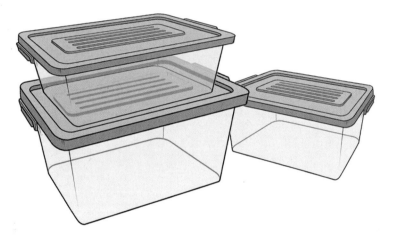

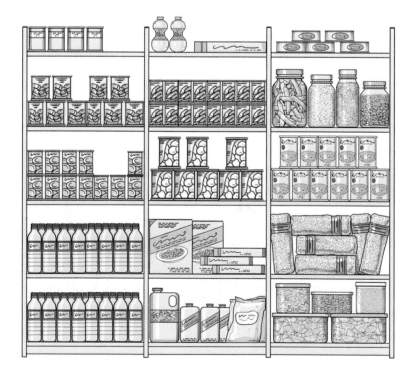

Stockpiling

Ordered stockpiling is imperative if you are to have a clear sense of what is in your survival larder, and if you are to ration the foods out coherently in a disaster. Keep your goods tidily organised on shelving units, and bring the items with the nearest use-by dates to the front of the shelf, replacing them as they approach (not pass) these dates.

Water storage

Every available means for collecting and storing water should be employed around your home/refuge. Rain water can be collected by fitting a diversion tube from a gutter downpipe into a water collector. Boil or purify all water before drinking.

Food Storage Lifespans

The following advice on emergency food comes from the Federal Emergency Management Agency (FEMA) library and gives you an idea of when to check and replace your stockpiled food:

Shelf Life of Foods for Storage
The following provides some general guidelines for replacement of common emergency foods.

Use within six months:
- Powdered milk – boxed
- Dried fruit
- Dry, crisp crackers
- Potatoes

Use within one year, or before the date indicated on the label:
- Canned condensed meat and vegetable soups
- Canned fruits, fruit juices, and vegetables
- Ready-to-eat cereals and uncooked instant cereals

- Peanut butter
- Jelly
- Hard candy and canned nuts
- Vitamins

May be stored indefinitely (in proper containers and conditions):
- Wheat
- Vegetable oils
- Dried corn
- Baking powder
- Soybeans
- Instant coffee, tea, and cocoa
- Salt
- Non-carbonated soft drinks
- White rice
- Bouillon products
- Dry pasta
- Powdered milk – in nitrogen-packed cans

Self-sufficiency

No matter how large your stockpile, if a disaster persists it will eventually dwindle. For this reason, you should also develop a basic knowledge of how to grow crops and manage livestock.

Keeping pigs

A 'pig ark' such as the one above can be purchased relatively cheaply, and it provides adequate shelter for one or two pigs. Ensure that the pigs also have constant access to a trough filled with clean water. Two pigs ideally require about half an acre of land, although they can be sustained on less.

Keeping chickens

A hen house needs to be big enough to allow the chickens space to exercise. It should also have a nesting box for the hen to lay eggs and plenty of security netting around it to protect the birds from foxes, rats and other predators. Try to place the coop out of sight to limit potential thefts.

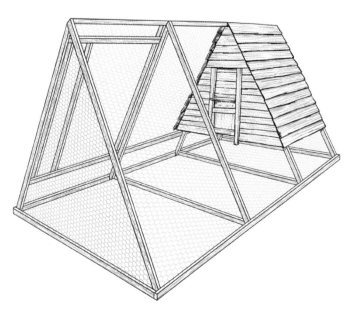

Allotment layout

Here we see a basic allotment layout, viewed diagramatically. Each growing area is dedicated to a particular food, including pumpkins, broccolli, onions, carrots and potatoes. Properly tended, such allotments are capable of providing an annual supply of fresh vegetables. Add the peelings to pig feed, or use them to make compost. Surplus supplies can be cooked and frozen, or used to trade for other goods.

Keeping chickens – advice from the UK's DirectGov Organization

Where to Keep Chickens
Chickens should be kept outdoors in a coop or shed. You can buy chicken coops from home improvement stores or online, or you could build your own. Your coop should have:

- At least 250cm (98in) squared floor area for each bird
- A perch for them to stand on while they sleep
- An exercise space, or 'run'
- A nesting box filled with wood shavings for the hens to lay eggs
- You should clean the chicken coop every week and put out fresh bedding.

Keeping Chickens Safe from Predators
Most people who keep chickens have some experience of predators – usually foxes – getting into the coop. Foxes can climb over or dig under fences, and squeeze through very small spaces. Some tips to keep your chickens safe include:

- Use wire mesh fencing all the way around and above the coop
- Fix wooden boards to the base of the fence
- Check the coop regularly to make sure it is secure
- Shut the chickens into their coop at night.

Feeding and Watering Chickens
You can buy ready-made food that has everything chickens need to keep them healthy. Grit is also an important part of a chicken's diet. The tiny stones help them break down and digest their food. Keep a supply of grit available and the chickens will help themselves to however much they need. Chickens need a constant supply of clean drinking water. Try to choose a container that the chickens can't step in or knock over.

Security: locks and shutters

Security should be part of your daily life and routine, for even in normal peaceful times our homes are under human threat. In a disaster situation, the human threat is vastly magnified.

Double entry doors

House burglary has increased worldwide over recent decades. Make double doors secure by fitting heavy-duty slide bolts to the non-active door. Ensure that these bolts slide into deep recesses in the door frame and floor. Multiple locks make it very difficult for someone to kick a door open, and the spread of bolts distributes the impact along the entire length of the doorjamb.

Hurricane shutters

Windows are by far the most vulnerable points of your house. Hurricane shutters, as the name suggests, protect windows from storm damage, but they can also be a useful disincentive to would-be burglars. The average time a burglar will attempt a forced entry before giving up is four minutes. When faced with such security, most burglars are likely to give up and move on.

Patio locks

Do not focus all your attention on the front of the house. Doors leading to the garden are often more secluded and should be protected. Patio windows especially can be extremely vulnerable to break-ins. At minimum, fit separate patio locks on the frames (shown to the right), but ideally the windows should be protected by security shutters.

Door security

Security should be part of your everyday routine, not just something that you expect to do in a disaster. When at the door, always use a peephole, lock and latch to control who enters your home, and don't be afraid of keeping people outside if you are not sure of their intentions. Peepholes and security chains can be easily added to doors.

Bolts and locks

Hinge bolts (shown near right) provide an extra degree of security around a door, giving multi-point locking and thus making the door more resistant to forced-entry attempts. Deadbolt locks (shown far right) provide far more secure locking than spring-loaded bolts; they can only be opened by rotating the lock cylinder, whereas a spring-loaded bolt can be forced open with pressure to the bolt itself.

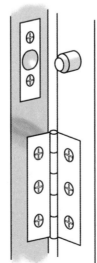
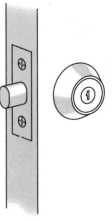

Security systems

Alarm systems are excellent additions to home security, with a control panel and sensors to monitor the property. Simply having an alarm on the side of your house will deter most criminals.

Security dogs

A guard dog not only provides you with companionship, it also gives you a superb natural burglar alarm and a powerful form of self-defence should an aggressor make it into your property. A dog's bark or the sight of dog toys may even be enough to put off some burglars. However, this should not be your only security measure.

Detector sensors

The security systems shown here can trigger alarms based on motion, heat (infrared) and forced entry.

A. Smoke detector
B. Wireless roof infrared
C. Multibeam infrared detector
D. PIR angle detector
E. Gas detector
F. Wireless monitoring system
G. PIR motion detector
H. Signal transfer unit
I. burglar alarm surveillance card
J. Glass break sensor

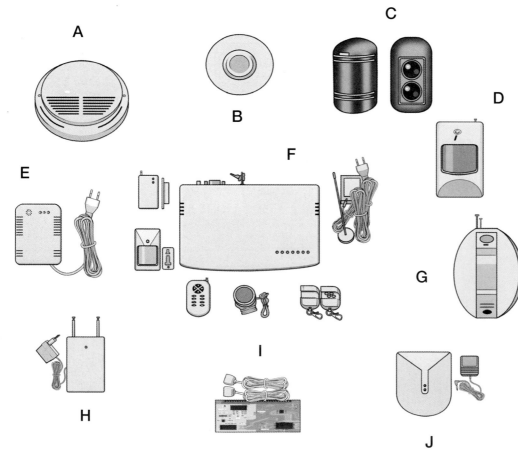

Knowing your escape routes

- Have fire drills with your family on a regular basis. Obtain a map of the area surrounding your home. Review the map and plot two or more evacuation routes that you may use when fleeing a fire.
- If a wildfire is threatening your area, listen to your radio for updated reports and evacuation information. If advised to evacuate, do so immediately.

- Wear protective clothing and footwear to protect yourself from flying sparks and ashes.
- Prepare an evacuation pack that you can pick up at a moment's notice. It should include: drinking water, a change of clothes and footwear, a blanket or sleeping bag for each person, a first aid kit (with any prescription medication), emergency tools, a battery-powered flashlight and radio, extra sets of keys, credit cards and cash.

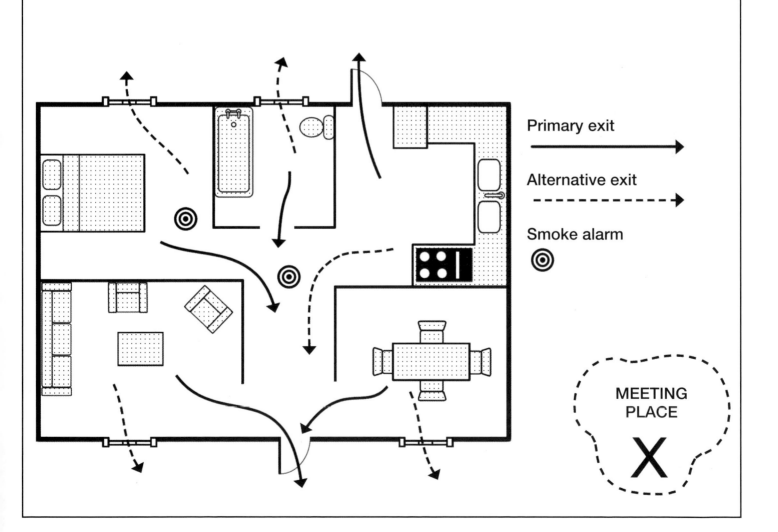

Primary exit

Alternative exit

Smoke alarm

MEETING PLACE

X

Securing against damage

There are certain precautions you should take in your home that will immediately contribute to your safety in the event of a natural disaster, such as flooding or fire.

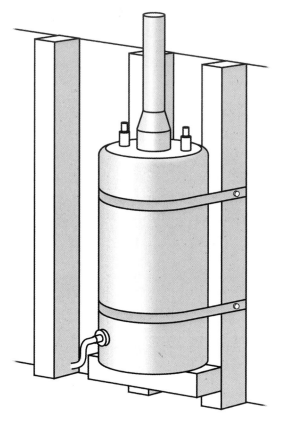

Secure water heater

In earthquake-prone areas, ensure that heavy objects are properly secured to walls and floors. Here we see a procedure for fixing a water heater firmly to an external wall, using a strong timber frame and nylon straps around the waist of the tank, which are attached to the frame.

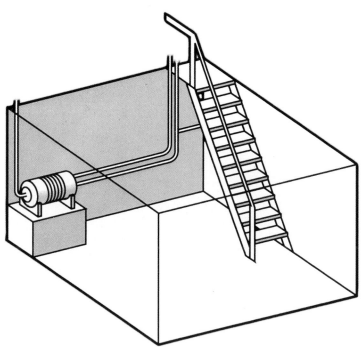

Basement flooding

If you live in an area prone to flooding, a wise investment could be a sump pump in the basement, which will drain out rising waters and control the flooding. Take care when cleaning up after floods, as the water may be contaminated.

Structural damage

Before going back into a damaged house, check the structure carefully to ensure that it is safe to be inside. In particular, don't go back in if you see deep and long cracks through the outer and load-bearing walls, dislodged roof beams and an asymmetrical structure.

FEMA Guidelines for Fire Prevention and Safety

Every home should have at least one working smoke alarm. Buy a smoke alarm at any hardware or discount store. It's inexpensive protection for you and your family. Install a smoke alarm on every level of your home. A working smoke alarm can double your chances of survival. Test it monthly, keep it free of dust and replace the battery at least once a year. Smoke alarms themselves should be replaced after ten years of service, or as recommended by the manufacturer.

Prevent electrical fires
Never overload circuits or extension cords. Do not place cords and wires under rugs, over nails or in high traffic areas. Immediately shut off and unplug appliances that sputter, spark or emit an unusual smell. Have them professionally repaired or replaced.

Use appliances wisely
When using appliances follow the manufacturer's safety precautions. Overheating, unusual smells, shorts and sparks are all warning signs that appliances need to be shut off, then replaced or repaired. Unplug appliances when not in use. Use safety caps to cover all unused outlets, especially if there are small children in the home.

Alternate heaters
- Portable heaters need their space. Keep anything combustible at least 1m (3ft) away.
- Keep fire in the fireplace. Use fire screens and have your chimney cleaned annually. The creosote build-up can ignite a chimney fire that could easily spread.

- Kerosene heaters should be used only where approved by authorities. Never use gasoline or camp-stove fuel. Refuel outside and only after the heater has cooled.

Affordable home fire safety sprinklers
When home fire sprinklers are used with working smoke alarms, your chances of surviving a fire are greatly increased. Sprinklers are affordable – they can increase property value and lower insurance rates.

Plan your escape
Practice an escape plan from every room in the house. Caution everyone to stay low to the floor when escaping from fire and never to open doors that are hot. Select a location where everyone can meet after escaping the house. Get out, then call for help.

Caring for children
Children under five are naturally curious about fire. Many play with matches and lighters. Fifty-two percent of all child fire deaths occur to those under age five. Take the mystery out of fire play by teaching your children that fire is a tool, not a toy.

Caring for older people
Every year over a thousand senior citizens die in fires. Many of these fire deaths could have been prevented. Seniors are especially vulnerable because many live alone and can't respond quickly.

Bunkers and shelters

Bunkers are the ultimate survival location. They are dedicated, sizeable, spaces, often reinforced against even nuclear attacks, and can be the safest and best option to survive a disaster.

Blast shelter

Ready-made blast shelters such as these are simply buried underground (leaving the ventilation ducts on the surface), and the commercial models provide one of the quickest routes to creating a secure refuge. The most advanced shelters come fitted with electromagnetic pulse protection, full nuclear/biological/chemical (NBC) systems, air filtration and communication systems.

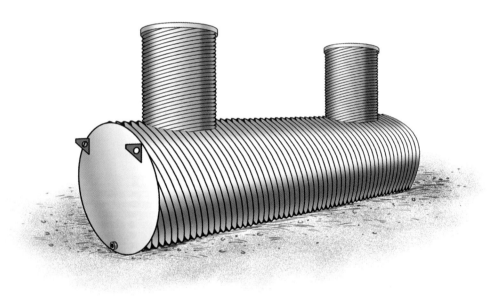

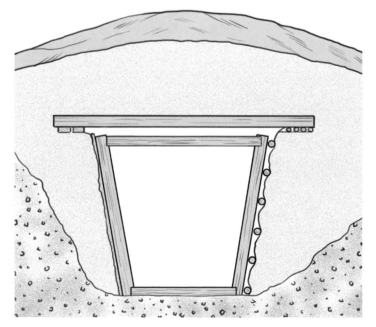

Expedient shelter

This shelter consists of an area approximately 1.3m (4ft 6in) tall, built from a sturdy timber frame, roofed with earth and a waterproof membrane.

Bunker location

In an emergency, you may feel that it is better to place your bunker very close to your home so that it can be inhabited quickly when a disaster occurs. However, extended family, friends and neighbours will likely know about the facility, and in times of crisis may turn up expecting help and shelter.

Shelter safety for sealed rooms

Ten square feet of floor space per person will provide sufficient air to prevent carbon dioxide build-up for up to five hours, assuming a normal breathing rate while resting.

However, local officials are unlikely to recommend the public shelter in a sealed room for more than two to three hours because the effectiveness of such sheltering diminishes with time as the contaminated outside air gradually seeps into the shelter. At this point, evacuation from the area is the better protective action to take. Also you should ventilate the shelter when the emergency has passed to avoid breathing contaminated air still inside the shelter.

(Further information: www.ready.gov/shelter)

Homemade bunker

This homemade bunker forms the ultimate survival retreat in case of a disaster. Buried beneath the grounds of the home, it includes features such as periscope viewing, blast-proof outer doors and plentiful storage shelving. Ensure that appropriate ventilation, sanitation and running water are fitted, and that entrances are concealed.

Social unrest

The world outside your home or bunker can be a dangerous one indeed, not least from desperate people looking to take advantage of the situation, or simply prepared to do anything to survive.

Riots

Riots can be precipitated by numerous different phenomena, from sporting events through to political protest. Major stores and wealthy-looking houses are often particularly vunerable to being targeted by rioters, so avoid such locations during times of civil disturbance, when even passing through the streets can be a dangerous activity.

Stop and search

During a disater, be prepared to encouter law enforcement and security services conducting stop-and-search operations. Emotions can be running high at this time, so ensure that you comply with all the orders given to you, especially if the searchers are armed. In certain disaster situations (if you have adequate supplies), it might be safer to remain at home.

Tear gas

If you are affected by tear gas, don't rub your eyes with your hands. Instead, get a friend to spray your eyes with water. Here, the person on the left is wearing glasses and has wrapped a water-soaked cloth around the eyes and nose, which are both good protective measures against the effects of the gas.

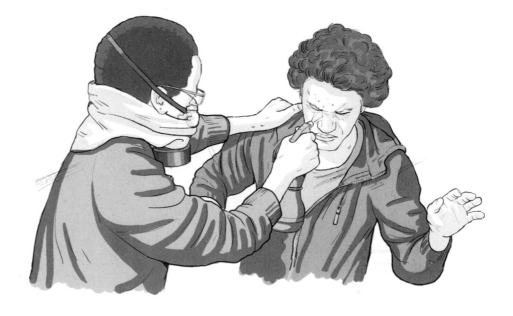

Dealing with a threat

When facing a threat, above all do not show fear, which is more likely to prompt rather than dissuade an attack. The man on the left here remains calm in the face of a potential attack, standing tall and not yielding. At the very least, this attitude will make the attacker think twice about continuing with any form of assault. If the attacker shows no signs of stopping or moves any closer, the defender will need to switch to a guard position in readiness to defend against any physical attack.

Survival on home ground

Social breakdown

Civil emergencies are often accompanied by anti-social behaviour, particularly looting. Stay well away from looting gangs, as they might be targeted en masse by an aggressive physical response from law-enforcement or military agencies. Crowds often have their own momentum that can turn nasty.

Military presence

When military forces are deployed onto the streets during a time of emergency, their rules of engagement (RoE) can range from stop-and-search to shoot-on-sight. Obey any curfews in place, and don't carry a firearm or weapon in open sight of military units as this may prompt them into an immediate armed response.

Riot procedure if trapped in a car

Cars and vehicles often attract the ire of rioters when they attempt to pass through the crowd. If your vehicle is confronted by rioters, follow these procedures:

- Keep moving through the crowd – don't stop.
- If you see an escape route with a clear exit, drive away from the crowd quickly and attempt to put as much distance between it and you as possible.
- Try to drive on minor routes that won't attract the majority of the rioters.

- If rioters surround your vehicle, don't stop but just keep crawling forward slowly, allowing the crowd to part naturally in front of you.
- Don't drive at speed towards military or police checkpoints – you might be seeking protection, but the authorities might simply think that you are a threat and open fire.
- Try not to get visibly angry with the rioters. If you make eye contact, smile or say encouraging words; don't give in to rage or shouting, which may exacerbate the problem.

Mugging

If you are faced with armed muggers, as seen above, compliance is generally your best response. It can be a wise precaution to carry some valuables that you don't mind losing, such as a cheap watch. Handling these over might satisfy the attackers and allow you to keep more important items.

Long-term survival

Surviving the initial disaster is very different from long-term survival. Even if the world has changed and it is no longer possible to rely on your old way of life, there are things you can do to survive.

Power generator

A petrol- or diesel-powered generator will enabe you to keep essential household equipment – including freezers and electric cookers – going in the event of a mains power outage. Ensure that it is run in a well-ventilated area to vent carbon monoxide, and kept hidden from external view.

Bicycle generator

One of the more energy-demanding ways to produce small amounts of electricity is by using a bicycle generator. Pedalling the bike powers a dynamo running off the back wheel, and the electricity yielded can be stored in rechargeable batteries for emergencies.

Characteristics of a nuclear explosion

A fireball, roughly spherical in shape, is created from the energy of the initial explosion. It can reach tens of millions of degrees.

A shockwave races away from the explosion and can cause great damage to structures and injuries to humans.

A mushroom cloud typically forms as everything inside of the fireball vaporizes and is carried upwards. Radioactive material from the nuclear device mixes with the vaporized material in the mushroom cloud.

Fallout results when the vaporized radioactive material in the mushroom cloud cools, condenses to form solid particles, and falls back to the earth. Fallout can be carried long distances on wind currents as a plume and contaminate surfaces miles from the explosion, including food and water supplies. The ionization of the atmosphere around the blast can result in an electromagnetic pulse (EMP) that, for ground detonations, can drive an electric current through underground wires causing local damage. For high-altitude nuclear detonations, EMP can cause widespread disruption to electronic equipment and networks.

Source/Further information:
Department of Homeland Security
(www.dhs.gov/index.shtm)

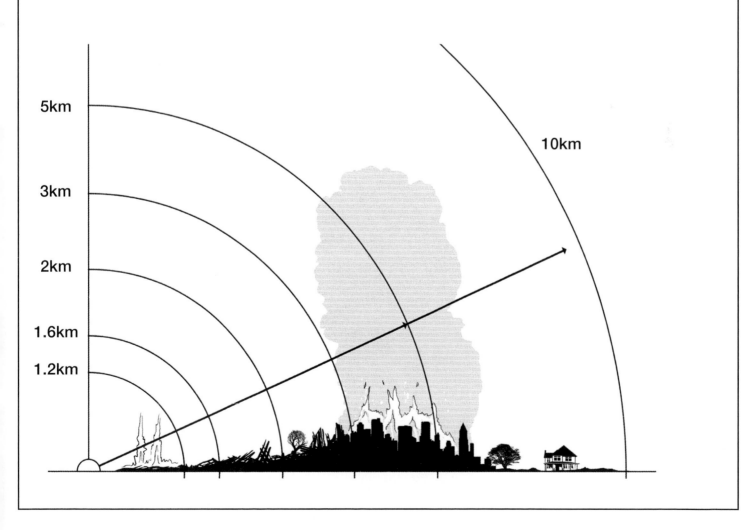

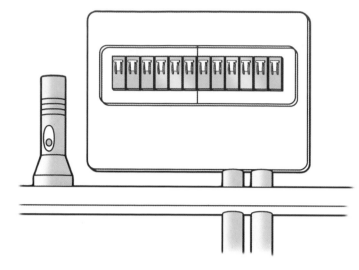

Power cuts

Be ready for power cuts at any moment. Always keep a torch by the side of the fuse board in your house, regularly replenishing the batteries. Ensure that each circuit on the fuse board is clearly labelled, so if the board trips you can easily identify the precise cause of the problem.

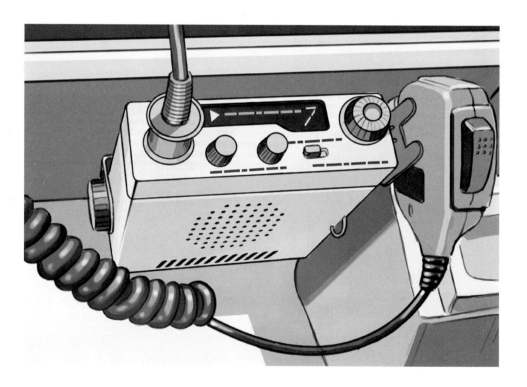

CB radio

A Citizen's Band (CB) or very high frequency (VHF) radio may seem old-fashioned in an age of mobile phones and digital technology, yet having one installed in your car can provide you with an effective means of short-range communication even when mobile networks have ceased to operate.

Survivalist Lighting Options

Candles
Tea light candles are useful, as they can be spread around a room in large numbers. Thick 'church' candles give much longer burn times, however. Place the candle in a storm lantern for portable lighting. One interesting point to note is that simply burning a couple of candles in a small room can raise the temperature of that room by several degrees.

Paraffin/kerosene lamps
Produced in a variety of types, from simple flat wick lanterns to pressurized types that produce levels of light to rival conventional light bulbs (at the expense of greater fuel consumption).

Oil lamps
A particularly ancient form of lighting, which can consist of little more than a fuel reservoir from which a wick projects through an opening in the body of the lamp.

Dynamo lights
Hand-cranked torches are available, which provide basic illumination without the need for batteries.

Chemical lights
In the form of 'glow sticks', chemical lights offer a useful source of emergency lighting. Snap and shake the stick. This will activate the light for up to 12 hours.

LED lights
LED lighting requires little energy to work compared to standard bulb technology, so battery life is dramatically extended. Purchase some of the new generations of LED camping lanterns, including directly rechargeable models.

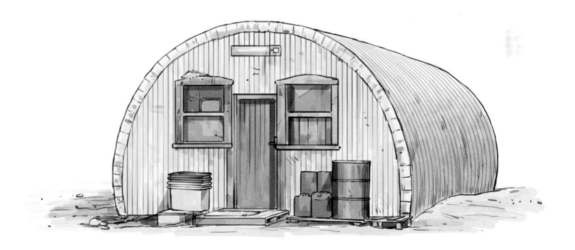

Corrugated shelter

If you are away from home, or if it is not safe to stay there, corrugated iron is a useful material for creating semi-permanent shelters. Such shelters can also be built in deep trenches, and subsequently covered with a thick layer of earth to provide additional warmth and blast protection.

Tornadoes and hurricanes

The severity of tornadoes and hurricanes is dictated by numerous variables, but the most important is the size of the affected region – anywhere from a few kilometres to more than 300km (188 miles).

Preparing your home

In the event of a tornado or hurricane warning, close all doors and storm shutters, tie down or secure anything that could become a missile, reinforce garage or sliding doors and take shelter in a 'safe' room or interior room. Tune your radio in for emergency advice. If you live in a mobile home, evacuate immediately.

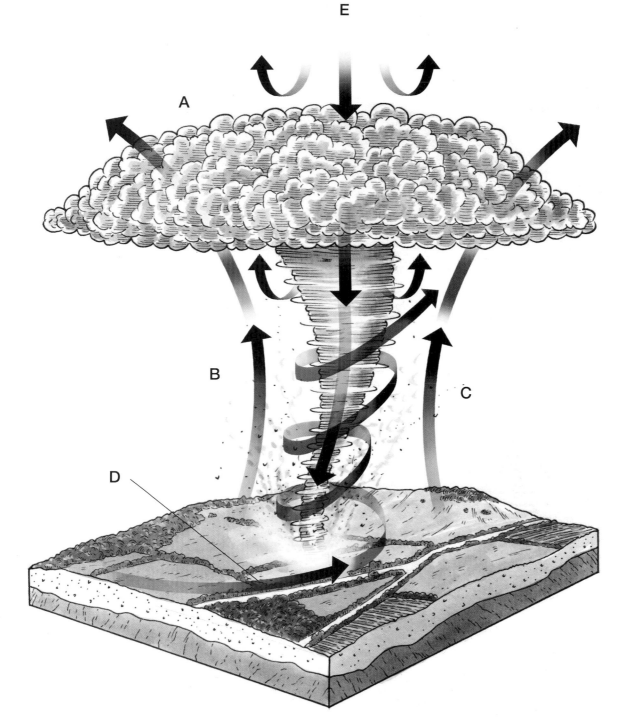

Anatomy of a tornado

Tornadoes are one of the most destructive natural phenomena on the face of the planet. They are capable of travelling at speeds of up to 480km/h (300mph), flattening houses, uprooting entire trees and flipping cars. Here we see the characteristic tornado funnel shape, the wind made visible by the ingress of water vapour and dust.

A. Wall cloud
B. Updraughts
C. Debris around funnel
D. Direction of storm
E. Downdraughts

How hurricanes form

The devastation caused by even multiple tornadoes tends to pale in comparison to that delivered by a hurricane. Hurricane winds are not as fast as tornadoes, but they can still reach up to 252km/h (157mph) at their most extreme. More importantly, an individual hurricane is typically in the region of 30–65km (19–40 miles) across, and sometimes can even be several hundred kilometres wide. The powerful destructive winds of a hurricane rotate around a central 'eye', which has the lowest atmospheric pressure of the storm system. While conditions within the eye are typically calm and relatively benign, the outer storm winds can hit prolonged speeds of up to and beyond 241km/h (150mph). Hurricanes not only deliver crushing winds, but also huge volumes of rain and devastating storm surges that can result in massive flooding across coastal districts. Hurricane Katrina's storm surge, which inundated large areas of Louisiana and Mississippi in 2005, meant that floods reached more than 8m (25ft) in height.

A. Layers of rain cloud   **B.** Eye of hurricane   **C.** Sea level lifted under eye   **D.** Warm air spirals upwards

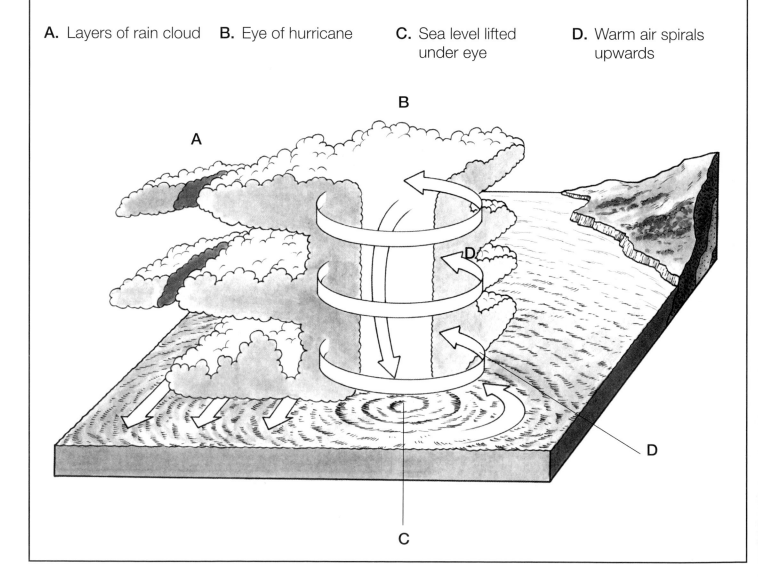

Protecting yourself

Tornadoes are capable of turning even the smallest objects into lethal projectiles. Even if you are in an area with few large objects, the most harmless looking branches or stones can be deadly when travelling at such high speeds. If you are caught in the debris fallout, cover your head with a thick coat for protection.

Seek shelter

If you find yourself outside when a tornado hits, the best thing you can do is remove yourself from the path of the wind. Look for any gullies or shelter, such as the ditch shown below, and remain there until the winds subside and you are sure it has passed. Seeking shelter under a tree is not advised, as branches could turn into dangerous missiles.

Extreme weather: droughts, tsunamis and volcanoes

The effects of extreme weather can be devastating. Peoples' homes and livelihoods – the work of many years – can be obliterated in a matter of seconds.

Drought

Surprisingly, droughts affect more people than any other natural hazard. Drought is a threat for many countries over the coming decades, with some seeing water shortage as the world's greatest security issue. If there are official drought warnings, take care to store enough bottled water in a cool and secure area.

Tsunami

The rule of all floods or tsunamis is to seek higher ground. In rare cases, this may prove to be the roof of your house. Dress warmly, attract attention with a piece of clothing used as a flag, and avoid power lines. If you are sure there is time, take food and water, plus extra clothing in case you get cold or wet.

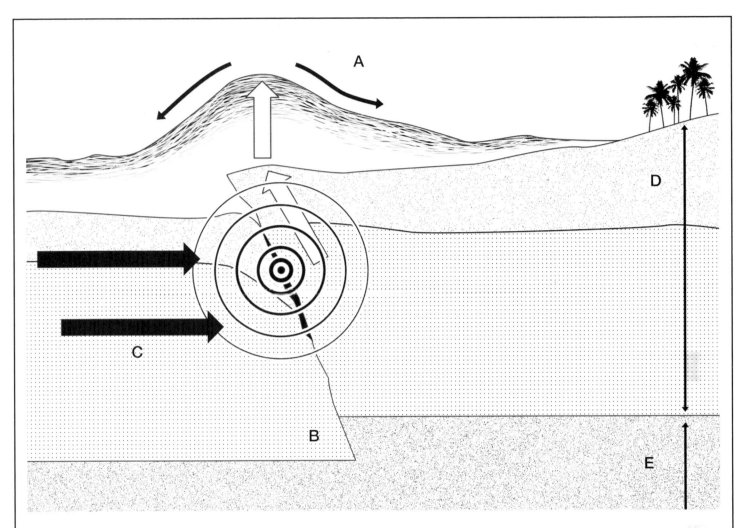

Tsunamis and how they work

An earthquake-related tsunami is generated when the slip of tectonic plates at a plate boundary causes a massive water displacement, generating a huge wave that can travel hundreds of kilometres to strike land. It is difficult to predict a tsunami from the behaviour of waves at sea, since tsunami waves might travel a long way at a height of no more than 1m (3ft) and therefore pass by ships unnoticed. When they reach land, however, they can be about 15m (50ft) high. Japan's worst tsunami involved a wave 24m (80ft) high. Tsunami alerts are issued on the basis of earthquake reports. Although this system can work well for places that are far enough away from the earthquake, it is often the case that the tsunami will have struck before the warning can be given. As you may not have long, plan an escape route to an inland location that is above the likely height of any approaching wave. Put together an emergency kit with food, water and first aid kit. Never head towards the beach to check if you can see a wave approaching. If you can see it, it is too late to escape.

A. Upward wave
B. Fault line
C. Earthquake tremors
D. Crust
E. Mantle

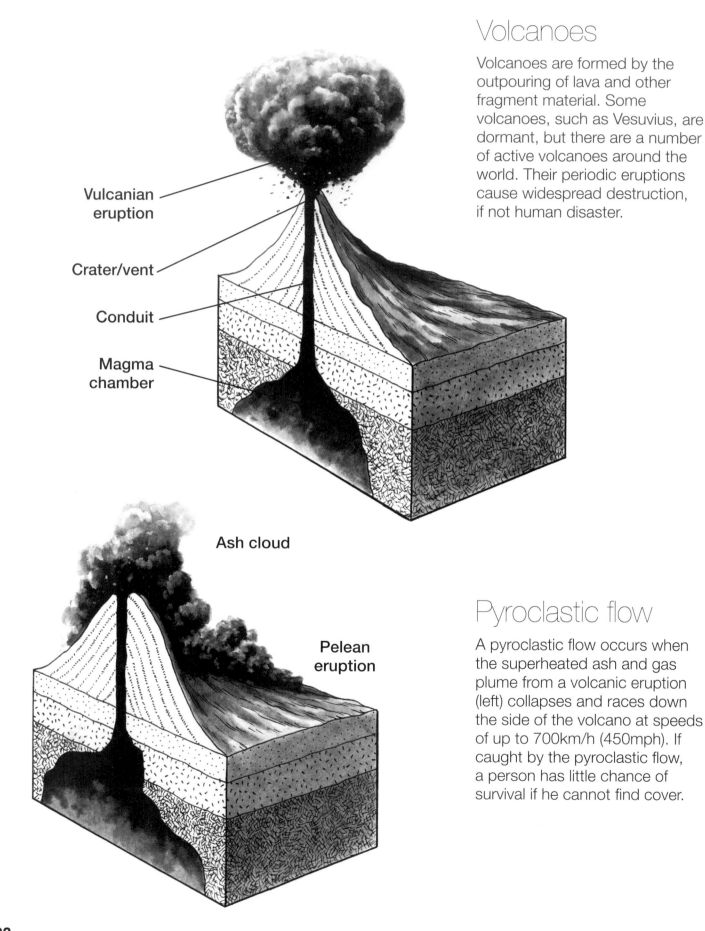

Volcanoes

Volcanoes are formed by the outpouring of lava and other fragment material. Some volcanoes, such as Vesuvius, are dormant, but there are a number of active volcanoes around the world. Their periodic eruptions cause widespread destruction, if not human disaster.

Vulcanian eruption

Crater/vent

Conduit

Magma chamber

Ash cloud

Pelean eruption

Pyroclastic flow

A pyroclastic flow occurs when the superheated ash and gas plume from a volcanic eruption (left) collapses and races down the side of the volcano at speeds of up to 700km/h (450mph). If caught by the pyroclastic flow, a person has little chance of survival if he cannot find cover.

Weather-proofing

Keep a flashlight and tools handy for switching off all utilities – and know how to do so. Install flexible gas and water connections on all gas appliances. Latches for kitchen drawers are useful to prevent them flying open in the event of an earthquake. Install smoke detectors on every level of your home, regularly checking and replacing the batteries.

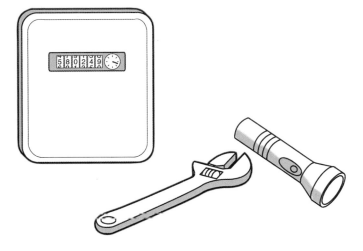

Avoiding accidents

Secure all heavy appliances – water heater, air conditioning unit, etc – to the walls. Remove heavy or glass objects from high shelves, especially those overhanging sleeping, seating or dining areas. Brace gabled roofs and install hurricane straps. Check chimneys for loose bricks or any potential fire risk and take heavy light fittings down.

Top 10 most active volcanoes

Seventy-five per cent of the world's active volcanoes are dotted along the 'Pacific Ring of Fire', a tectonic belt around the perimeter of the Pacific Ocean. The greatest explosion in human history was delivered by the volcano Krakatoa on 27 August 1883, equivalent to the blast of 200 megatons of TNT. The most active volcanoes today include:

1. Chaitén, southern Chile
2. Mayon, Phillippines
3. Mount Etna, Sicily
4. Mount Nyiragongo, Democratic Republic of the Congo
5. White Island, off east coast of New Zealand's north island
6. Mount St Helens, Washington, USA
7. Kilauea, Big Island, Hawaiian islands
8. Soufrière Hills, Montserrat, Caribbean
9. Popocatépeti, Mexico
10. Sakurajima, Osumi Peninsula, Japan

Flooding

Hurricanes, tornadoes, regular storms and seasonal rains often bring with them the blight of flooding. Take precautionary measures if you live in proximity to any natural watercourse.

Flooding

Flooding is not only a major structural issue. As well as weakening walls, floors and foundations, flood waters tend to carry with them serious health hazards, such as water-borne diseases. For this reason, try to avoid wading through the water unless you are wearing appropriate protective clothing.

Flooded roads

Fast-flowing water carries with it great power. If it is running higher that the wheel arches of a car, it can easily push the vehicle uncontrollably in the direction of the flow. Only cross running water if you are certain that you can make the other side safely. Avoid travelling through floods if at all possible.

Flood protection

Flood protection is a fairly basic process. Sandbags are a critical line of defence; when the sand becomes wet, it provides a waterproof barrier around doors and windows. Other apertures, such as ventilation ducts, can be sealed with plastic and tape to provide an extra layer of defence.

Force of water surges

Storm surges happen when tropical cyclones cause an offshore rise of water. High winds push on the ocean's surface, causing the water to pile up higher than the ordinary sea level. The sudden rise in water level can create tidal waves that flood coastal areas. These illustrations show the clear importance of staying on the upper levels of the house if tidal waves or floods are a definite threat.

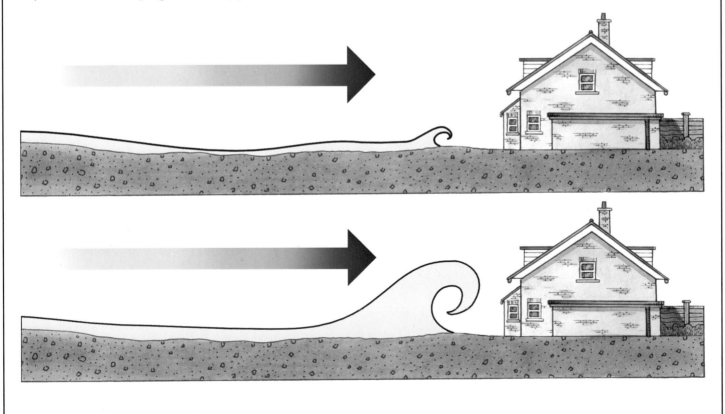

Earthquakes

The earth beneath our feet is ever changing. We stand on a relatively thin crust of vast tectonic plates that 'float' on the hot, viscous mantle beneath. This movement can cause earthquakes, some of unimaginable power.

Earthquake protection

The 'duck, cover and hold' adage applies to earthquake protection when indoors. Shelter under a strong table or other form of overhead protection to shield yourself from falling masonry and objects. Stay under cover as long as the tremors continue. If outside, keep away from trees, buildings or any other structure that might fall on you. Do not attempt to run away from an earthquake, as it is difficult to pinpoint where its main effect lies and you are more likely to run into danger. If you are in a vehicle, drive to a clear space away from underpasses, lamp posts or trees. Stay in the vehicle until the shaking stops.

Seismic waves

The seismic waves of an earthquake ripple outwards from the hypocentre, which is located on the geological faultline – fractures in the surface of the Earth created by the meeting of two geological plate boundaries – and which forms the origin of the earthquake. The epicentre is the point on the earth's surface immediately above the hypocentre, and is typically the location where the seismic waves are at their strongest. For the survivalist, fault lines are a blessing in that they provide a clear warning of where earthquakes can occur, but a curse in that the interval between earthquakes is often measured in many decades, which can breed complacency. Various scales are used to measure the severity of earthquakes, and the greater the release of tension, the more severe the damage.

A. Seismic waves
B. Epicentre
C. Hypocentre
D. Fault line

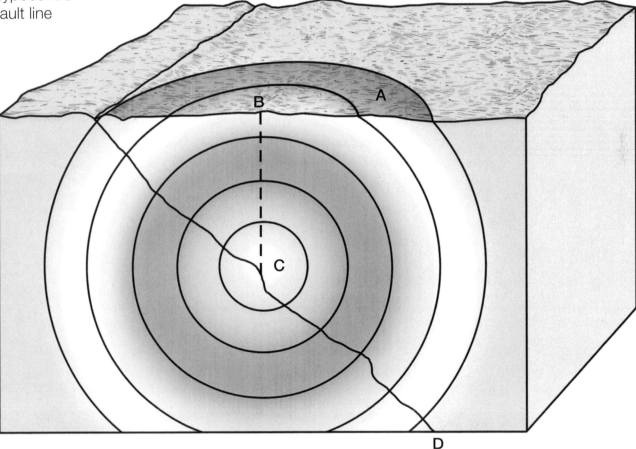

Survival on home ground

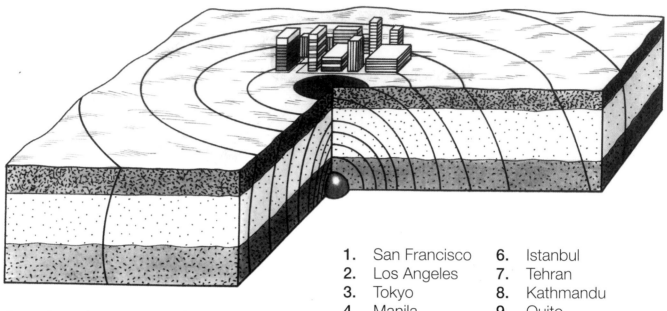

1.	San Francisco	**6.**	Istanbul
2.	Los Angeles	**7.**	Tehran
3.	Tokyo	**8.**	Kathmandu
4.	Manila	**9.**	Quito
5.	Mexico City	**10.**	Anchorage

Cities in danger of an earthquake

Earthquakes are some of the most destructive natural phenomena on earth, and also have equally destructive side-effects, such as tsunamis. As with tsunamis, earthquakes can, in theory, occur anywhere in the world, but they are more likely to occur in areas where separate tectonic plates come together, and it is here that they will have the most destructive effects.

Preparing for an earthquake

Avoid leaving large items of unstable furniture near key exits in your home. If they fall, this could impede a rescue or escape route, leaving you trapped inside the house. Secure such items to the walls where possible.

Modified Mercalli Earthquake Intensity Scale

Level and description

I. Not felt except by a very few under especially favourable circumstances.

II. Felt only by a few persons at rest, especially on upper floors of buildings. Delicately suspended objects may swing.

III. Felt quite noticeably indoors, especially on upper floors of buildings, but many people do not recognize it as an earthquake. Standing motor cars may rock slightly. Vibration like passing of truck. Duration estimated.

IV. During the day felt indoors by many, outdoors by few. At night some awakened. Dishes, windows, doors disturbed; walls make cracking sound. Sensation like heavy truck striking building. Standing motor cars rocked noticeably.

V. Felt by nearly everyone, many awakened. Some dishes, windows, etc., broken; a few instances of cracked plaster; unstable objects overturned. Disturbances of trees, poles, and other tall objects sometimes noticed. Pendulum clocks may stop.

VI. Felt by all, many frightened and run indoors. Some heavy furniture moved; a few instances of fallen plaster or damaged chimneys. Damage slight.

VII. Everybody runs outdoors. Damage negligible in buildings of good design and construction; slight to moderate in well-built ordinary structures; considerable in poorly built or badly designed structures; some chimneys broken. Noticed by persons driving motor cars.

VIII. Damage slight in specially designed structures; considerable in ordinary substantial buildings, with partial collapse; great in poorly built structures. Panel walls thrown out of frame structures. Fall of chimneys, factory stacks, columns, monuments, walls. Heavy furniture overturned. Sand and mud ejected in small amounts. Changes in well water. Persons driving motor cars disturbed.

IX. Damage considerable in specially designed structures; well-designed frame structures thrown out of plumb; great in substantial buildings, with partial collapse. Buildings shifted off foundations. Ground cracked conspicuously. Underground pipes broken.

X. Some well-built wooden structures destroyed; most masonry and frame structures destroyed with foundations; ground badly cracked. Rails bent. Landslides considerable from river banks and steep slopes. Shifted sand and mud. Water splashed (slopped) over banks.

XI. Few, if any, (masonry) structures remain standing. Bridges destroyed. Broad fissures in ground. Underground pipelines completely out of service. Earth slumps and land slips in soft ground. Rails bent greatly.

XII. Damage total. Practically all works of construction are damaged greatly or destroyed. Waves seen on ground surface. Lines of sight and level are distorted. Objects are thrown into the air.

Source: Farzad Naeim, *The Seismic Design Handbook* (New York, Van Nostrand Reinhold, 1989)

Fire

Fires in the home and wildfires are a common hazard and can lead to thousands of deaths each year. Many of the deaths are caused by the asphyxiating effect of smoke rather than by burns.

How to prepare your home against forest fires

Wildfires can strike at any time and affect even urban areas, as fires in California and Australia have shown in recent years. People in fire prone areas should plan ahead and be prepared to evacuate with little notice. Protect yourself and your property by making a fire safe zone around your home, removing combustibles and waste from an area at least 9m (30ft) around the house and any outbuildings. Remove any branches that overhang the roof or chimney, as well as any leaves and needles from gutters. Hose with water any wooden areas around the outside of your home, including the roof if it is made of wood. Shut off any natural gas, propane or fuel supplies and move combustible materials, such as curtains or furniture, away from the window.

Clothing on fire

If your clothing catches fire, smother the flames immediately by falling to the floor and rolling over. This cuts off the oxygen supply that fuels the flames. If someone else's clothes catch fire, the same rule applies. You could also smother the flames with a fire blanket or heavy fabric, but avoid using anything that might be flammable.

Pan fires

Turn the heat under the pan off as soon as possible. Smother pan fires by throwing a damp towel over them, but never throw water directly on to the pan. Leave the pan covered for at least half an hour, otherwise it could reignite when exposed to the air. Vent the room to avoid smoke inhalation.

Home fire

- When moving around the house in a fire, stay close to the ground to avoid the smoke.
- Before opening a door, place the back of your hand against the exit to see if it is hot. This will tell you whether the fire is raging the other side or if it is safe to open the door.

Action if caught in a fire

If you are caught in a fire out of doors, remember that fire is unpredictable and will change direction rapidly according to the wind. Look for shelter in a clear area or among rocks. If possible, take refuge in a pond, lake or river. Breathe air close to the ground to avoid scorching your lungs or inhaling smoke. If you decide to dash to safety, cover or dampen as much of your body as possible.

Outdoor survival

Outdoor survival is essentially about making judicious decisions. If you find yourself exposed in the wilderness, every decision you make should increase your chances of survival, and not put further strains on your resources and health.

In essence, the goals of outdoor survival are fairly simple – food, water, shelter, rescue. Within these goals are a broad range of survival skills and techniques, from building a snow cave through to making an effective camp fire.

In this chapter, we will explore a core range of survival techniques. Ideally, you should familiarize yourself with them before heading out into the wilderness. Learning a complex skill is best not done in the wild! Nevertheless, the most vital survival step you can take is, always, think before you act.

A wilderness expert builds the frame of a camp fire, with tinder at the base, ready to light, and a frame of kindling over it.

Constructing shelters

In a survival situation, you must find or build shelter to protect you from the elements. Never assume that if you are in a warm and dry climate you will need less shelter, or even none at all.

Hot climates

The priority of the hot-weather shelter is to keep the glaring sun off your body. The more you are in direct exposure to the sun, the more you will lose body fluids and become dehydrated. Here a dinghy is converted into a shelter simply by propping it up using the oar, creating a cooling pool of shade beneath.

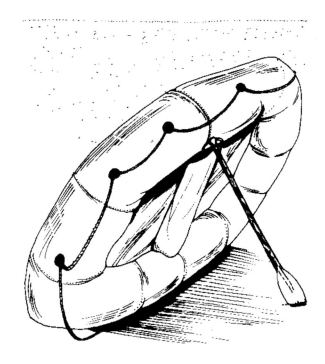

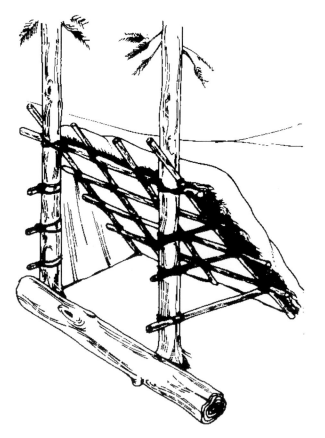

Supports/choosing a site

In hot climates especially, never build more than you have to. The more you exert yourself, the more you will deplete your body's supplies of fluids and essential salts, leading to dehydration. Two trees growing in close proximity have been used to provide the support for a basic shelter. When you have found adequate supplies of water and food, the shelter could be rebuilt as required.

Sheltering from the weather

Shelters should protect you from the main forces of nature: sun, rain, snow and wind. Failure to make a shelter dramatically lowers your chances of survival; making one should be a priority.

Exposure to direct sunlight increases the risk of heatstroke

Exposure to wet and cold increases the risk of hypothermia

A-frame shelter

A-frame shelters are relatively easy to construct, and when properly covered with foliage (plus any other materials, such as a groundsheet), they are warm and weatherproof. The A-frame shown above uses a main horizontal branch that is lashed to two more branches on each end to give extra support, and to which cover can be attached. If you don't want to make end supports, simply prop the horizontal branch between two low tree forks.

SAS tips: where not to build a shelter

SAS soldiers often have to build shelters quickly when on operations behind enemy lines. They know they must avoid the following spots:

- On a hilltop exposed to wind; it will be cold and windy.
- In a valley bottom or deep hollow; they could be damp and are prone to frost at night.
- On a hillside terrace that holds moisture; they are invariably damp.
- On spurs of land that lead to water; they are often routes to animals' watering places.
- Below a tree that contains a bees' or hornets' nest or dead wood. Dead wood could come crashing down on you in the next high wind.
- Under a solitary tree; it can attract lightning.

Types of shelter

If no natural shelter is available, or you want to create a more permanent survival home, then you will need to build your own. The key is to work in harmony with nature, not against it.

Underground shelter

Shelter is extremely important in the desert, both to protect you from heat during the day and to keep you warm during the sometimes intense cold of the night. Natural shelters can be scarce, limited to the shade of cliffs and the lee sides of hills, dunes or rock formations. This underground shelter is ideal for use in arid zones. Note how the airspace created in the top of the shelter provides a layer of still-air insulation that protects against the heat of the sun. Build your shelter to take advantage of a breeze because it will keep you cool. Look out for poisonous snakes and insects who may seek out shady places.

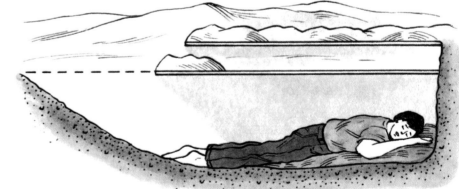

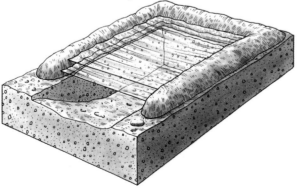

Desert shelter

This simple desert shelter is a more basic version of the one shown above. Follow a tip from the French Foreign Legion and build your shelter during the early morning or at night to conserve valuable energy.

Moulded snow dome

This is quick to construct and requires minimal effort. However, you do need some large cloth or poncho with which to build it. Pile up bark or boughs (not too large) and cover the pile with material. Then cover the material with snow (leaving an entrance gap). When the snow has hardened, remove the brush and cloth. You can make an entrance block by wrapping small sticks inside a piece of cloth and then tying it off. Insulate the shelter's floor with green boughs.

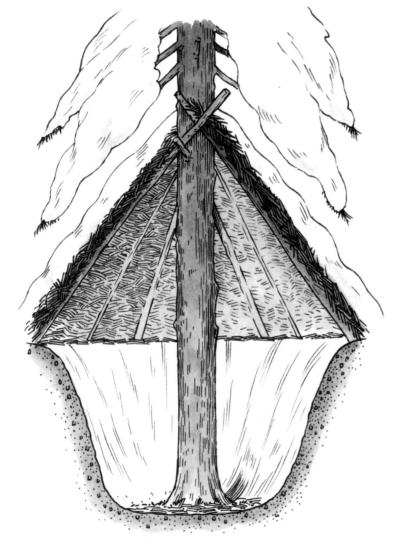

Tree shelter

The tree shelter utilizes the trunk of a tree as a robust central support. Fir trees are ideal for this sort of shelter because the canopy of branches forms a natural barrier, which allows the majority of rainfall to slide right off. Select a large tree with thick lower branches. Dig out a pit around the tree trunk and make a roof with cut branches and boughs. Line the walls and floor with the same materials to insulate on all sides. This is a temporary shelter for use below the tree line. When making this shelter, try not to disturb any snow on the branches.

Materials for an A-frame shelter

You will need the following: one 3.5–5.5m (12–18ft) long sturdy ridge pole with all the branches, projections and rough edges cut off; two bipod poles 2m (7ft) long; materials to cover the frame; branches to form a framework; and material for lashing items together.

Shelters and fire safety

Shelters built from wood and vegetation are very vulnerable to fire. Obey the following precautions:

- Build the shelter upwind of the campfire so that any hot embers and sparks are blown away from the shelter.
- Do not construct a sleeping platform too close to a fire.
- Do not allow a fire to blaze while you are sleeping.
- Never build fires within shelters.
- Ensure that nothing heavy or bulky restricts exit from the shelter, in case you have to abandon the shelter should it catch fire.

Construction

Lash the two bipod poles together at eye-level height and place the ridge pole (with the large end on the ground) into the bipod formed by the poles, and secure. The bipod structure should be at an angle of 90° to the ridge pole, with the bipod poles being spread out to an approximate angle of 60°.

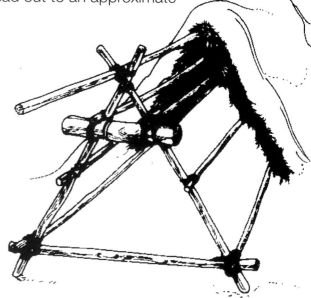

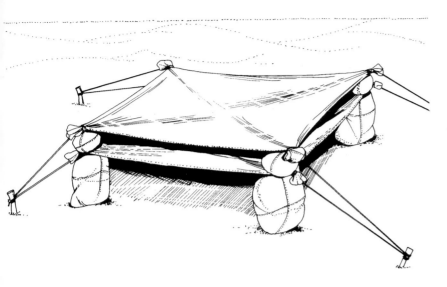

Open shelter

Even though this shelter is open around the sides (something that can be remedied using vegetation, soil or rocks), the double-sheet construction is ideal for providing protection against direct sunlight. You should place the floor of the shelter about 46cm (18in) above or below the desert surface to further increase the cooling effect when inside.

Willow-frame shelter

The willow-frame shelter takes some effort and skill to build, but is worth the investment if you are to spend any length of time in the wilderness. Construct a framework and cover it from the bottom up with boughs. Make sure the stakes are firmly embedded in the ground to prevent wind damage. You can cover the whole shelter with snow in winter.

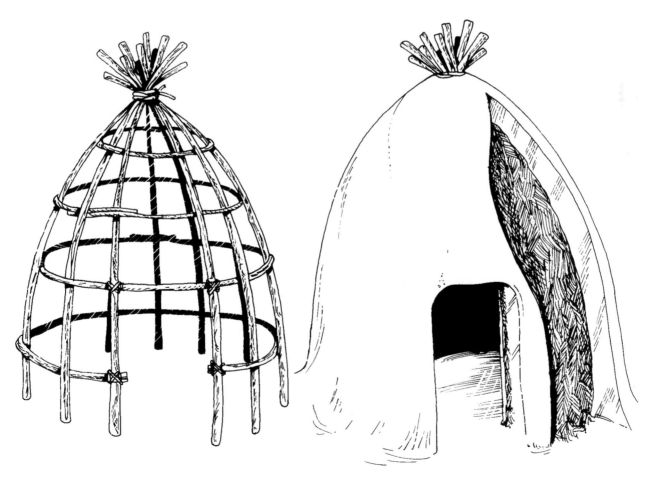

Making fire

Fire is vital to survival. It boosts morale, keeps you warm, dries your clothes, and can be used for signalling and cooking food. It is imperative that you can build, start and maintain a fire.

Hand drill

The hand drill method of starting a fire requires considerable practice to master, and a lot of effort. Maintain a steady rhythm and don't take a break between repetitions, otherwise the wood will cool down and you will have to start over. Note the small pile of tinder placed next to the drill, and ensure that you have ample kindling and fuel to add to your tinder once the fire has started.

Fire plow

The fire plow (left) creates smouldering embers through friction generated by the stick rubbing up and down the groove of the hearth. Make the strokes long and fast, and use strong pressure.

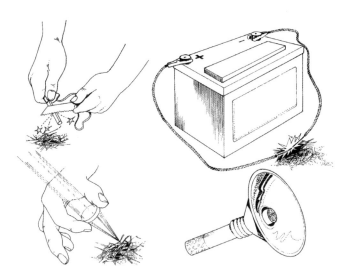

Fire without matches

When people think of starting fires, they often think of hand-drill or bow-drill methods. Yet there are many other techniques, including friction, sparks from a battery, using a magnifying glass and placing tinder in a flashlight reflector.

Bow and drill fire

A bow and drill system works best with woods such as willow, larch, cedar, poplar, sycamore and mulberry. Avoid woods that are very hard or very soft.

A. You need four components – hand socket, bow, drill and hearth

B. Apply even downward pressure while working the bow from side to side

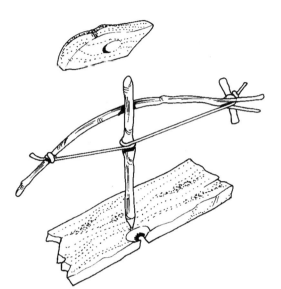

C. The drill will eventually produce coals in the hearth

D. Drop the coals onto a pile of tinder

E. Blow gently to create a flame

Types of fire

There are many different types of fire, all used for specific conditions and purposes. Learn how to site and build them all, in readiness for any kind of survival situation.

Fire pit

The fire pit is a classic soldier's campfire. Fire pits are safe to maintain and can prevent flames from catching on nearby foliage. Additionally, wrapped parcels of food can be placed in the pit for roasting, while the opening above can be used for grilling, boiling and drying.

Tipi fire

This is an excellent type of fire for both cooking and heat, but you need to have ample supplies of fuel to maintain it. Place some tinder in the middle of the fire site and push a stick into the ground, slanting over the tinder. Lean a circle of kindling sticks against the slanting stick, with an opening toward the wind to let in a draft. Light the fire with your back to the wind and feed the fire from the downwind side.

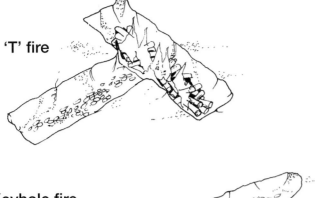

'T' fire

Keyhole fire

Safety fires

These safety night fires are useful constructions which prevents the fire from accidentally spreading. The 'T' fire and keyhole fires are especially useful for cooking.

Special forces fire-building

If the ground is wet or covered in snow, build a fire platform out of green logs or stones – don't make the fire directly on the ground.

- Choose a sheltered site for your fire, as strong winds make fire-starting difficult, or can make an established fire burn too fast.
- If you can't avoid a wind, put your back to it when lighting a fire to shelter the tinder.
- Do not build a fire up against a rock. Instead, build it so that you can sit between the rock and the fire – the rock behind you will reflect heat onto your back. If no 'reflector' is naturally available, build one out of rocks and earth.
- Remember to gather tinder, kindling and fuel in good quantities before attempting to make a flame.
- At night, when you are about to go to sleep, place two large, green logs against the fire to ensure that the fire is kept away from you and your shelter.

Rock fire

In areas of dense, dry bush, it may be a good idea to build your fire within a circle of stones, to keep the flames contained and controlled. The heated rocks can be wrapped and used to warm sleeping bags or even cook food if they are hot enough. This technique is also useful in windy conditions. Blocks of ice or snow can be used in arctic conditions.

Setting up camp

There are many things to consider when choosing a place to set up camp, as well as ensuring your camp is safe, secure, easy to locate and equipped with everything you need for a comfortable stay.

Bracketing

Bracketing is a useful technique for finding your way back to a fixed point, such as your camp or shelter. Take note of features that lie on either side of your chosen destination. When you reach one of the bracketing features, you will know which way to turn next.

Safe camp fires

While you might be tempted to build a shelter close to a tree or other form of natural shelter, bear in mind that you should never build a camp fire closer than 10ft (3m) to either your camp or any natural kindling, such as overhanging branches, foliage or tree stumps.

Deep trench latrine

A trench latrine should be dug to a depth of around 1–2m (3ft 3in–6ft 6in). The cover, made from logs lashed together, should be drawn over the hole when the pit is not in use. Note that body wastes in the pit should be covered over with a thick layer of earth after every visit.

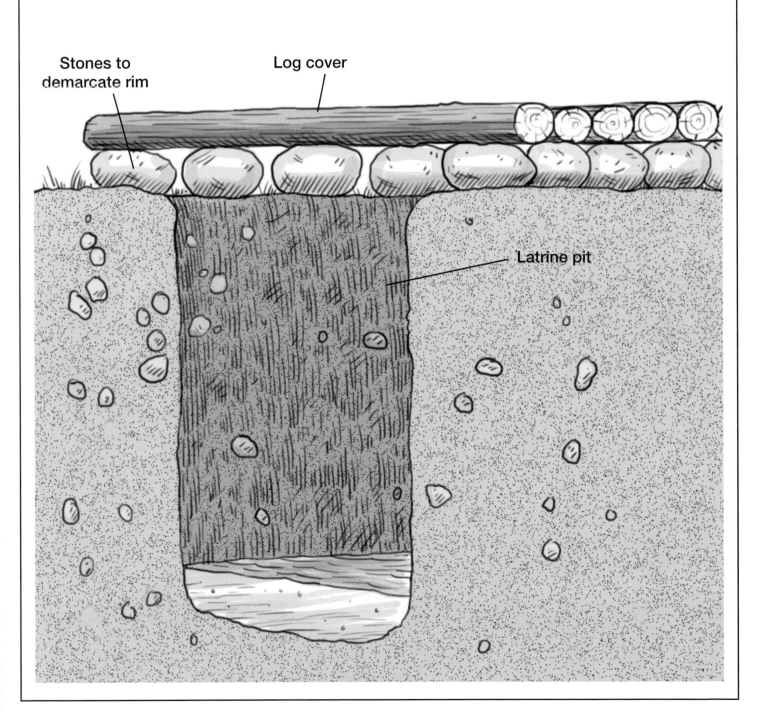

Stones to demarcate rim

Log cover

Latrine pit

Tools

For thousands of years, humankind produced a workable range of tools, using materials such as stone, wood and bone. In a survival situation, there is no reason why you cannot do the same.

Making a wooden bowl

This wooden bowl is made by burning the centre of a block of wood with embers from a fire, then carving out the burnt material to form a receptacle. Soft woods, such as sycamore, birch and hazel, are easy to carve, but they will not last as long as hard woods.

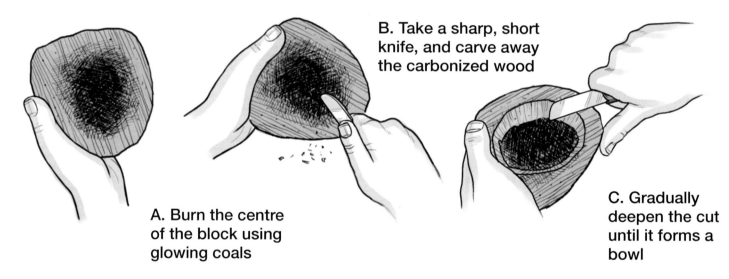

B. Take a sharp, short knife, and carve away the carbonized wood

A. Burn the centre of the block using glowing coals

C. Gradually deepen the cut until it forms a bowl

Improvised axe

This improvised axe is made by binding a chipped stone axe head into a partially split wooden shaft. Once the head is in place, make the structure more solid by wrapping it with a shear lash. For a sharp tool such as an axe, flint, quartz, obsidian, chert or other stones with similar glassy qualities are ideal, as they can be shaped to take a surprisingly sharp edge.

As well as stone, cutting tools can also be made out of bits of junk and refuse. A piece of glass or the lids from tin cans (especially those lids made by can openers which cut inside the rim, rather than beneath), for example, can be inserted into a split stick and tied securely in place to make a sharp knife.

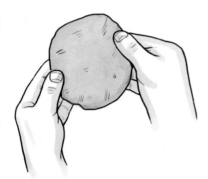

A. First fashion a thick clay base

B. Use coils of clay to create the walls

Making a clay pot

If you find clay of a smooth, non-crumbly consistency, you can use it to make a basic drinking cup or storage pot. Let the pot dry out after construction, then stand it close to a hot fire to harden it. Rubbing pine resin on the inside of the container and allowing it to dry will provide additional waterproofing.

C. Build up the walls to the required height

D. Wetting the clay, smooth out the surfaces of the pot

Bark container

Bark has long been used by traditional communities to manufacture containers, the bark being both flexible and, when properly treated with resin, waterproof. The best type of bark for this use is green birch from young, healthy trees, which is flexible and easily bent into shape.

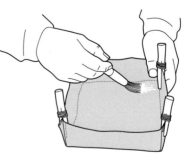

A. Trim the sheet to the required size

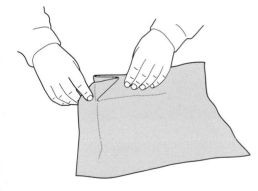

B. Fold up the corners

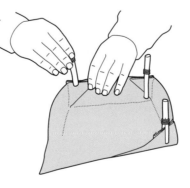

C. Glue with resin and peg into place to set

D. Paint the container with resin to waterproof

Knots and loops

Regardless of your destination, taking a decent rope with you is a sound policy. Modern ropes are made from strong synthetic materials, but natural, improvised ropes can also work well.

Knots

The overhand knot is the most well-known knot, but the other knots shown have wider utility. Reef knots, for example, are used for tying ropes together, and the figure-of-eight loop is a good anchoring knot. All of these knots should be relatively strong, yet easy to tie and untie.

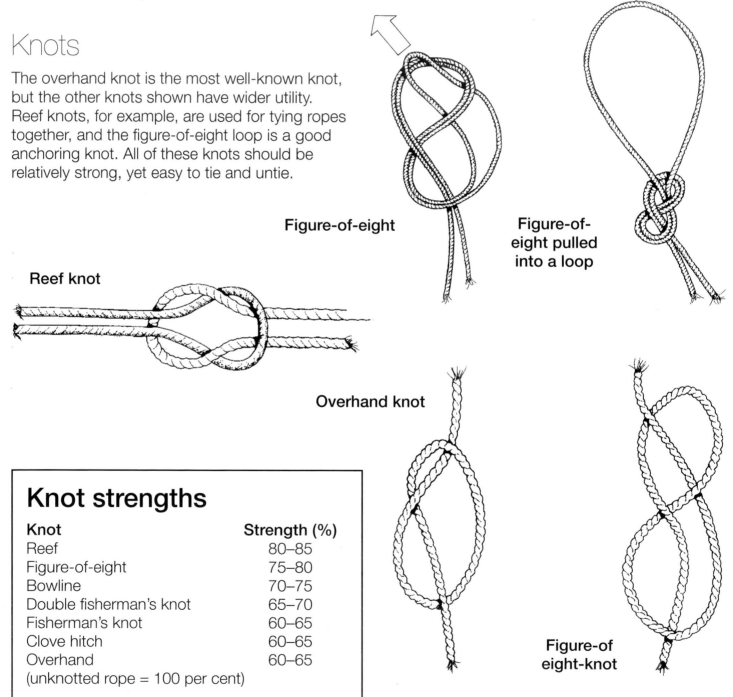

Figure-of-eight

Figure-of-eight pulled into a loop

Reef knot

Overhand knot

Figure-of eight-knot

Knot strengths

Knot	Strength (%)
Reef	80–85
Figure-of-eight	75–80
Bowline	70–75
Double fisherman's knot	65–70
Fisherman's knot	60–65
Clove hitch	60–65
Overhand	60–65
(unknotted rope = 100 per cent)	

Fixed loop

As its name implies, the fixed loop forms a stable, strong loop that is useful for tasks such as carrying logs or similar heavy items. Remember, however, that any knot is only as strong as the rope material itself. Use enough loops for the weight of the object.

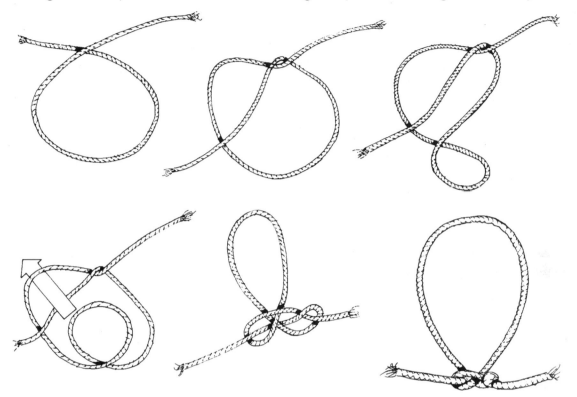

Loop-making

The bowline is used to form a loop at the end of a rope, and is also very quick to untie. The more complex triple bowline loop works as a sling chair or as a carrying harness (with two of the loops worn over the arms).

Triple bowline

Lashes

An essential survival skill, lashings are used for building shelters, equipment racks, rafts and other structures. The most commonly used are the diagonal lash, square lash and shear lash.

Diagonal lash

Used to secure logs at right angles. Tie a clove hitch around the two logs at the point of crossing. Three turns are taken around the two logs (lying beside not on top of each other), then three more crosswise turns over the previous turns. Pull the turns tight. Two frapping (diagonal) turns are made between the two logs, around the lashing turns. The lash is finished with a clove hitch around the same pole the lash was started on.

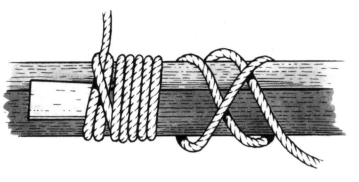

Round lash

Use this to lash two poles together alongside each other. Start with a clove hitch around both poles and then bind the rope around them. End with a clove hitch at the other end of the knot. You can force a wedge down between the lashing and the poles to tighten the lashing.

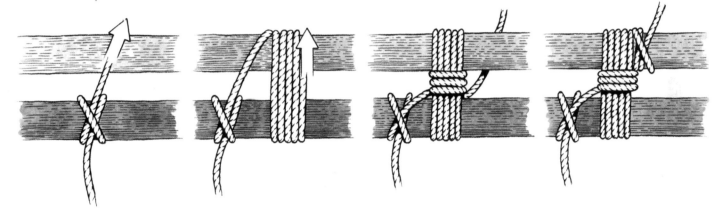

Shear lash

Used for lashing two or more logs together. Place logs side by side and start the lash with a clove hitch on the outer log. Logs are then lashed together with the rope turns loosely laid beside each other. Make frapping turns between each log and finish on the opposite side.

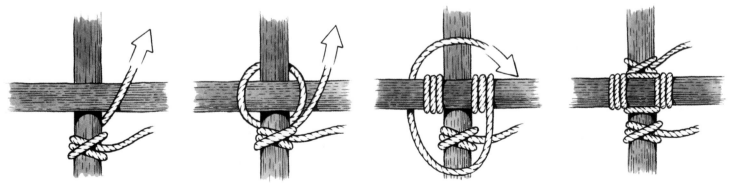

Square lash

Used to secure logs at right angles. Tie a clove hitch under the crosspiece. Take the rope round three or four turns outside of the previous turn. Take the rope over and under both logs, going anti-clockwise. Then make a full turn and end with a clove hitch where the lash was started.

Supplies and storage

The most accessible sources of water in the wilderness are those you have brought with you. There are a variety of containers available. Look for impact-resistant storage with leak-proof tops.

Water-carrying frame

Water is heavy stuff, so strike a balance between taking plenty of fluids with you and managing weight loads. A water-carrying frame can be made by cutting a Y-shaped wooden bough, leaving forks on the uppermost branches of the Y. Using cord, you can strap a water container to the bough, tying the whole structure to your body like a backpack.

Storage containers

It is not only water that should be stored safely in the wilderness. Any foods not already in pest-resistant packaging should be transferred to plastic or glass containers with an air-tight seal. Pack them right to the top to reduce the air content inside.

Water storage

There are many different types of water storage vessel available, from vacuum flasks through to high-capacity military hydration bladders. Remember that water adds considerably to weight, so increases in fluid weight may mean you have to reduce other elements of pack.

A

B

Building a reservoir

A personal water reservoir can be created by digging a large circular hole in the earth (A), and then lining it with a waterproof sheet (B). (The waterproof sheet will prevent the water from dispersing into the earth.) An improvised lid will help keep animals out, slow water loss to evaporation, and also prevent the green bloom of algae which occurs in any water exposed to sunlight for several days. Do not drink water from the reservoir which is over three or four days old, as it will usually have stagnated, breeding germs and bacteria. If you intend to dig a reservoir, ensure that you pack water purification tablets to cleanse water before drinking.

Finding water

Finding water is the most important priority in any survival situation, ranking well above food. The reason for this is simple – without water, we stand a high chance of dying within just a few days.

Dew collector

Dew collectors can be improvised from sheets of plastic, although commercial versions like the one seen here are far more efficient. Condensation gathers on the sides of the collector, eventually running down into the central reservoir. Dew collectors are especially useful as the fluids collected can be safely drunk without being filtered or purified first.

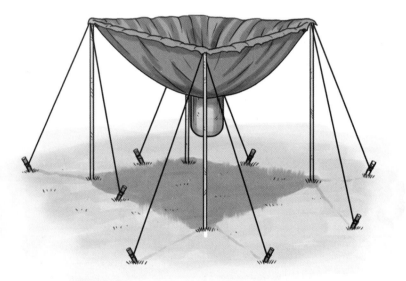

Rain collector

If rainfall is scarce, you want to maximize the amount of water you collect every time there is a downpour. This simple rain collector will channel large volumes of rainwater down into a container, although it will usually need constructing in advance of rainfall beginning. Look for signs such as gathering clouds.

Solar still

The solar still works best if placed in damp ground containing moisture. Dig a hole of about 1m (3ft 3in) across and 60cm (2ft) deep. Place a container in the bottom to catch the water. Insert a tube into the container for drinking. Spread a sheet of plastic over the hole and weigh down the perimeter with heavy stones, leaving no gaps. Put another stone in the middle of the sheet, causing it to dip down over the container. Leave for 24 hours, allowing water vapour to collect.

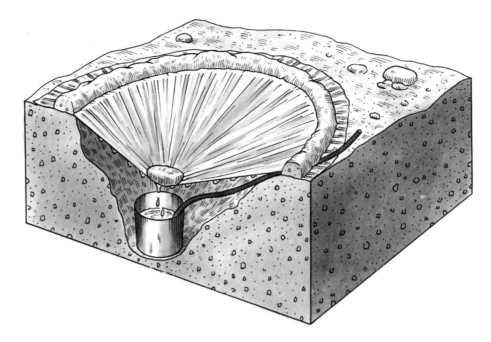

Digging for water

Digging down into damp earth can often lead to significant water deposits. Create a hole several feet deep and about 1ft (30cm) wide and allow the water to seep through the earth, collecting in the hole. Always filter and purify such fluids before you drink them. In flat, agricultural land, look for irrigation ditches between fields.

Transpiration bag

A transpiration bag will typically only produce small amounts of water, but they can be life-saving. Make sure that the plastic bag is tied tight at the neck, and that the bag contains no holes. Any gaps will result in water vapour escaping to the outside rather than condensing inside. Also, never use poisonous vegetation, as this will produce poisonous water.

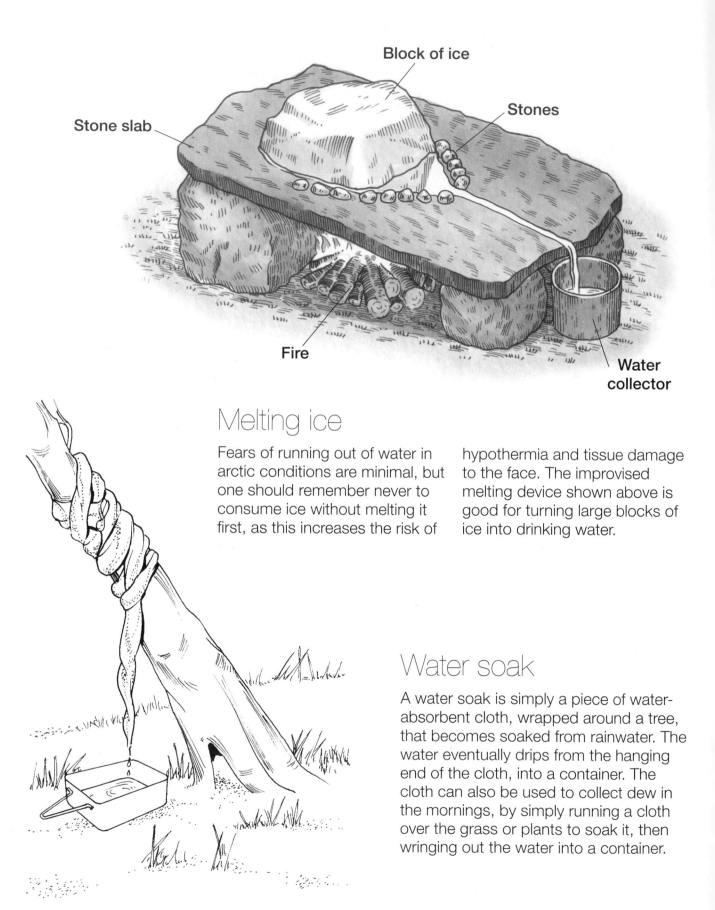

Block of ice

Stones

Stone slab

Fire

Water collector

Melting ice

Fears of running out of water in arctic conditions are minimal, but one should remember never to consume ice without melting it first, as this increases the risk of hypothermia and tissue damage to the face. The improvised melting device shown above is good for turning large blocks of ice into drinking water.

Water soak

A water soak is simply a piece of water-absorbent cloth, wrapped around a tree, that becomes soaked from rainwater. The water eventually drips from the hanging end of the cloth, into a container. The cloth can also be used to collect dew in the mornings, by simply running a cloth over the grass or plants to soak it, then wringing out the water into a container.

Water from a dry riverbed

The US Army's *Survival* manual lists 'the foot of concave banks of dry rivers' as a key place to look for water in arid regions. A trick of African tribesmen is to use a long reed to suck up water from the earth – target the outside bend of the river, which is usually the last place from which the surface water evaporated, or beneath a section heavily shaded by trees. Alternatively, dig down into the earth until you strike water.

Water from a banana tree

Some plants also contain water within themselves. Banana trees are a good source of drinkable water. Cut down the tree at the point shown, and water will fill up the stump. The first three fillings will taste unpleasant, but subsequent water should be drinkable. A banana tree stump can supply enough water for up to four days.

Filtering and purifying

Remember, all water needs to be clean before drinking. Ensure that water is safe to drink by filtering and purifying it carefully, no matter how thirsty you may be and how clean the water looks.

Poisonous water signs

Cattails, rushes and the lack of water flow seen in the image to the left all indicate that the water is stagnant. The foam and bubbles on the surface are the result of decomposition or chemical pollution.

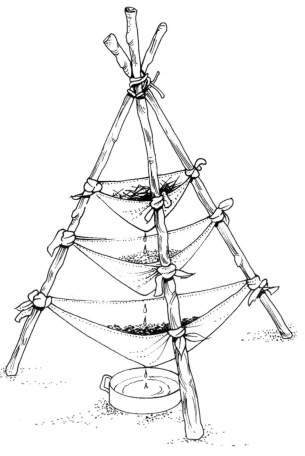

Water filter frame

A water filter frame uses pouches of contrasting natural materials to remove unwanted particles from natural water. Pour the water into the uppermost pouch, and allow it to filter slowly down into the container at the bottom. Filtered water should also be purified with chemicals, such as iodine, potassium permanganate and chlorine (follow instructions carefully for dosage and usage), or by boiling water for a minimum of 10 minutes.

Water filter pump

Portable water purification pumps were first developed by the US military during the 1980s. They are excellent tools to take on survival expeditions or to keep close in case of emergencies, both in the home and outside. Their advantage is that they instantly clean natural water, rendering it drinkable as it passes through in-built filters, without the need for boiling.

Hanging water filter

This hanging water filter works in the same way as the water filter frame, by allowing the water to pass through the layers of filtration. The contrasting layers of rock and sand inside the cloth bag of this water filter will each strip out particles of debris from the water, leaving it clean enough to be bottled for purification.

Fluid loss

Special forces soldiers are taught that our bodies are in a constant process of losing body fluids:

- Urine output – approximately 1.5 litres (2.6 pints) per day.
- Defecation – approximately 0.2 litres (0.4 pints) per day.
- Sweat/skin diffusion – approximately 0.5 litres (0.9 pints) per day.
- Daily average loss in temperate climate, normal levels of exertion – 2–3 litres (3.5–5.3 pints).
- Tropical/desert conditions, heavy exertion – water replacement should be around 19 litres (33.4 pints) per day.

Identifying dangerous plants and fungi

Ingesting certain plants and fungi can be deadly. In a survival situation, you must have a knowledge of the most common types of poisonous plants and fungi so you can diligently avoid them.

Water hemlock

Water hemlock and hemlock are two of the most deadliest plants. Water hemlock has purplish stems; a hollow-chamber rootstalk; small, toothed, lobed leaflets; and clusters of small white flowers. It carries an unpleasant odour and is always found near water. Hemlock is found growing in grassy waste places all over the world.

Destroying angel

Death cap

Poisonous fungi

Fungi can be deadly if you are not sure what you are eating. Both mushrooms shown here are extremely poisonous and even fatal. They share many similarities in appearance to field mushrooms, so if in any doubt, avoid fungi at all costs.

Strychnine plant

The strychnine plant occurs in tropical areas of Asia. It contains a lethal poison that attacks the nervous, muscular and respiratory systems within minutes, the effects increasing cumulatively over time.

Strychnine plant

Foxglove

Universal edibility test

Use this simple US Army test for establishing whether a plant is safe to eat. Note: It CANNOT be applied to fungi.

- Test only one part of the plant at a time.
- Break plant into its base constituents: leaves, stem, roots, etc.
- Smell the plant for strong or acid odours.
- Do not eat for eight hours before starting the test.
- During this period, put a sample of the plant on the inside of your elbow or wrist; 15 minutes is enough time to allow for a reaction.
- During the test period, take nothing orally except pure water and the plant to be tested.
- Select a small portion of the component.
- Before putting it in your mouth, put the plant piece on the outer surface of the lip to test for burning or itching.
- If after three minutes there is no reaction, place it on your tongue; hold for 15 minutes.
- If there is no reaction, chew a piece thoroughly and hold it in your mouth for 15 minutes. DO NOT SWALLOW.
- If there is no irritation whatsoever during this time, swallow the food.
- Wait eight hours. If any ill effects occur, induce vomiting and drink plenty of water.
- If no bad effects occur, eat half a cup of the same plant prepared the same way. Wait another eight hours; if no ill effects are suffered, the plant as prepared is safe to eat.

Foxglove

Poisoning from foxglove, or digitalis, can be serious or even fatal to humans. The leaves, seeds and flowers of the plant are toxic and should never be eaten. Avoid touching foxgloves as it can cause skin irritations. Identify the plant by its tubular flowers, which are often pink or purplish in colour, and its tall, spiky appearance.

Edible plants and fungi

In any prolonged survival emergency, a balanced diet is just as important as in everyday life. Plant foods are amongst the most accessible survival foods, as long as you know which are safe to eat.

Wild fig

Conveniently packaged inside a protective skin, the fruit of figs is safe to eat, nutritious and very tasty. Fig trees can grow in most temperate climates, but fruit trees such as guava, mango, papaya and banana are more common in tropical climates. As a rule, single pieces of fruit hanging from a stem are usually safe to eat.

Oak leaves and acorns

Oak trees are often familiar and can be recognised by their deeply lobed leaves and acorns. They can grow to very large sizes and can provide a generous source of acorns. Shell the acorns and boil in several changes of water (or soak in cold water for several days). Roast the acorns to eat them, or use cooked and ground acorns as a substitute for flour or coffee.

Guidelines for selecting edible fungi

You must be extremely careful selecting fungi for consumption. Use the following SAS tips for when you are collecting fungi.

- Avoid at all costs any fungi with white gills, a cuplike appendage at the base of the stem (volva) and stem rings.
- Avoid any fungi that are decomposing or wormy.
- Unless positively identified, avoid altogether.

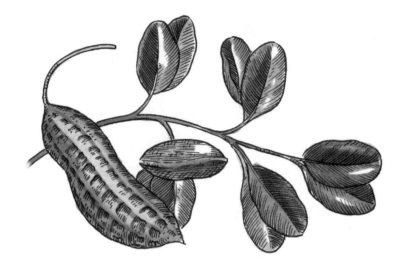

Peanuts

An excellent source of nutritious protein and healthy fats, peanuts are a survivalists' dream food. They can be eaten in the wild straight from their shells, and can be identified by their wrinkled brown pods. Consider taking jars of peanut butter on survival expeditions. It is tasty, high in essential calories, and provides energy boosts.

Stinging nettles

Although they need careful handling to avoid being stung by the fine, irritating hairs that cover the stems and leaves, nettles are excellent sources of nutrition. Recognise them from their oval leaves that are toothed around the edges. Look for young plants measuring 15–20cm/6–8in high, or young offshoots. Boil for at least 15 minutes to destroy the stinging.

Edible fungi

Eating fungi requires great care. Certain varieties are lethally poisonous. The universal edibility test (UET) cannot be applied to fungi and poisons are not killed during cooking. Saying that, if you can identify fungi with certainty, edible forms of fungi are excellent survival foods. They are usually high in vitamins and minerals, and contain more protein than other vegetables. Softer varieties can be eaten raw, or in soups and stews.

A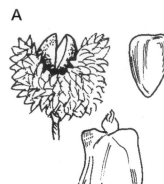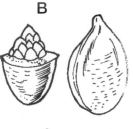

B

C

D

Nuts

A source of protein and healthy fats, nuts are excellent survival foods, many of which can be picked, shelled and eaten straight away. Use a knife, pointed away from your flesh, or heavy object to break open the shells. Beech tree nuts and almonds can be eaten or crushed down to produce a useful oil.

A. Beech nut
B. Almond
C. Walnut
D. Sweet chestnut

Berries

When deciding whether berries are edible, use the following rules: white and yellow berries are usually poisonous; 50 per cent of red berries are poisonous; and blue and black berries are usually safe to eat.

Wild sorrel

Sorrel grows to about 3ft (1m) and can be found in grassy areas and wasteland. Look for long, arrow-shaped leaves and very small, red and green flowers set on spikes. The leaves can be eaten raw, but boiling makes them much more palatable. It also ensures that any germs or bacteria are thoroughly killed off.

Giant puffball

A fungi of a singular appearance, the giant puffball can grow up to 150cm (59in) in diameter, although it is the younger, white puffballs that are edible. The mushrooms have a limited life as they will begin to decompose after a few weeks. Cut open a puffball; if the inside is pure white, it should be safe to eat. If you see any yellowish spores, do not eat the fungi.

Eating seaweed

One plant you should never overlook is seaweed. It is a form of marine algae found on or near ocean shores. There are also some edible freshwater varieties. Seaweed is a valuable source of iodine, other minerals and vitamin C. Large quantities of seaweed in an unaccustomed stomach can produce a severe laxative effect. When gathering seaweeds for food, find living plants attached to rocks or floating free. Seaweed washed onshore for any length of time may be spoiled or decayed.

You can dry freshly harvested seaweeds for later use. Its preparation for eating depends on the type of seaweed. You can dry thin and tender varieties in the sun or over a fire until crisp. Crush and add these to soups or broths. Boil thick, leathery seaweeds for a short time to soften them. Eat them as a vegetable or with other foods. You can eat some varieties raw after testing for edibility.

– US Army, FM 21-76, *Survival*

Eating and cooking plants

Even the most austere desert or polar environment can offer significant plant food sources, with most being rendered edible and much more palatable to eat if they are cooked.

Edible roots

Roots are amongst the plant world's most versatile foodstuff when it comes to cooking. Treat them exactly as you would potatoes – boil, mash or fry them. A particularly good combination is to parboil the root, then roast it on hot stones until soft. Whichever method you choose, make sure that all roots are cooked thoroughly because some contain harmful substances when raw.

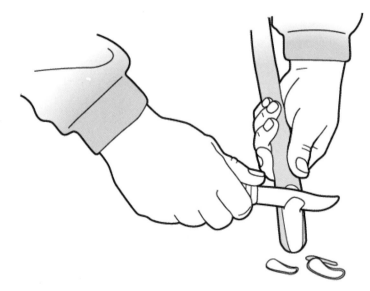

Digging and preparing roots

Roots can be extremely hard to remove from the ground. You can dig up shallow roots by sharpening a stick into a flat, blade-like end. Dig down the sides of the roots, and lever them out with the stick. Wash roots to clean off debris, but try not to peel them – the most nutritious elements are often found in the skin.

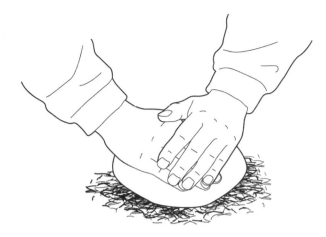

Drinks from plants

As well as being eaten, some plants can make nutritious and tasty drinks. Even the water used for cooking plants will contain many nutrients, and should never be discarded. Use it as the basis for soups or stews, or as the water for tea. Nettles can be used to make a satisfying tea. Add wild herbs, such as mint or chamomile, or berries for extra flavour.

Infusion method (1)

Pine needles can be used for producing drinks through the infusion method. Use two teaspoons of pine needles per cup. The infusion can be drunk while hot or left to cool.

Infusion method (2)

Crush the needles with a large stone to release the flavour. Then, tip the needles into boiling water and allow the mix to sit for up to 10 minutes, stirring occasionally. Finally, strain the fluid through a piece of cloth into a vessel and drink.

Tree bark

The tree bark of several species can provide a fine source of sustenance. Discard the outer bark because it contains high concentrations of tannin, and instead mine the tree for its inner bark. Identify one of the tree species listed below and peel off a section of outer bark near the bottom to reveal sap-rich inner bark (more nutritious sap will be present in the summer than the winter). This bark can be eaten raw or, for easier digestion, boiled. This is a sweet-tasting and delicious meal. When cut into, some trees ooze resin or gum. These sugary substances can be eaten to provide a strong burst of energy. A more refined substance obtained is the syrup obtained from the bark of birch and maple trees. To get useable amounts of sap-like substances, you may have to tap a tree for several days.

Trees with edible inner bark:
Aspens (Populus tremula); birches (Betula); hemlocks (Tsuga); maples (Acer); pines (Pinus); poplars (Populus); slippery elm (Ulmus rubra); willows (Salix).

Types of animal food

Meat is by far the best source of protein and fat, both of which are essential for energy and body warmth. Therefore, it is likely that you will need to kill and eat animals in most survival situations.

Game birds

Game birds such as the ones shown here are desirable birds to hunt because of the quality – and often the quantity – of their meat. However, the easiest birds to catch are birds of prey and carrion birds, mainly because the hunter can easily exploit their attraction to meat.

A. Swan
B. Canada goose
C. Gadwell
D. Mallard
E. Teal

White-tailed deer

Deer are one of the world's most popular animals to hunt, and also one of the most demanding, being highly sensitive to changes in their environment. The white-tailed deer is widely distributed through the Americas, but is also found in northern/eastern Europe and New Zealand.

Cuts of meat from a cow

The diagram illustrates the portions of meat into which a large animal carcass is usually divided. The best steak cuts are the fillet (H), rump (G) and sirloin (F) while the silverside (I) yields good roasting joints. Tougher meats which require slow stewing, roasting or boiling are topside (J), hind flank (P), flank (D), brisket (N), clod (L), chuck and blade (B) and leg (K). Of course, all these parts are perfectly edible in a survival situation. Ensure meat is always cooked well.

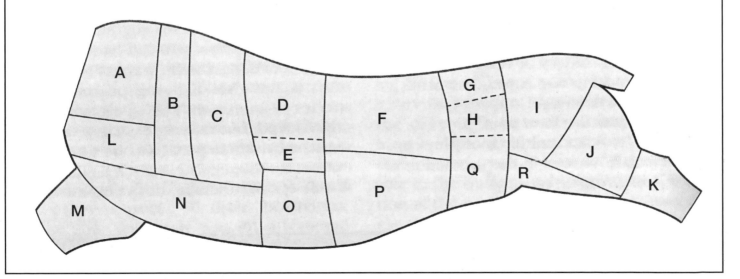

Outdoor survival

Northern caribou

Caribou are precious kills for the hungry hunter. A single large specimen can deliver about 45kg (100lb) of edible meat. The responsible hunter should aim not to waste any meat from a kill, so think carefully about butchery and storage before you hunt such a creature. In a survival situation, make full use of smoking techniques.

Wild pig

Wild pigs provide excellent meat, especially in the winter, when their fat reserves are high. The quantity from a single animal is also generous. But they are very aggressive and difficult to catch, prone to attacking especially if their young are near. Therefore, the best time to hunt is usually when they are asleep.

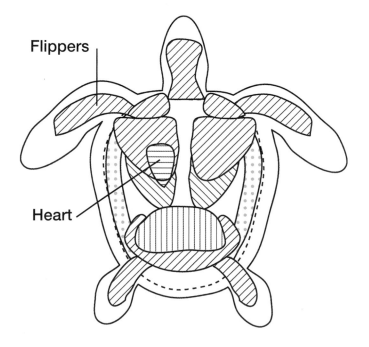

Flippers

Heart

Turtle anatomy

An excellent source of lean protein, turtle meat can be a useful survival food. It can, however, be an effort to catch and dress a turtle. Younger turtles should take less energy to subdue and prepare, as the shell will be thinner and easier to remove. Most of the muscle meat is located around the flippers. The heart can also be eaten, but the rest of the organs should be used for bait only. Females can be identified by their lack of protruding tails (shown here). Look for eggs, which can also be eaten.

Silvery gibbon

Monkeys are eaten by indigenous peoples throughout the tropical world. Tackle only the smaller varieties, though, and never large chimpanzees or gorillas, which can be extremely violent. Spear traps baited with fruit are effective methods with which to trap monkeys, although a wounded monkey can scream at deafening volume.

Bear hunting

Bear hunting is a strictly controlled activity in most countries. When permitted, it should be pursued with extreme caution, as the bear is a dangerous opponent when wounded. Use a powerful rifle of about 7.62mm (0.3in) calibre.

US National Parks advice: Encountering a bear at close range

Bear warning behaviour
If the bear clacks its teeth, sticks out its lips, huffs, woofs or slaps the ground with its paws, it is warning you that it is nervous about your presence and that you are too close. Heed this warning and back away.

Do not panic! Do not run!
Do not run, shout or make sudden movements. You don't want to startle the bear. Do not run! You cannot outrun a bear. Running may trigger a chase response in the bear. Bears in Yellowstone chase down elk calves all the time. You do not want to look like a slow elk calf.

Back away slowly
Immediately but slowly back away. Often times, slowly putting distance between yourself and the bear will defuse the situation.

Prepare your bear spray
Draw your bear spray from the holster, remove the safety tab and prepare to use it if the bear charges.

Should you climb a tree?
Climbing a tree to avoid an attack might be an option but is often impractical. Remember all black bears and most grizzly bears can climb trees (if there is something up the tree that the bear really wants). Running to a tree or frantically climbing a tree may provoke an un-aggressive bear to chase you. Many people have been pulled from trees before they can get high enough to get away. Remember, you have probably not climbed a tree since you were 10 years old – it is harder than you remember. In most cases climbing a tree is a poor decision.

www.Nps.Gov/yell/naturescience/upload/surprise_encounter.Pdf

Gutting a deer

It's the ambitious survivor who will attempt to hunt a large deer, but the massive quantity of meat they provide may well make it worth the effort. However, you must know how to prepare the kill for eating.

Bleeding a deer

Bleeding animal carcasses helps preserve the meat by reducing the fluid content. A deer is bled suspended by its rear legs from a wooden frame, its carotid artery in the neck slashed. The frame must be of very solid construction to take the deer's weight; the bough of a tree may be a more convenient alternative.

Nutritional value of blood

Animal blood is an excellent source of vitamins and minerals, so it should not be wasted. However unpalatable it may seem, in a survival situation consuming animal blood will provide you with essential micronutrients, including iron and salt. It can be added to soups, stews or sauces, or used to make sausages.

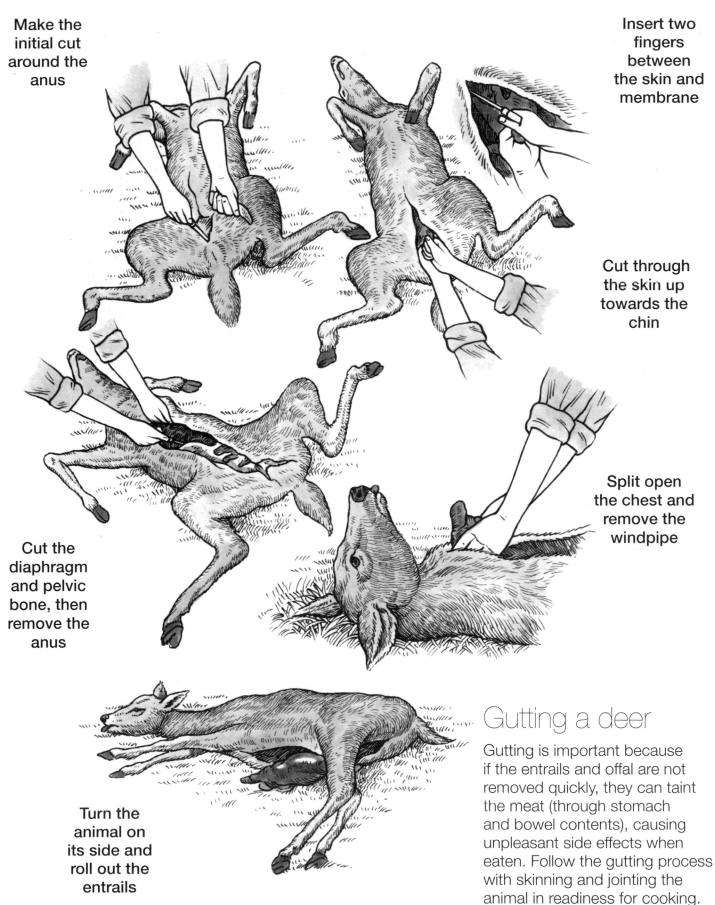

Make the initial cut around the anus

Insert two fingers between the skin and membrane

Cut through the skin up towards the chin

Split open the chest and remove the windpipe

Cut the diaphragm and pelvic bone, then remove the anus

Turn the animal on its side and roll out the entrails

Gutting a deer

Gutting is important because if the entrails and offal are not removed quickly, they can taint the meat (through stomach and bowel contents), causing unpleasant side effects when eaten. Follow the gutting process with skinning and jointing the animal in readiness for cooking.

153

Skinning a rabbit

Rabbits and hares are the all-time survival favourite. Easy to trap, kill and prepare, rabbits are plentiful, make tasty and nutritious wilderness meals, and can be found in most climates.

Dispatching a rabbit

Royal Marines are taught this technique for disatching a rabbit in their basic training. Hang the trapped or injured animal downwards, gripping its back legs. Then, chop hard with the edge of the free hand down into the rabbit's neck. If performed swiftly, the blow will kill the animal instantly.

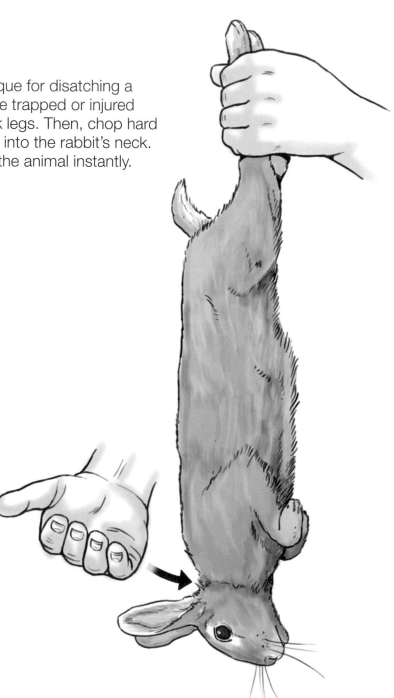

Tools

In addition to any weapons required to kill the animal, there are certain tools that make preparing a carcass much easier. These include:

- A large, very sharp hunting knife to cut through flesh, tendons and bone.
- A small, thin-bladed knife to skin the carcass.
- A sharp, pointed knife to cut meat and trim the carcass.
- A container for collecting and storing blood.
- Containers for edible offal and waste entrails.

In a survival situation, an alternative to a knife is a piece of sharp stone (split slate or flint is particularly good) or pieces of discarded steel (such as tin lids), sharpened to an edge on a rock.

Cut around the skin of the hind legs

Skinning a rabbit

Hanging the rabbit to bleed and skin makes the skinning process easier. When skinned, cut off the rabbit's rear feet and head before cooking. Use the bones for stock as the basis of a rich stew, and keep the skins, which can be sewn together to make warm clothing.

Draw the pelt off the body towards the head

Once near the neck, cut off the forelegs at the knee

Pull the pelt off the rabbit over its body

155

Filleting a fish

Fish can be invaluable for the survivor. There are fish in the seas, rivers, and lakes all over the world. They are an excellent source of protein, vitamins and fats, and can be caught easily.

Fishing as a food source

Fishing is probably a survivalist's best method of acquiring meat foods in a survival situation, as it places low demands on energy for potentially excellent yields. Decent amounts of fish can be caught with little more than a fishing hook, some weights and a fishing line. Setting up a nightline enables you to continue fishing at night. Remember to change the bait regularly and do not leave the line out past daybreak – predators will steal your catch.

Filleting a fish

All but the tiniest fish need to be gutted before cooking.

1. To fillet a fish for cooking, first slit the fish from the anus to just behind the gills and remove the internal organs by pulling them out with your fingers.
2. Wash and clean the flesh, then trim off the fins and tail.
3. Cut down to, but not through, the spine.
4. Cut around the spine, finishing behind the gills on both sides.
5. Insert your thumb along the top of the spine and begin to pull it away from the flesh. The ribs should come out cleanly with the spine.
6. If the flesh does not come away cleanly and you find that you are wasting too much good meat by attempting to fillet the fish, simply gut the fish, wash it thoroughly, and cook whole. When cooked, the meat should fall away from the bones.

Trapping birds

The following are some useful special forces methods for catching birds.

- Bird lime – boil holly leaves and grain in water to produce a glue-like substance. Spread the bird lime along branches commonly used by birds for perching; when the birds land here they will become stuck.
- Put fish hooks into pieces of bird food – remember to secure the fish hook to a branch or other anchor using fishing line.
- Tie straight lengths of fishing line across flight paths commonly taken by birds – flying birds may hit the lines and fall injured to the ground for you to collect.

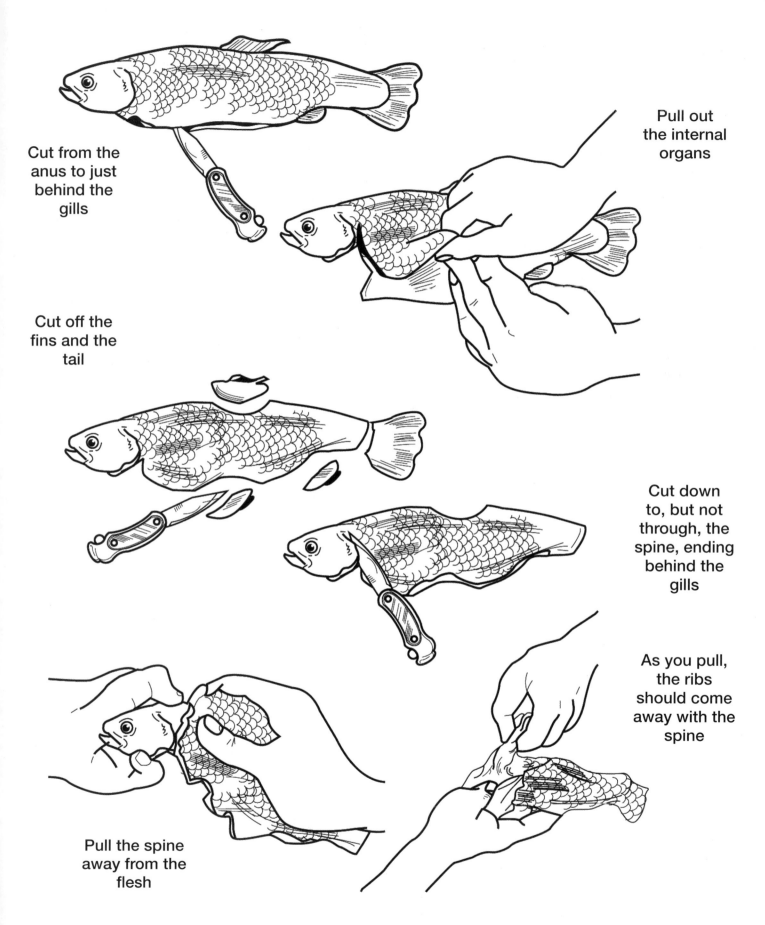

Cut from the anus to just behind the gills

Pull out the internal organs

Cut off the fins and the tail

Cut down to, but not through, the spine, ending behind the gills

As you pull, the ribs should come away with the spine

Pull the spine away from the flesh

Food from insects

As unpalatable as they sound, insects and molluscs can make excellent survival foods, being particularly high in protein. They also have the advantage of being present in large numbers.

Molluscs

Snails make excellent food, but first starve the creatures for 24 hours before eating, to ensure that they excrete their internal poisons. To cook, drop them live into boiling water and cook for 10 minutes. Avoid snails with highly colourful shells, as they might be poisonous.

Edible insects (1)

Below we see three types of termites, all edible, and a grasshopper. All provide decent levels of protein, and the larger termites also offer high levels of fat for their size. Grasshoppers and crickets are a decent food source. Kill with a leafy branch, pull off the wings, antennae and legs, then roast or boil.

'Sexual' termite

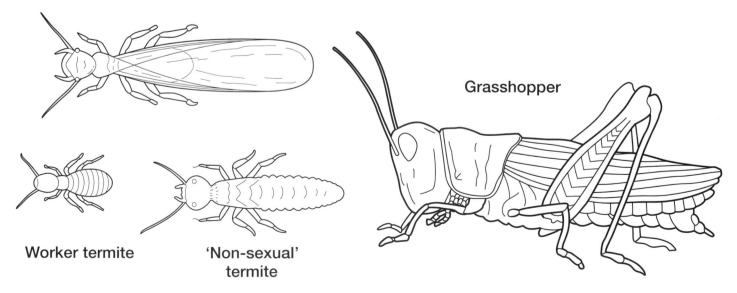

Worker termite

'Non-sexual' termite

Grasshopper

Effort and risk

While insects are often found in large quantities, they also yield very little meat. Some also come with risks. Don't go straight for a bee or wasp nest – instead make a smoky fire directly beneath the nest, which will kill the bees. Never assault a hornets' nest, as hornets are extremely aggressive and possess far more powerful stings than bees or wasps.

Edible insects (2)

Ants, crickets and grasshoppers are all edible, as are bees and wasps, along with their pupae, lava and honey. Prepare the bees for cooking by removing the poison sting and sac, the wings and the legs. Extract the honey, keeping the honeycomb to provide a waterproof wax.

Eating termites

Termites can be collected in quite large volumes by pushing a long, thin stick into the side of a mud termite nest, and withdrawing it – aggressive termites will have their jaws clamped on the stick. Alternatively, smash off a piece of the nest with a stone and drop it into water, letting the termites float out to the surface for collection. They are tasty and nutritious creatures and can be eaten cooked by almost any method. To eat them, remove the wings and legs first.

Cooking food

Cooking your kill makes any survival eating experience safer and more palatable. In fact, sitting down to enjoy the fruits of your labour can be the most satisfying part of a wilderness trip.

Roasting spit

Here we see a chicken cooked on a traditional roasting spit. Choose a green wood for the spit, as this is less likely to catch fire. Note that the mount for the spit is made simply from two forked branches, stuck securely into the ground. A fire trench is made here simply by folding back the sod.

Pan support

Shown here is a simple system for hanging a pan directly over a fire, by using a long branch and two rocks: one to hold the end of the branch down, the other as a support to control the height of the pan over the fire. Remember that with any metallic pan the handle will become very hot during the cooking time, so have a thick cloth at the ready to lift it off.

Cooking table

It is useful to note which cuts of meat are best suited to a certain cooking method. Otherwise you might end up frying tough cuts that are then chewy and unpalatable, while those same cuts would have made a delicious stew. Note that some cuts benefit from aging, while others should be eaten straight away.

Animal part	Information
Liver	An excellent source of micronutrients, the liver should be eaten as soon as possible. Avoid eating if it is mottled or covered in white spots. It can be eaten raw or fried quickly.
Kidneys	Kidneys are very nutritious. Eat them quickly, cooking them with herbs or adding them to soups or stews.
Heart	Roast the heart or add it to stews. Eat it soon after the animal is killed.
Stomach (tripe)	A delicacy in some European countries, tripe should be cooked with herbs. Eat it soon after the animal is killed.
Tail, feet, bones and head	Boil these up for stock, which can be used for soups, stews or even as a nutritious drink. The cheeks and tongue can both be eaten, but remove the tongue's skin first.
Fast-cooked meat	Cuts from the hind, such as fillet, sirloin and rump steaks, can be preserved to eat after stocks of offal have gone. They require little cooking and can also be dried in strips.
Slow-cooked meat	Forequarter meat is tougher and benefits from slower cooking. It includes leg meat, such as topside, silverside and shin, flank or brisket from the belly, neck, chuck or rib meat.

Hot plate

A basic but efficient griddle can be produced with just a couple of wooden slabs and a metal plate. Leave a large air gap between the fire and the plate, and you can restrict the air flow to the fire with additional logs to control the temperature of the hot plate for grilling foods.

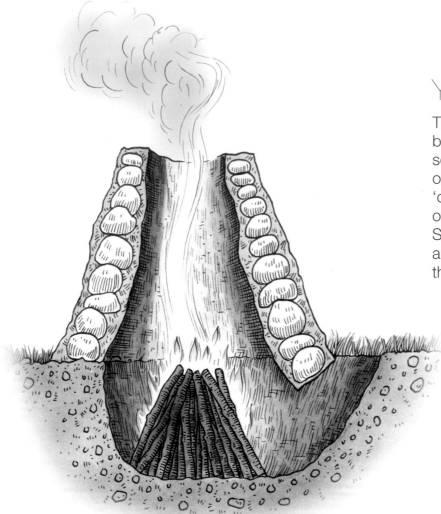

Yukon stove

The Yukon stove is a good structure to build if you intend to stay in one place for some time. Cook over the open chimney or by inserting wrapped foods into the 'oven' at the bottom. The stove is built over a ditch which contains the fire. Stones and mud keep the stove stable and the heat intense. Note the channel at the side, used to control air flow.

Hobo stove

The hobo stove is a classic special forces method of improvised cooking. If you can acquire one, a simple oil drum can be converted into a stove. Cut a fuel port and ventilation holes in the bottom, as well as one in the side. The top of the drum can be used for frying. As with the Yukon stove, place wrapped foods inside the stove for roasting.

Baking in mud

Baking in mud is a gentle way of cooking fish and other meats. The outer layers of mud and leaves protect the food from burning, even when placed in the fire. When it burns down, the food inside should be cooked.

Wrap the fish in a thick layer of green leaves

Tie the leaves in place with cordage

Cover the parcel with a thick layer of mud or soil

Make a large fire on and around the parcel and let it burn down

Cooking on hot rocks

Heated rocks can make a grill surface for cooking strips of fish, meat and vegetables. Make an even pile of large, smooth rocks (A). Pile twigs and branches on top of the rocks to build a substantial fire, then let it burn down (B). Brush the remaining embers from the rocks using branches (C). Lay the food directly onto the rocks to cook (D). This method is especilly good for thin strips of food, which will cook quite quickly and taste very good. While the rocks will retain their heat for some time, they will not cook thick pieces of meat or fish adequately (however rare you like your meat, do not forget that this is a survival situation).

A

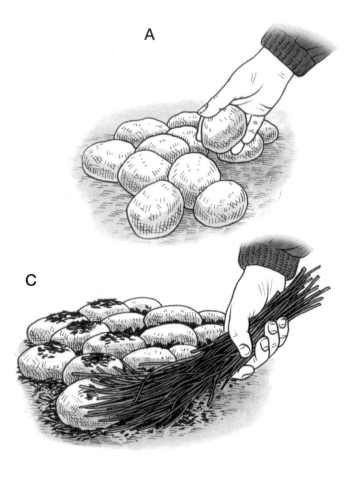

C

B

D

Survival cooking

Note that cooking in a survival situation is not the same as preparing food that you have purchased from a store or butcher's shop. Meat or fish should never be served rare, and if you have any lingering doubts about food, extend the cooking time until you are sure it is thoroughly cooked and that any remaining bacteria is destroyed. Never eat rabbits with lumps or weeping eyes for fear of myxomatosis, which cannot be killed by cooking, and never eat fish that you found already dead.

Mud oven

If you have a large, fireproof pot – ideally one with a lid – a mud oven can be built as an ideal survival roasting machine. Dig a narrow trench in the ground and lay a fireproof pot along it, leaving enough room for fuel for a fire. Look for a pot with a lid to act as the oven door. Jam a stick into the ground at the base of the pot.

A

B

Cover the body of the pot with a thick layer of soil. Using a combination of wet and dry soil will make this easier to build. The wet mud will soon dry out and create a clay-like oven that will insulate the pot. When you have finished covering the pot, remove the stick. The remaining hole acts as a chimney. The mud oven is useful for longer wilderness trips and can even be constructed in the garden.

Light a fire beneath the pot, leaving sufficient room for this to be done, and for spent fuel to be replaced at a later stage. Fit the lid in place and hold it on with a stick to stop heat escaping. The fire will heat the interior of the pot to ovenlike temperatures. It can now be used to cook meat, fish and vegetables. The insulation means that the oven will stay hot for a longer time, meaning that larger quantities of food can be cooked together.

C

Preserving meat

If you kill more animals than you can eat, food will need to be stored for later consumption. Freezing meat is ideal, but if you are unable to access equipment, preserve the meat by other methods.

Smoking

A smoking frame (left) lets the smoke move evenly around the food. Use green leaves on the fire to generate a thick smoke, but do not use conifer wood – it ruins the flavour.

Carrying a carcass

For carrying a heavy carcass over long distances, try using the method pictured here. Tie the torso as close to the pole as possible to reduce swinging effects.

Drying frame

Make a simple drying frame for air-drying meats and vegetables, but watch it closely in case animals attempt to steal your food. Cut the meat into long, thin strips and hang them to dry in sunlight or by fire. In this state, the meat will last a long time. You can chew on them or cook them in water to rehydrate them.

Length of storage

The most effective way to preserve food is by keeping it cool. The sooner you get your meat into a fridge or freezer, the longer it will last. The following storage times are based on a constant temperature of below 32°F (0°C).

Product	Length of recommended storage
Steaks and chops	Four to six months
Ground beef, lamb or pork	Two to three months
Poultry (legs, thighs, wings)	Six to nine months
Oily fish (salmon, tuna)	Two to three months
White fish (cod, haddock)	Four to six months
Cooked meats	Two to three months

Storing a kill

An animal which is caught and killed should be butchered immediately if possible. If this is not an option (perhaps there are predators in the area), then it can be placed in a tree to hide or protect it temporarily from ground-dewlling predators. Do not throw the animal up into the tree, as you will need to climb up to retrieve it afterwards. While this method cannot protect the carcass from all predators, it significantly reduces the risk of your hard work in trapping and bringing down the animal being wasted.

Hunting and trapping

For some, the idea of killing wild creatures is unsettling. There is no hiding the fact that hunting is a violent pursuit, aimed at transforming a healthy animal into a dead one ready to eat. Yet survival situations often necessitate that people become hunters if they are to live.

Those unfamiliar with hunting, however, can underestimate just how hard it is to track, stalk and kill prey, or to trap it. Animals have superb senses and have been using them to survive since the day they were born.

This chapter, therefore, looks at a broad range of hunting options and tools, from hunting with a rifle through to trapping with a snare. In the wilderness, you have to use every advantage at your disposal just to secure one kill.

A rifle-armed hunter checks the ground for signs of his prey. During a hunt, most time will be spent just in the process of tracking and stalking.

Making and using hunting weapons

The most important considerations are to choose the right weapon for your prey, use that weapon fluently and maintain it in good condition. In a survival situation, your weapon can save your life.

Steady shot

A monopod can provide a useful frontal support for a rifle when taking a standing shot. Monopods can be purpose designed or improvised in a survival situation by fashioning a support from branches tethered with rope. Ensure the monopod is set on firm, non-slip ground.

Modern slingshot

This modern catapult features a useful sight (the two graduated prongs extending inwards from the catapult arms) and stabilizers to balance the weapon in the hand. With regular practice, such a slingshot can hit and kill suitable prey at distances of 30m (100ft) and more.

Making a bow and arrow

Constructing a recurve bow takes practice and a high-quality piece of wood. Suitable woods for making a bow include yew, red oak and osage. Select a piece of wood without any weak points, such as prominent knots.

A good bow is the result of many hours of work. You can construct a suitable short-term bow fairly easily. When it loses its spring or breaks, you can replace it.

Select a hardwood stick about 1m (3ft 3in) long that is free of knots or limbs. Carefully scrape the large end down until it has the same pull as the small end. Close examination will show the natural curve of the stick. Always scrape from the side that faces you, or the bow will break the first time you pull it. Dead, dry wood is preferable to green wood. To increase the pull, lash a second bow to the first, front to front, forming an

'X' when viewed from the side. Attach the tips of the bows with cordage and only use a bowstring on one bow.

Select your arrows from the straightest dry sticks available. The arrows should be about half as long as the bow. Scrape each shaft smooth all around. You will need to straighten the shaft. You can bend an arrow straight by heating the shaft over hot coals, but do not allow it to scorch or burn. Hold the shaft straight until it cools.

You can make arrowheads from bone, glass, metal or pieces of rock. You can also sharpen and fire-harden the end of the shaft. You must notch the ends of the arrows for the bowstring. Cut or file the notch; do not split it. Fletching (adding feathers to the notched end of an arrow) improves its flight characteristics, but is not necessary on a field-expedient arrow.

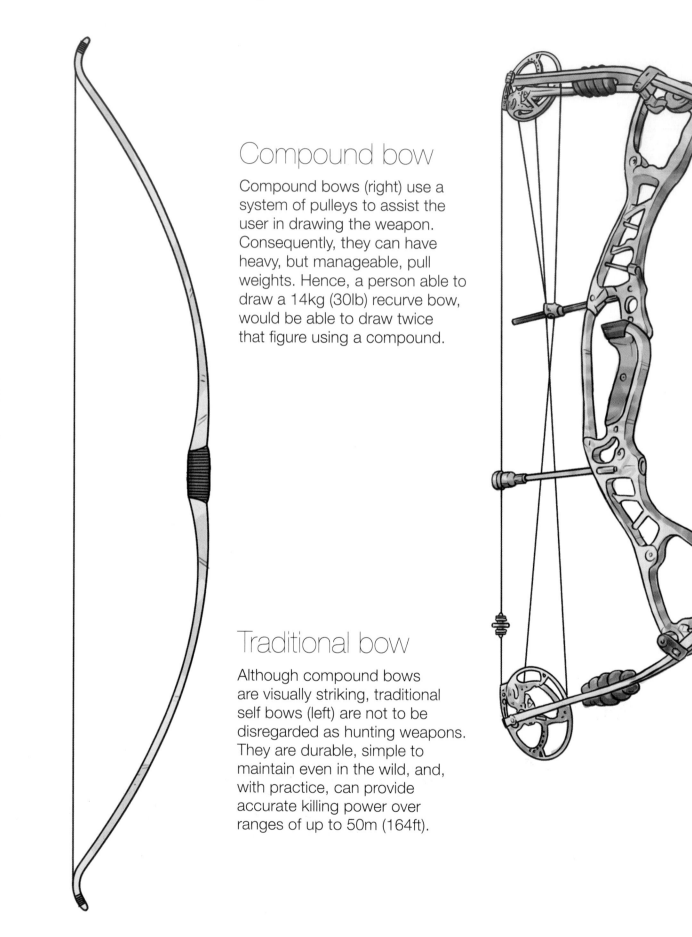

Compound bow

Compound bows (right) use a system of pulleys to assist the user in drawing the weapon. Consequently, they can have heavy, but manageable, pull weights. Hence, a person able to draw a 14kg (30lb) recurve bow, would be able to draw twice that figure using a compound.

Traditional bow

Although compound bows are visually striking, traditional self bows (left) are not to be disregarded as hunting weapons. They are durable, simple to maintain even in the wild, and, with practice, can provide accurate killing power over ranges of up to 50m (164ft).

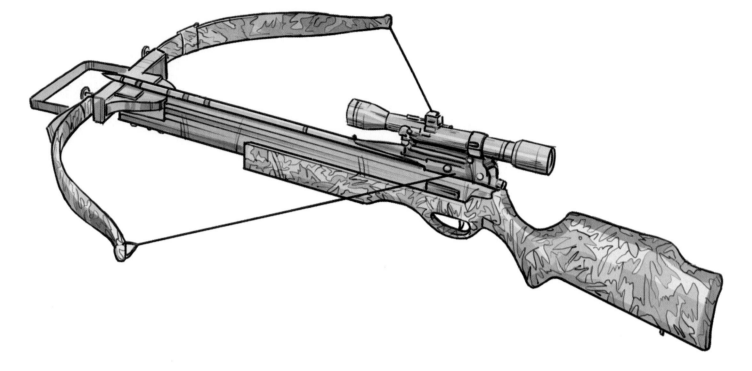

Crossbow

Crossbows are an alternative to the bow and arrow, and are typically easier to master as they are held rather like a firearm and, once cocked, require little physical control to aim and release. Modern varieties can be fitted with optical sights and are available in both recurve and compound varieties.

Slingshot

The slingshot – or sling as it is more commonly known in the UK – is a classic and very ancient hunting weapon. It is also cheap, convenient and almost noiseless in use, ideal for situations where gunshot will startle potential prey. Select small, smooth stones about 2–3cm (0.8–1.1in) across as ammunition and use for ranges of up to 20m (65ft).

173

Firearms

Firearms remain ideal survival equipment because centuries of weapons evolution has made them into near-perfect hunting tools, especially for taking down large prey at safe distances.

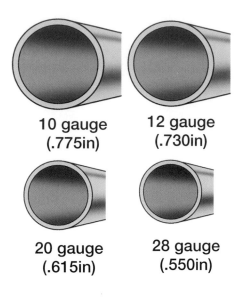

| 10 gauge (.775in) | 12 gauge (.730in) |
| 20 gauge (.615in) | 28 gauge (.550in) |

Shotgun gauge

Gauge is a rather archaic measure based on the weight of the largest lead ball that will fit in a weapon's bore. The smaller the gauge number, the bigger the gun.

Types of round

The right ammunition for hunting is partly a matter of choice and the type of prey you will be hunting. Here we see a variety of ammunition types, including two pistol rounds (9mm and .44 Magnum) two rifle cartridges (7.62mm and 5.56mm) and a shotgun shell. The pistol cartridges have little utility in a hunting setting.

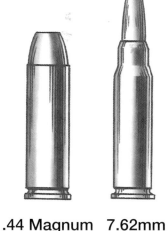

9mm   .44 Magnum   7.62mm   5.56mm   12-gauge shotgun shell

Pre-charged air rifle

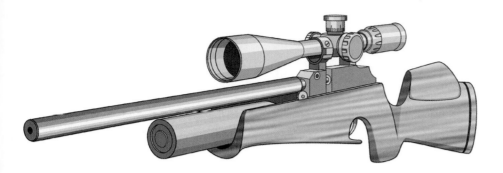

This pre-charged air rifle has a state-of-the-art design. The gas cylinder beneath the free-floating barrel provides consistent power delivery and a multi-shot magazine allows for shots at multiple targets. The stock is contoured for a precise fit against the cheek.

Spring gun

The advantage of 'break-barrel' weapons is that they are inexpensive compared to other types of air rifle, but also robust and reliable. Here is the classic break-barrel air rifle design, the rear of the barrel visible beneath the simple adjustable rear sight above. Don't over-oil the pellet aperture – just a thin film around the moving parts will suffice.

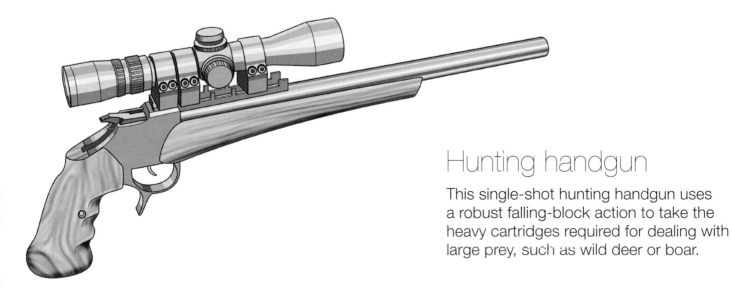

Hunting handgun

This single-shot hunting handgun uses a robust falling-block action to take the heavy cartridges required for dealing with large prey, such as wild deer or boar.

M40A1 rifle

The M40 rifle and its subsequent variants have been the standard sniper weapons of the US Marine Corps since the 1960s and 1970s. Many of its more modern features, such as a weather-resistant fibreglass stock, are also found on hunting rifles. Typical of bolt-action rifles, it is generally rugged, reliable and outstandingly accurate up to a mile.

Lever-action rifle

An alternative option for rifle configuration is the lever action, most famously embodied in the Winchester/Henry series of rifles. Lever-action rifles are extremely robust field guns with a high ammunition capacity in the under-barrel magazine. They are best suited to standing or kneeling shooting, as reloading in the prone position can be awkward.

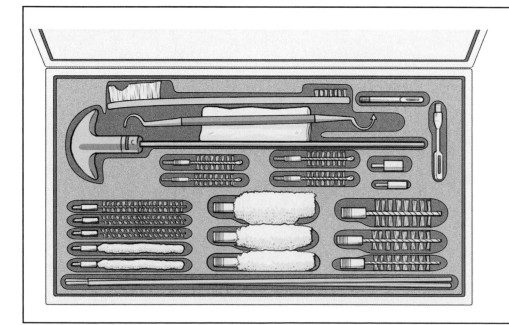

Gun cleaning kit

A good gun-cleaning kit should contain everything you need to keep a weapon in working order. The phosphor bronze brushes are particularly useful for cleaning off stubborn propellant and lead deposits from the inside of the gun's barrel. You might also use a pull-through cleaning device to draw through the barrel of your rifle for a quick clean in the field.

Double-barrelled shotgun

This modern over-and-under 12-gauge shotgun has an adjustable comb on the stock, a rubber recoil pad for comfortable shooting and an automatic ejection system. The shotgun is unsurpassed as a weapon for tackling moving game.

Side-by-side shotgun

Shotguns are smoothbore firearms with a unique type of ammunition. Side-by-side shotguns have been traditionally popular for field shooting. This gun features double triggers, allowing the user to select which barrel is fired. Each barrel will be choked differently at the muzzle, and therefore will have different performance characteristics over range.

Diseased animals

Soldiers and survivalists must stay healthy in the field, hence they avoid eating any diseased animal if at all possible. Signs of illness include problems in movement, disturbed behaviour, poor-quality fur or skin, a distorted or discoloured head, isolation from a herd or pack and enlarged lymph nodes in the cheeks (relevant only to larger animals, such as deer). If you are forced to eat such animals, boil the meat thoroughly and cover any cut or sore on your own body when preparing the meat.

Sign

Sign – indication of the recent presence of birds or animals – is the element that dictates tracking, enabling you to piece together an animal's movement, then follow the track to make your kill.

Displacement of sign

When quarry moves from one type of surface to another, it leaves signs of its movement, such as displacement (shown right), watery prints on rocks, muddy marks on vegetation and sandy residue on grass. These signs can be used to track animals to their present location or to choose a convenient place to wait for the animal along one of its trails.

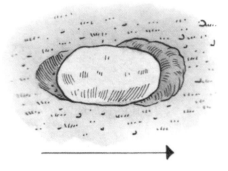

Reading sign

A combination of sign can let you know that an animal is close by. Its territorial area, its dietary preferences and even the species (if a print is clear) can be discerned with practice. Three pieces of linked sign will give you a useful direction of travel.

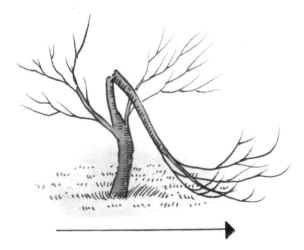

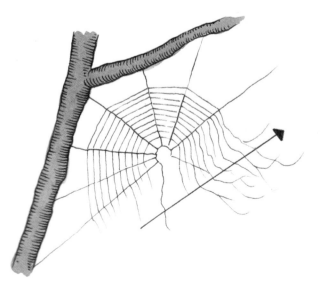

Pointing the way

Some sign can literally point the direction taken by the animal. Hoof or paw prints will be heading in the direction taken. Additional sign include broken branches, which will show the direction the animal was moving when they were broken. Incomplete cobwebs or broken foliage act as indicators in the same way.

Time

Remember that sign is affected by the passage of time. The edge of a print will become more crumbly over time, filling up with dirt and leaves. Water displacement will dry and tracks in dry, sandy soil will soon disappear.

Vegetation

Flattened grass usually returns to the vertical within three to four hours of being trampled. If the entrance to a den or burrow is overgrown, it is a good indication that it is no longer occupied by an animal.

Other sign

When hunting, as well as visual sign, strain every sense to pick up indicators of animal life or movement. For example, sounds of birds taking flight could mean they have been disturbed by an animal passing close by.

Shot placement on a deer

Accurate shot placement is critical to bring down a deer effectively. Generally, always aim for the shoulder area.

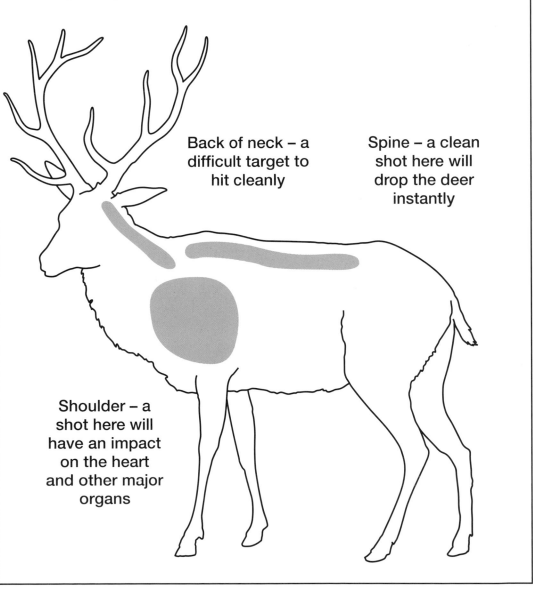

Back of neck – a difficult target to hit cleanly

Spine – a clean shot here will drop the deer instantly

Shoulder – a shot here will have an impact on the heart and other major organs

Animal tracks

Tracks are the sign par excellence. After all, you might successfully follow sign to find an animal, only to discover that it is not what you wished to hunt – recognizing tracks can prevent this.

Tracks

Here are some typical animal tracks which might be encountered in the wilderness. Note that the value of tracks varies with their age. Look for indicators that the tracks are fresh, as well as other sign, to avoid wasting time and energy on a redundant trail. Although it might be tempting to follow any trail, consider your equipment. If it is not suitable for the prey you are hunting, then keep looking.

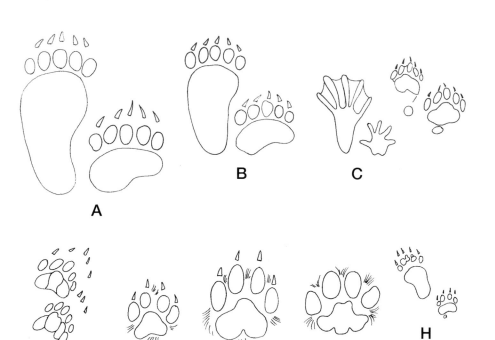

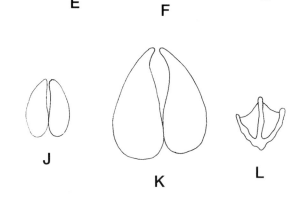

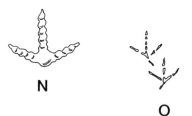

A. Grizzly bear
B. Black bear
C. Beaver
D. Badger
E. Dog
F. Wolf
G. Cougar
H. Squirrel
I. Hare
J. Deer
K. Moose
L. Goose
M. Duck
N. Wild turkey
O. Shore birds

Droppings

Tracks are often accompanied by animal droppings. These can be very useful to gauge the dirrection of the trail, as well as its age. Droppings that have been recently passed retain heat and scent, becoming dry and scentless with age.

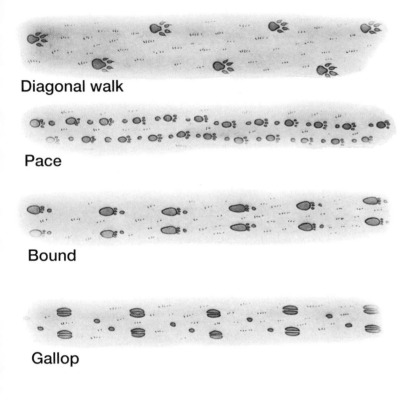

Diagonal walk

Pace

Bound

Gallop

Animal gait

To the left are the four main types of animal gait. It is not only the shape of tracks that provides you with information, but also the arrangement of the tracks in relation to each other. Different animals have different gaits – compare the bear at the top with the rabbit at the bottom.

Tracking

Deer
Deer often strip bark, twigs and buds. In winter, bark is chewed off in patches. In summer, it is taken off in long strips. Deer may also scratch their antlers against trees to remove their velvet. Branches or saplings trimmed off at a level height often indicate the presence of grazing deer.

Rabbits
Rabbits tend to stay close to their warrens. They are most active in the early morning and at night, though in darker climes they can remain active throughout the day. Rabbits may change fur colour in the winter.

Squirrels
Piles of discarded nutshells beneath a tree might indicate a squirrel's nest above. Squirrels also strip patches of bark and dig up small patches of ground for shoots.

Wild pigs
Wild pigs root through the earth and turn over large patches of soil. They also bathe in muddy hollows. If the splashes of water over the side of the hole appear fresh, then the pig may have visited recently.

Stalking

Once you make visual contact with an animal, you then have to move into range to deploy your weapon. Keep downwind of the prey, move as silently as possible, and use all available cover.

Stalking

When stalking an animal, make no abrupt movements and keep the body profile as low as possible. Keep balanced to ensure that you can freeze at any point in the stalk if the animal spots you. Jerking quickly to prevent yourself from falling might startle the animal.

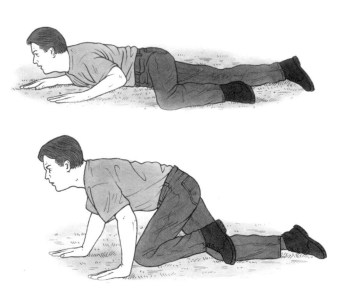

Natural camouflage

Animals can recognize human shape or unnatural colours and textures, and may instinctively run from them. Hiding among foliage is excellent for breaking up body shape. You could also add pieces of vegetation or strips of natural coloured fabric to your clothing, headgear and equipment to break up smooth outlines.

Team hunting

Hunting as a team throws up issues when it comes to stalking, although it is advised if you are in a remote or unfamiliar region. Each member of the team will need to consider the position of his team mates, as well as be and alert for any wildlife while staying silent himself.

Blending in

Here the shapes of the trees are mirrored by the hunter, making him less visible. If you choose not to wear specialist camouflage, opt for natural, muted shades of clothing such as khaki, browns or greys. Never wear bright colours not found in nature.

Upright stalking

Take steps about half your normal stride when stalking in the upright position. Such strides help you to maintain your balance. You should be able to stop at any point in that movement and hold that position as long as necessary. Curl the toes up out of the way when stepping down so the outside edge of the ball of the foot touches the ground. Feel for sticks and twigs that may snap when you place your weight on them. If you start to step on one, lift your foot and move it. After making contact with the outside edge of the ball of your foot, roll to the inside ball of your foot, place your heel down, followed by your toes. Then gradually shift your weight forward to the front foot. Lift the back foot to about knee height and start the process over again. Keep your hands and arms close to your body and avoid waving them about or hitting vegetation. When moving in a crouch, you gain extra support by placing your hands on your knees. One step usually takes one minute to complete, but the time it takes will depend on the situation.

– US Army, FM 3-05.70, *Survival* (2002)

Low movement

Crawling

Crawl on your hands and knees when the vegetation is too low to allow you to walk upright without being seen. Move one limb at a time and be sure to set it down softly, feeling for anything that may snap and make noise. Be careful that your toes and heels do not catch on vegetation.

Prone stalking

To stalk in the prone position, you do a low, modified push-up on your hands and toes, moving yourself forward slightly, and then lowering yourself again slowly. Avoid dragging and scraping along the ground as this makes excessive noise and leaves large trails for trackers to follow.

– US Army, FM 3-05.70, *Survival* (2002)

Dead ground

When stalking prey, use as much natural cover as the ground affords. The hunter depicted below is using a deep gulley to move up close to a deer, although the animal's posture suggests it might be alert to sound and smell warnings already. If you fear your prey might suddenly bolt, stay as still as you can and wait it out. There is a chance the animal will relax and look away, in which case you can continue the hunt.

Moving undetected

The basic principle of stalking is to stay low at all times, either in a crouch or a crawl. Practice crawling before you go out into the field, and make sure that the rifle muzzle stays clear of the dirt. It is a wise idea to practice without holding a rifle or any gear until you feel that you can move more assuredly and fluidly. Do not forget to keep your rifle in line with your body whenever possible.

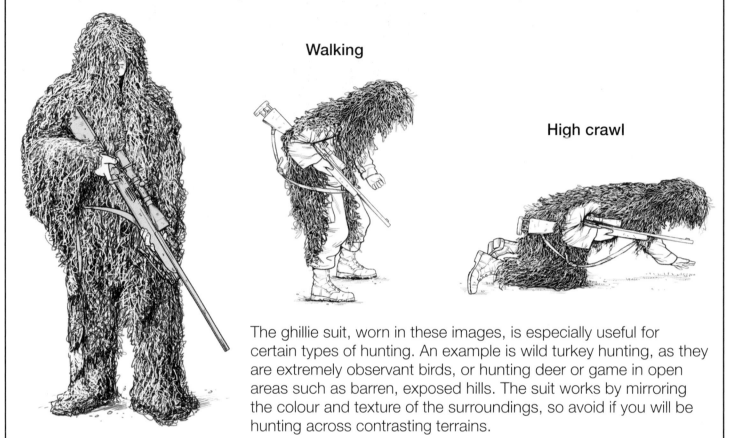

Walking

High crawl

The ghillie suit, worn in these images, is especially useful for certain types of hunting. An example is wild turkey hunting, as they are extremely observant birds, or hunting deer or game in open areas such as barren, exposed hills. The suit works by mirroring the colour and texture of the surroundings, so avoid if you will be hunting across contrasting terrains.

Low crawl

Weapon protection

Note here how the hunter, clad in his ghillie suit, is cradling his rifle in the crook of his elbows, keeping the weapon out of the mud as he inches forward towards his prey.

Blinds and hides

A hide is a camouflaged static position in which you can remain hidden while waiting for prey to appear – in essence, letting them come to you. They are especially useful for aggressive animals.

Tent hide

This modern hunting hide is essentially a camouflaged tent with apertures for the gun. Even if your hide is made of camouflage material, think carefully about its location in the environment – aim to make it blend as seamlessly as possible into the backdrop.

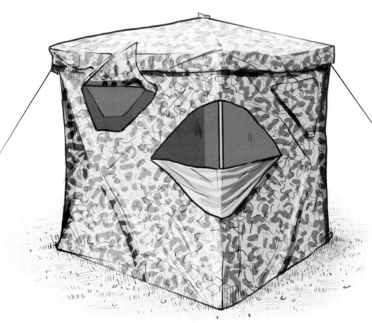

Ground blind

A ground blind is a camouflaged hide used for hunting. If the blind is intelligently positioned so that it blends in naturally with its surroundings, local animals will become used to its presence and will easily venture within bow, rifle or shotgun range. Note the positioning and use of foliage to disguise the smooth lines of the blind.

Loopholes in a hide

This hunter has created a foliage hide with near total concealment. However, he has left loopholes in the front of the position for the rifle barrel; these also need to be big enough to allow unobstructed views through the telescopic sight. Remain as still as possible to avoid rustling leaves when moving.

Field hide

This basic hide is used by the hunter for pigeon shooting. Whatever your hide design, ensure that you can stay in it with reasonable comfort for several hours. A light folding camp stool and a flask of hot drink can make all the difference to a lengthy hunting experience.

Belly hide position

Here we can see military fighting positions with applications for the hunter. In this image, the soldier has created a roof of logs over a shallow scrape position, camouflaging the logs with foliage and leaving a thin opening for the rifle. While such hides are not as comfortable in the long term, they blend in to become almost undetectable.

Hunting with dogs

Gun dogs can be formidable allies when it comes to hunting in the field. Depending on the breed, a good gun dog can track down prey, flush it out of hiding and even perform the entire hunt itself.

Hunting dogs

Pictured here are three different types of hunting dog, each with contrasting performance characteristics. Spaniels (top) are classically adept at flushing birds from undergrowth, while labradors (middle) at easily trained to collect downed prey. Cross-breed hounds (lurchers, bottom) use their tremendous speed to run down fast-moving animals.

The right breed

Today there are no fewer than 161 dog breeds recognized by the American Kennel Club (AKG). Out of this spectrum of animal types, there are dogs in which natural hunting instincts have been refined and physiques appropriately enhanced by selective breeding, each of which offers a combination of aptitudes and abilities for the modern-day hunter.

The right dog

In the same way as choosing a gun depends on the type of hunting you want to perform, choosing a sporting dog involves weighing up the pros and cons of each breed, and selecting one that will work efficiently for you as well as being a good companion in the field and home. Remember that the dog will need to be fully socialized with people and animals.

Basic obedience

Getting your dog to obey the 'stay' command is vital to its obedience and hunting training. Gradually extend the time period the dog can stay seated, using both hand and voice commands, so that eventually the dog will obey either.

Fox hounds

Fox hounds are the ultimate pursuit pack animal, able to follow a fox by scent over many miles without tiring. Once hounds find their prey, they can trap it for the hunter or kill it themselves. (It should be pointed out that hunting with dogs, or at least letting the dog kill the prey, is illegal in many countries).

American Kennel Club – recognized sporting breeds

- American water spaniel
- Boykin spaniel
- Brittany spaniel
- Chesapeake Bay retriever
- Clumber spaniel
- Cocker spaniel
- Curly-coated retriever
- English cocker spaniel
- English setter
- English springer spaniel
- Field spaniel
- Flat-coated retriever
- German shorthaired pointer
- German wirehaired pointer
- Golden retriever
- Golden setter
- Irish setter
- Irish red and white setter
- Irish water spaniel
- Labrador retriever
- Nova Scotia duck trolling retriever
- Pointer
- Spinone Italiano
- Sussex spaniel
- Vizsla
- Weimaraner
- Welsh springer spaniel
- Wirehaired pointing griffon

Hunting birds

The list of feathered prey for hunters is enormous, ranging from diminutive and solitary birds to great flocks of large geese. Bird shooting is a very specific type of hunting, reliant on shotgunning.

Overhead bird

The shooter catches the pheasant as it is climbing up and overhead. He swings up through the line of the bird's climb and pulls the trigger just as the bird disappears behind the muzzle. If you intend to prepare and eat your bird, remember to look out for lead shot in the carcass.

Shot spread

With shotgunning, you are aiming to place the target bird in the centre of your shot spread, maximizing the number of impacts (below). Remember that the bird will be in motion, so aiming ahead into its path will increase the likelihood of you hitting your target.

Approved shot types for wildfowling

The shot types that are approved as nontoxic for waterfowl hunting in the US are shown here.

Approved shot type*	Percent composition by weight	Field testing device**
Bismuth-tin	97 bismuth and 3 tin	Hot Shot7***
Iron (steel)	Iron and carbon	Magnet or Hot Shot7
Iron-tungsten	Any proportion of tungsten and >1 iron	Magnet or Hot Shot7
Iron-tungsten-nickel	>1 iron, any proportion of tungsten and up to 40 nickel	Magnet or Hot Shot7
Tungsten-bronze	51.1 tungsten, 44.4 copper, 3.9 tin and 0.6 iron, or 60 tungsten, 35.1 copper, 3.9 tin and 1 iron	Rare earth magnet
Tungsten-iron-coppernickel	40-76 tungsten, 10-37 iron, 9-16 copper and 5-7 nickel	Hot Shot7 or rare earth magnet
Tungsten-matrix	95.9 tungsten, 4.1 polymer	Hot Shot7
Tungsten-polymer	95.5 tungsten, 4.5 nylon 6 or 11	Hot Shot7
Tungsten-tin-iron	Any proportions of tungsten and tin, and >1 iron	Magnet or Hot Shot7
Tungsten-tin-bismuth	Any proportions of tungsten, tin and bismuth	Rare earth magnet
Tungsten-tin-iron-nickel	65 tungsten, 21.8 tin, 10.4 iron and 2.8 nickel	Magnet
Tungsten-iron-polymer	41.5-95.2 tungsten, 1.5-52.0 iron and 3.5-8.0 fluoropolymer	Magnet or Hot Shot7

* Coatings of copper, nickel, tin, zinc, zinc chloride and zinc chrome on approved nontoxic shot types also are approved.

** This column is for information only, it is not regulatory.

*** The Hot Shot field testing device is from Stream Systems of Concord, CA.

It is important to check hunting, firearm, ammunition and trapping regulations for every country you might want to hunt in, as well as whether or not any hunting is seasonal or requires a permit.

Pull-through technique

Applying the pull-through technique, this hunter starts with his gun behind the bird, then swings in a smooth arc straight through the target, only pulling the trigger as the gun swings ahead of the bird's beak.

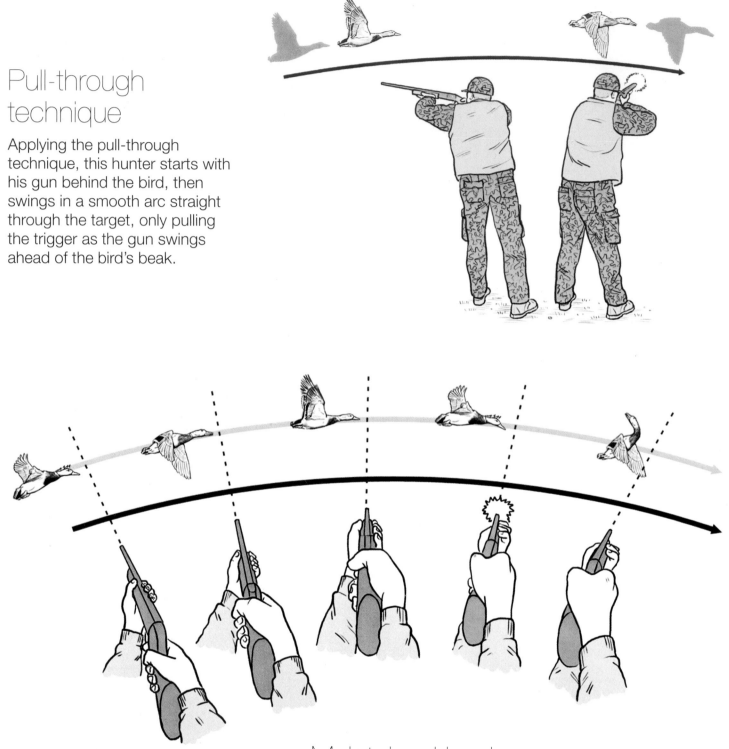

Maintained lead

When taking this shot, the hunter keeps his gun out ahead of the bird at all times, and keeps the barrel moving smoothly even as he pulls the trigger. British shooters have a catchphrase to clarify the sweep of the gun across the target and moment of firing: 'Butt, Belly, Beak, Bang.'

Correct stance

When shooting any longarm gun, lean forward into the shot, allowing your body weight to brace the recoil. Don't lean back, as this is an unstable position with a poor eyeline down the barrel. The kickback of the shot could easily unbalance you if you are in this position. Ensure that the butt of the shotgun is sitting firmly against your shoulder.

Taking high shots

When a target is directly overhead, shown on the right, drop your weight naturally onto your back foot, to prevent you straining to arch your back over. Make sure, however, that you keep your cheek down firmly on the stock. Note that with any type of shot, you should keep both your eyes open, as stereoscopic vision helps you to make more accurate lead and range adjustments.

Hunting land animals

The hunting techniques you use in the field have to be tailor-made for the species you intend to kill. Always remember the key point – an animal's senses are far more advanced than your own.

Mountain hunting

A red deer presents itself in a mountainous habitat. Deer hunting in these environments can be arduous, so make sure that your clothing is up to scratch and acquire an essential knowledge of survival techniques.

Mountain goat

Mountain goats can climb up near-vertical slopes with astounding agility. When hunting these creatures, be careful not to follow them into dangerous terrain. You might easily find that you are in more danger than the prey you were tracking. Become as familiar as you can with the area you plan to hunt. If possible, always tell someone where you will be hunting and when you will return.

Head shot

For small game at close ranges, a head shot can be one of the best options for a quick dispatch, and means that no meat is lost.

Spotting scope

Although binoculars have become more common for hunting use, some hunters still prefer telescopes such as this one above. They pack up in compact fashion, and can provide high magnification when viewing distant targets.

Moose

The North American moose may appear a docile prey, but exceptional powers of scent and hearing, and the ability to make a speedy getaway, means that it should not be underestimated. Their size means that they are a most satisfying kill, rendering a good deal of meat. Utilize as much of the animal as you can, including skin and bones.

Blood trail

A blood trail (above) is clearly etched into the snow. The heaviest concentration occurs over the point of impact, and it thins as the animal moves off. Hitting your target does not mean you have shot to kill. There are actually very few places that mean an instant kill. Never let a wounded animal wander off.

Deadfalls and special purpose traps

Traps and snares are essential tools for any survival hunter. Trapping involves constructing and setting a mechanism that will kill or hold an animal should it upset the trigger system.

Bird snares

Birds can be snared, even on the wing. These snares hang down into gaps that birds might fly through and become ensnared. Simple lengths of fine wire can also work: they injure the birds when struck, and the damaged birds then fall to the ground for collection.

Channelling

'Channelling' refers to arranging foliage and other materials to direct an animal straight into your trap. Here, for example, a snare is positioned at the end of a steadily narrowing avenue of plants. Utilize natural channels or tunnels that can lead to a trap, or construct your own.

Noosing wand

This improvised 'noosing wand' has various applications. It can be used to trap roosting birds (a hunting practice that requires much stealth and patience) or it can be used to control injured prey for dispatch. Such a tool can be easily improvised in the wild using rope or wire attached to a long branch, ideally longer than arm's length.

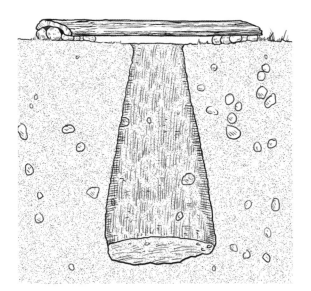

Leghold traps

Mechanical leghold traps are banned in many countries for the ordeal they put captured animals through. As with any trap, make sure that use is legal and that you follow responsible hunting practices, such as checking the trap regularly.

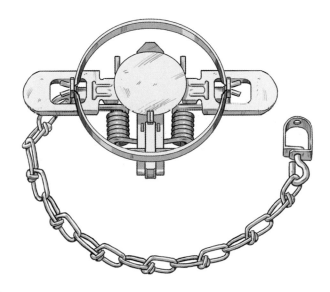

Pit traps

In this trap, designed for small mammals and reptiles, a flared pit several feet deep is covered by a slightly raised platform. Animals crawl under the platform for shelter, but fall into the pit and are trapped, unable to climb the walls.

Tips for siting and setting traps

- Handle the trap as little as possible with your bare hands because animals will pick up your scent and be wary. Bury a manufactured trap in the ground for a few days to remove the smells of artificial production. Also, set you trap well away from the smells of your camp, such as woodsmoke and cooked foods.
- Don't stand or work on the animal trail you are trapping. Instead, keep to one side.
- If you have broken branches to camouflage your trap, smear mud over the white inner wood so that it does not stand out brightly against the green foliage.

- Mark your sets so that they can be found easily after a snowstorm or other heavy weather. However, make the marks some way from the actual trap (carving directional arrows onto prominent trees can be good).
- Place some bait in the intended trapping site before actually setting the trap to see if it disappears. If it does, then the location is suitable for the trap.

Hunting and trapping

Traps and placement

This professional animal trap (right) is placed on a specially constructed crossing point over a river, channelling the prey into the trap. The trap shown above is set to spring shut when an animal enters it in search of bait. Often used for squirrels, the prey is caught alive, so it is unlikely to attract animals who scent its blood.

Making deadfall traps

Deadfalls need much practice to perfect, and be careful never to position yourself under the deadfall weight during construction – a falling heavy log will kill you as easily as your prey. Many traps can be made from wood and natural cordage, although having high-quality thin rope, string or wire (ideally three- or four-strand flexible brass wire) provides you with the greatest chances of a catch.

Deadfall traps

Deadfalls kill by a falling weight – usually a heavy log or stone – activated either by trip wires or by bait. Best used for medium-sized mammals and larger ground-feeding birds, the deadfall trap can be based around a single heavy object, such as a tree trunk (top), or multiple lighter objects (bottom) to deliver a broader impact area.

Spring deadfall trap

In this deadfall trap, a branch held under tension can deliver a more rapid movement of the weight-support branch. Do not be tempted to use an overly large or heavy weight, as this can crush the meat and even the bones, making the animal unusable as a source of food.

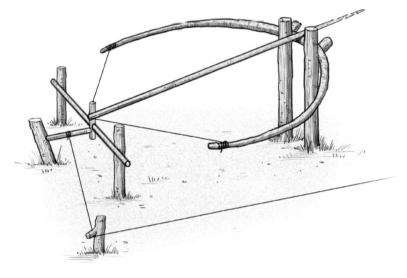

Bow trap

This bow trap holds a bow and arrow under tension until an animal activates the tripwire. Placement is critical here – the arrow's flight must intersect precisely with the position of the animal. Read up as much as you can about different types of prey and the best traps to ensnare them before any survival situation. This will also help you decide where to lay your traps.

Making a water trap for termites

A smooth-sided pot is inserted up to the rim in the ground with water in the bottom. A board or similar covering is placed over the pot propped up on four rocks to create a gap between the board and the earth. The insects crawl beneath the board in search of shelter and moisture and then drop into the pot and are trapped.

Snares and spear traps

Snares are a wire or string loop that kill or trap animals. While they are one of the cruellest forms of hunting, in a survival situation, they can make a great difference to efficient gathering of food supplies.

Simple snare

A snare such as this is simple to construct requiring only rope or wire, and, depending on the strength of the wire, can hold prey indefinitely. However, such traps are very cruel on the snared animal and should be checked frequently, both to minimize suffering and prevent the prey being stolen.

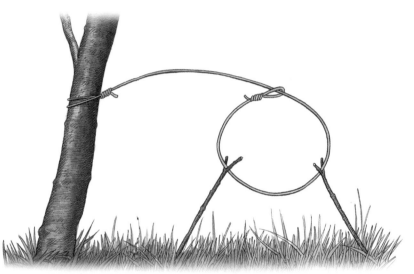

Bird net

Use a large net, strung between two trees, to ensnare flying birds. The net needs to be made of fine wires rather than thick rope, because if it appears to be too solid, birds will naturally avoid it and take safer routes through the trees.

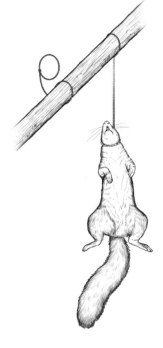

Squirrel pole

A squirrel pole consists of a series of small nooses placed along a long branch. The pole is positioned in a tree, and when the squirrels run along it, they hopefully become entangled in one of the nooses, and hang there for you to retrieve later.

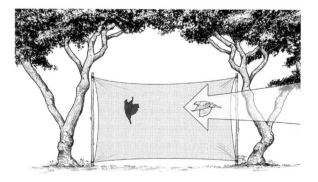

Spring snare

The spring snare is a classic trap type. Ensure that the trigger mechanism in not notched so firmly that the animal eats the bait without activating the trap. Also ensure that the trap not only holds the animal off the ground, but also away from the tree to avoid predators snatching your prey.

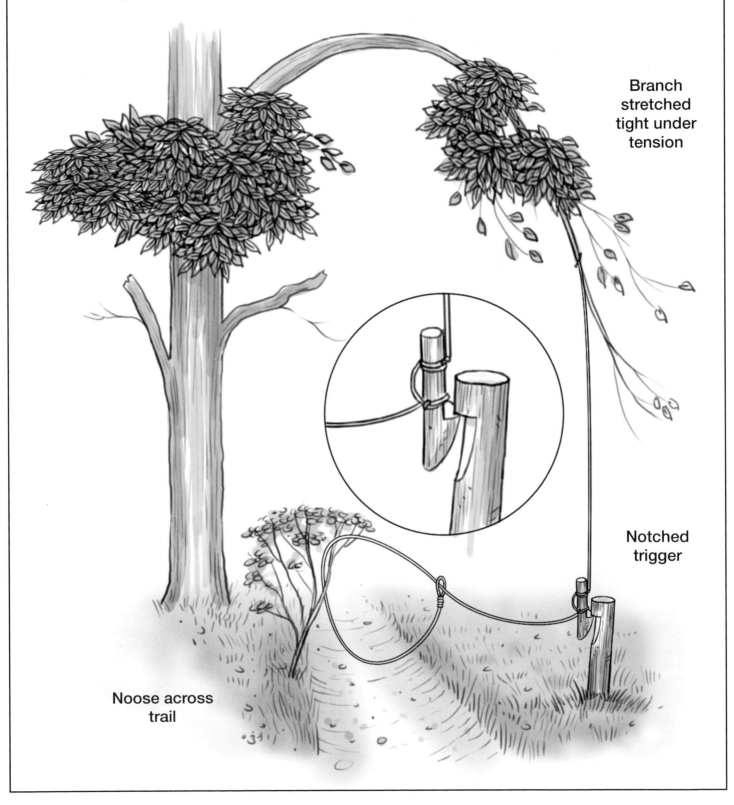

Branch stretched tight under tension

Notched trigger

Noose across trail

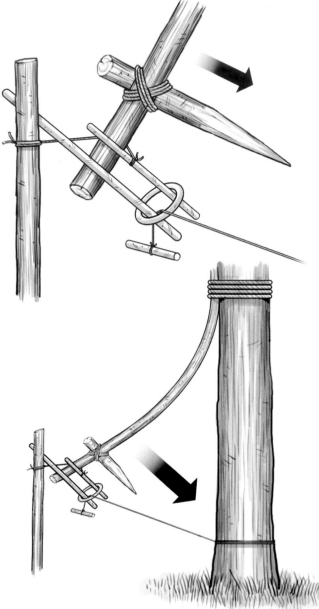

Spear trap (1)

Spear traps should be employed to kill medium-sized to large mammals. For this spear trap, the whip branch is held by two short sticks fitted through a slip ring. The slip ring is made of any smooth material such as bound creeper, leather or any other material which will not snag on the sticks. When an animal moves the tripwire, the toggle on the end of the tripwire pulls away the slip ring and the spear is released.

Spear trap (2)

This spear trap is of simple construction, especially if you have rope, though the release mechanism may take practice to perfect. The important point is to align the sweep of the spear when it is released with the positioning of the tripwire, otherwise the spear is likely to miss the prey.

Snare positioning and construction

The crucial aspect of using a snare is positioning. Using your tracking skills, identify routes regularly used by animals, although avoid watering areas, as animals tend to be more alert in these locations. If you are hunting as well as laying snares, be aware that gunshots will panic nearby animals and increase their wariness, so it might be best to keep hunting and trapping zones separate.

Use the natural resources around you to make a counterweight snare. Natural foliage means the snare is discreet.

Snares can also be constructed out of natural materials, such as this one to the right, which makes use of the tree's 'v'.

Channelling your prey into the snare by blocking other paths increases the chance of trapping animals.

When making a snare around a habitat's entrance, touch it as little as possible so your scent does not warn the animal.

Fishing kit

Fish can be a great source of food in a survival situation, and can be obtained from either salt- or freshwater sources. Make catching them simple by familiarizing yourself with the equipment.

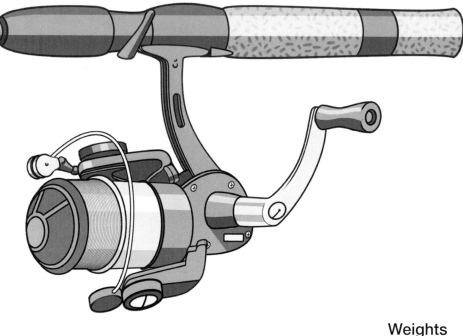

Fishing rod

Commercial fishing rods are a cheap and excellent investment for any survivalist. As a first purchase, opt for a 3–4m (10–12ft) rod, which will give you the flexibility to cope with a variety of fishing scenarios, from river bank to harbour wall. Practice fishing to build up patience and skill.

Types of fish hooks

You can adapt your survival tin by taking a variety of hooks, weights and lures for fishing. Ensure that you have a plentiful supply. You can also buy lightweight folding fishing nets, which, when set across a narrow section of river and weighted at the bottom, can catch large quantities of fish in a matter of minutes.

Weights

Sinkers

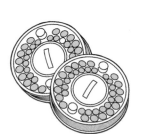

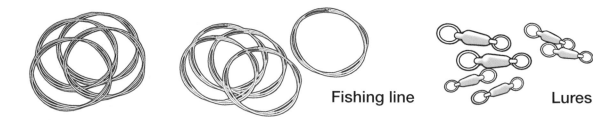

Fishing line

Lures

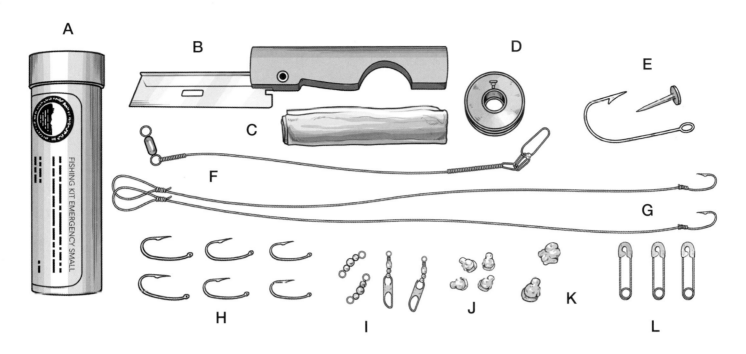

Fishing kit

Here we have a useful emergency fishing kit, consisting of various lines, hooks, weights and bait, all contained within an easily portable tube. Get used to carrying such pocket-sized survival kit around with you and in the car; it can make a crucial difference in an emergency.

A. Tube
B. Knife
C. Net
D. Sinker
E. Hooks
F. Line
G. Hooked line
H. Hooks
I. Bait
J. Weights
K. Weights
L. Safety pins

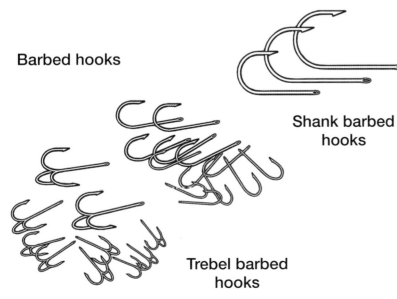

Barbed hooks

Shank barbed hooks

Trebel barbed hooks

Avoiding unsafe fish

Do not eat fish that appears spoiled. Cooking does not ensure that spoiled fish will be edible. Signs of spoilage include:

- Sunken eyes.
- Peculiar odour.
- Suspicious colour. (Gills should be red to pink. Scales should be a pronounced shade of grey, not faded.)
- Dents stay in the fish's flesh after pressing it with your thumb.
- Slimy, rather than moist or wet body.
- Sharp or peppery taste.

Eating spoiled or rotten fish may cause diarrhoea, nausea, cramps, vomiting, itching, paralysis or a metallic taste in the mouth. These symptoms appear suddenly, one to six hours after eating. Induce vomiting if symptoms appear.

– US Army, FM 21-76, *Survival*, p.95

Improvised fishing equipment

Line fishing requires nothing more than a fishing line, a hook and bait. If none of these is available, you will have to manufacture them, which can be done quite simply with basic equipment.

Rod fishing

In a survival situation, rod fishing can be performed with little more than a branch, a length of line and a hook (see opposite page), which can attract attention and greatly increase your chances of a catch. Note how this fisherman stays low on the bank, reducing his visibility to the fish.

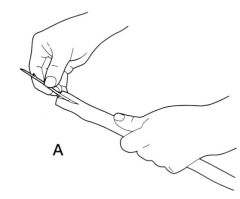

A

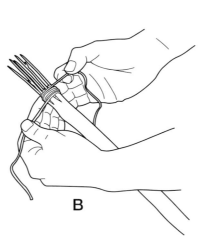

B

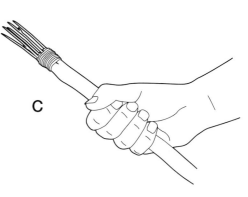

C

Spiked harpoon

Spearing fish can be surprisingly profitable with the right tools and technique. Make the head of a harpoon out of multiple thorns (A), set with spacing material between them to create a spear head of large diameter (B). Bind the thorns securely with cord (C). For a multi-point harpoon, tie sharp thorns to the end of the stick with them splayed in different directions to increase the strike area.

Making and using fishing hooks

Making your own fishing hooks is a simple process if you find yourself in a survival situation without equipment. Improvised fishhooks can be made out of thorns, bent nails or pins, or pieces of sharp wood tied at right angles to the line. Note that any wooden hook will need to be replaced if it softens in the water after several hours. Try to match the bait with what the fish feed on normally.

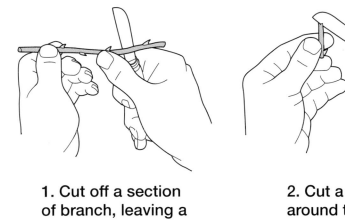

1. Cut off a section of branch, leaving a thorn at one end

2. Cut a notch around the end, opposite the thorn

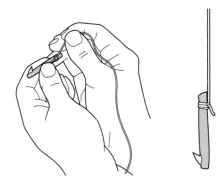

3. Securely tie fishing line around the notch

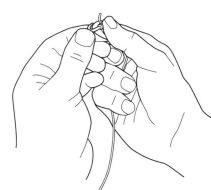

4. Bend a piece of thin metal into a hook shape

5. Tie on the line, adding a small feather if possible

6. The feather acts as a lure to attract fish

Easily accessible baits include worms, insects, minnows, berries, maggots or scraps of food (including meat, cheese and vegetables). Live bait gives the advantage of moving underwater, attracting the fish's attention, but fish can be curious about feathers (shown in the example above and often readily available) or shiny objects such as pieces of aluminium foil and metal.

Fishing

Fishing places reasonably low demands on energy for potentially excellent yields, leaving you free to hunt and forage for other foods, seek clean water supplies or work on your shelter.

Line of sight

The refraction of light through water enables a fish to see at non-line-of-sight angles over the riverbank. Stay low to avoid being seen, avoiding a position right at the edge of the river or pond. Also ensure that your shadow does not fall on the surface of the trauter.

Lures

For improvised lures, use pieces of brightly coloured fabric taken from foul weather gear or life raft canopy (A); for spinners, cut a sliver from a can and this will catch the light much like a spinner (B). Flying fish heads and tails can be threaded on to hook shanks to provide life-like lures (C).

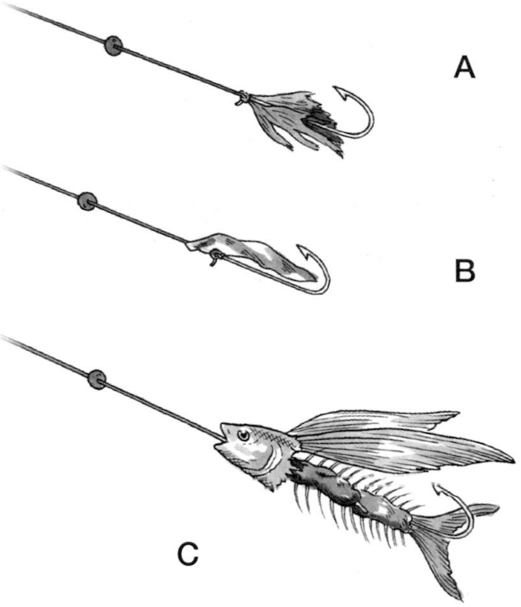

A

B

C

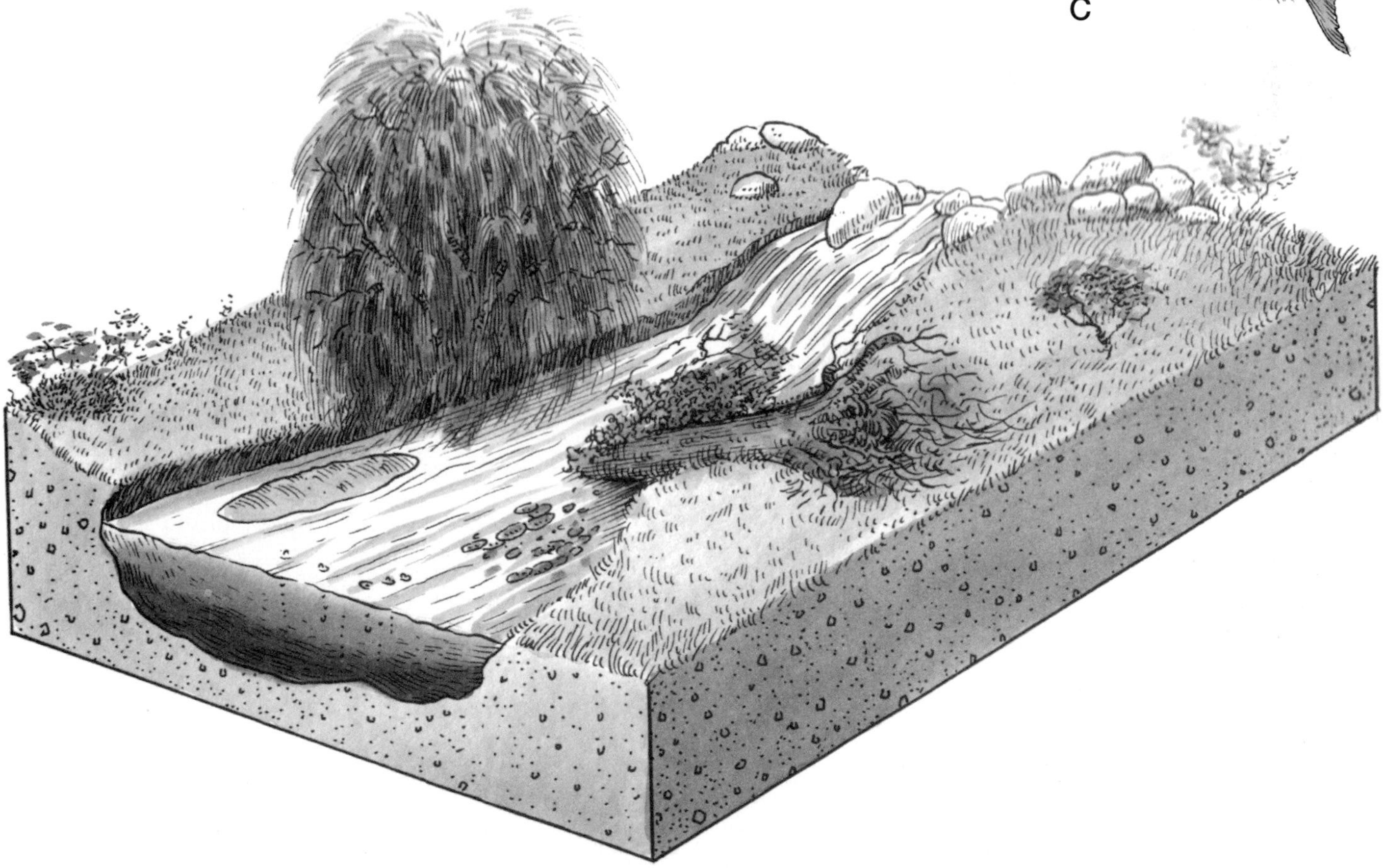

Finding fish

Fish enjoy swimming in areas where they feel protected or where they have some respite from strong currents. This illustration indicated several locations which might provide good fishing. Look for overhanging branches, floating weeds, boulders and fallen trees.

Trapping and netting

Traps and nets can provide much bigger yields than line fishing, and can be set up relatively easily, making them ideal for a survival situation where every lost calorie can count.

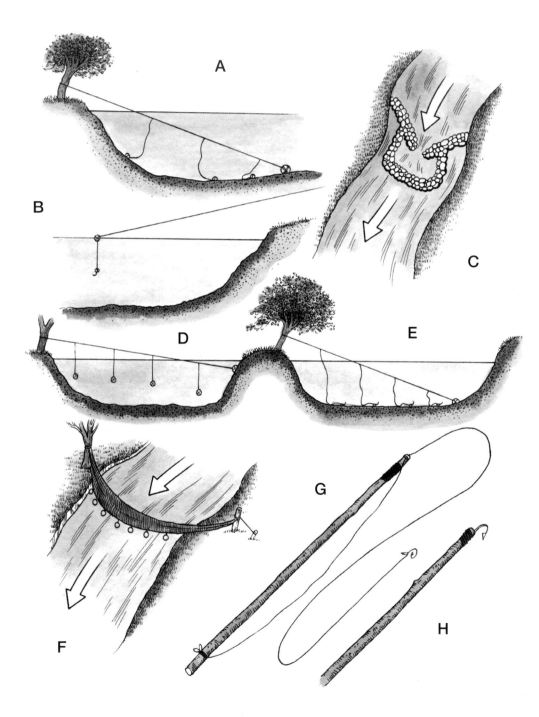

Techniques

An innovative use of fishing lines and terrain modifications will maximize your chances of good yields. Hooks can be set to sit on the river bottom (A and E) or suspended in the water at varying levels (B and D). A stone fish trap (C) and a gill net (F) can bring especially large catches, and an improvised gaff hook (H) is useful for landing large fish from the bank. Try not to catch more than you can eat, and avoid leaving rotting fish lying around.

A. Weighted line
B. Line and float
C. Stone fish trap
D. Suspended hooks
E. Hooks resting on river bed
F. Gill net held down by stones
G. Dry-fly fishing rod
H. Gaff hook

210

Bottle trap

The bottle trap works on similar principles to the fish trap illustration shown below, except that this device can be constructed simply from a common plastic drinks bottle, the neck and nozzle cut off and inverted inside the bottle body. While the size restricts prey, it is a useful additional trap.

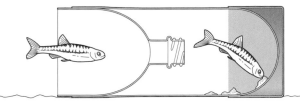

Basket trap

The basket trap is a more advanced option of the bottle trap above, requiring a good supply of flexible thin branches and some cordage. It can be reused and offers a larger yield than the bottle trap. Note the rocks piled up on either side of the trap, to channel the fish through into the basket.

Running line

A running line is a way of fishing while you occupy yourself with other tasks. You can fix as many hooks and line as needed, but do not overfish a water course as this might deplete valuable sources of food for the future, and check the lines regularly for any catches.

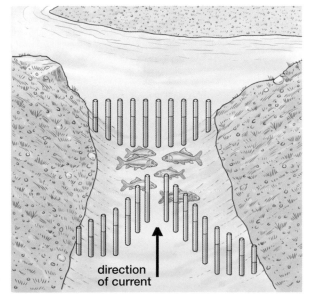

direction of current

Fish trap

Large quantities of fish can be caught in purpose-designed traps. Here, the hunter uses sticks embedded in the riverbed to channel the fish through a narrow aperture into a holding area. Note that the current should flow into the mouth of the funnel, which makes it harder for the fish to swim back out of the trap.

Fishing from a dinghy – constructing a gaff hook

If you have a wooden paddle, use your file to carve grooves for the lanyard and the safety lines. Use duct tape and cable ties to hold the gaff hook in place but remember the hook must be able to swivel so that the fish's fight won't snap the shank. Attach safety lines to the hook and wear the lanyard because you can't afford to lose important equipment.

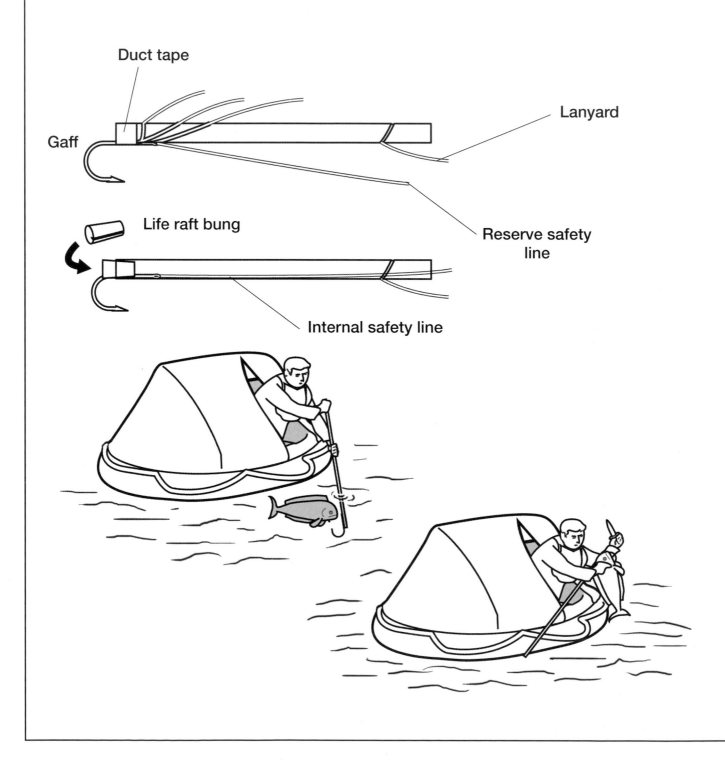

Duct tape

Gaff

Lanyard

Life raft bung

Reserve safety line

Internal safety line

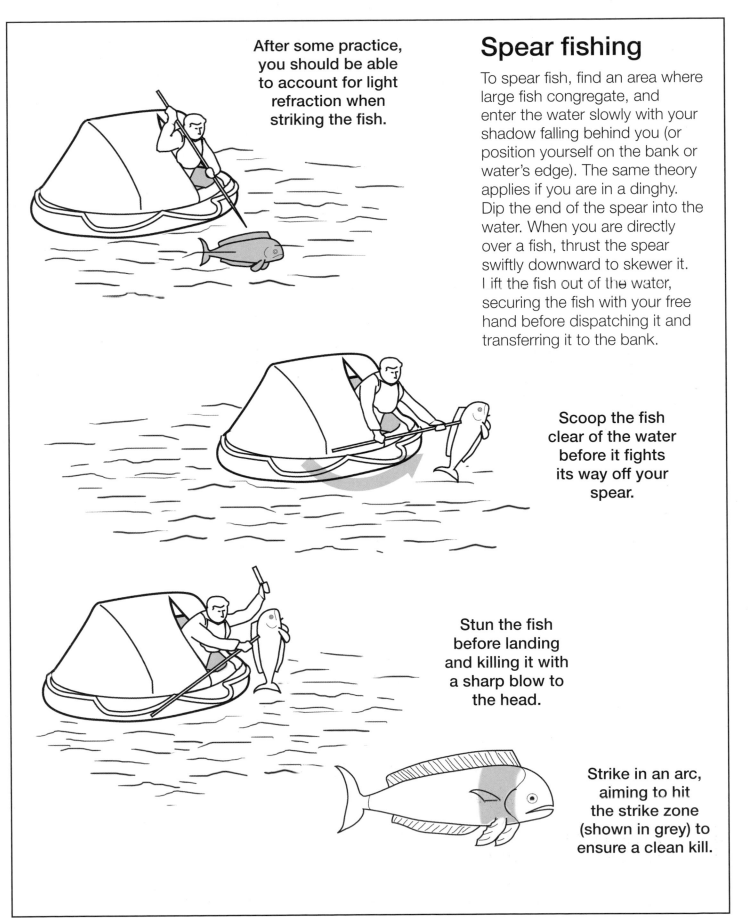

After some practice, you should be able to account for light refraction when striking the fish.

Spear fishing

To spear fish, find an area where large fish congregate, and enter the water slowly with your shadow falling behind you (or position yourself on the bank or water's edge). The same theory applies if you are in a dinghy. Dip the end of the spear into the water. When you are directly over a fish, thrust the spear swiftly downward to skewer it. Lift the fish out of the water, securing the fish with your free hand before dispatching it and transferring it to the bank.

Scoop the fish clear of the water before it fights its way off your spear.

Stun the fish before landing and killing it with a sharp blow to the head.

Strike in an arc, aiming to hit the strike zone (shown in grey) to ensure a clean kill.

Defending yourself

Physical violence has uncertain outcomes for all involved. Even the most confident fighter can be undone by a chance blow, so for this reason alone violence is best avoided.

Yet the fact remains that there are occasions in which you must defend yourself with brutal commitment. If another individual, possibly armed and intent on taking your life, makes an attack, you have to respond in kind, stopping him or her as quickly and decisively as possible.

To be effective, self-defence requires two elements. The first is a knowledge of fundamental unarmed and armed combat techniques, practised frequently so that they can be delivered instinctively under high-stress conditions. Second, you must fight with real spirit and aggression – if the attacker is not holding back, neither should you.

The man on the right is practising techniques of defending against knife attack. Note how he controls the blade by performing a lock against both the wrist and the elbow.

Recognizing impending violence

The fundamental rule of defence is to fight only if you have to. Training yourself to recognize the signs of impending violence means that you will be more likely to avoid walking into fights.

Defusing a situation

Your first aim should be to defuse a situation without violence. State clearly but without fear that you don't want to fight. Try to lighten the situation by making the aggressor laugh. Do not be afraid of losing face and move away from a violent situation if possible.

Violent posturing

Signs of impending violence can take many forms, including staring, finger beckoning and outright preparation for a fight. If someone approaches you with these signals, attempt to stop them with firm language, but also put yourself in the guard position in readiness for defence.

Not backing down

If you find yourself in a situation where violence looks likely, you may have to resort to reciprocal intimidation and threat. If the aggressor states he wants to fight, accept his offer with menace, saying that you want to fight him alone. Without the backing of his friends he might climb down. Alternatively, pretend that you are bordering on psychopathic. Make violent threats, screaming wildly and even dribbling saliva. It sounds extreme, but the attacker might back down if he believes himself in serious danger.

Safety on the streets

The chances of your being exposed to violence at all dramatically decrease with some basic common-sense precautions. Watch where you are walking at all times. Avoid dark or deserted side roads, alleyways, streets bordered by wasteland or bushes, or derelict areas. Position yourself close to the curb when walking alone. Attackers prey on signs of weakness, so do not display any. Pull yourself up to your full height, walk athletically and confidently, and maintain strong eye contact if directly threatened.

Defending yourself

Localized dangers

Beware of areas such as deserted car parks, unfamiliar or poorly-lit alleys, or subways or underpasses. Such areas are often very quiet, especially at night, and contain lots of places for an aggressor to conceal himself, making anyone who walks through them alone an easy target. Note that protection should extend to your vehicle. Try to park away from any bushes or hiding place, lock and secure your vehicle with a pedal jack and ensure that no valuables are left on display.

Remain alert

Falling asleep on public transport makes you vulnerable to pickpockets and other opportunists or deviants. It also means that you are more likely to depart from your planned route, meaning that you might find yourself in unfamiliar territory. When travelling, aim to ensure that you are never a target for attack. Read a book or newspaper to keep yourself awake and alert. If the vehicle is deserted, sit near the driver.

Attack and defence

If violence is unavoidable, remember that the attacker has the advantage of retaining the initiative; the defender must react rather than doing what he wants to do. If you are forced onto the defensive from the opening attack, find a way to counterattack as soon as you are able to.

Importance of defence

Initially, attacks must be defended. Defence should be used intelligently and as part of a fight-and-win strategy. A soldier who panics and simply covers up will, at best, just prolong the beating.

Evade and counterattack

The attacker in the image to the left has launched a powerful but wild swinging punch at the head. This is one of the most common of all unarmed attacks and is devastating if it lands, but is relatively easy to defeat. Ducking under the punch means that the opponent is off balance and open to attack – in this case, a kick to the side of the knee (see above).

Hand techniques

Hand techniques and striking tools are the mainstay of military unarmed combat. They can put a man down swiftly and powerfully without the need to become entangled in grappling.

Finger jab

The finger jab to the eyes is very good for causing irritation and disorientation in an opponent. It might even put a stop to many fights. Bear in mind that under civilian law, once an assailant is unable to continue fighting, hurting him further is illegal. Don't forget that it no longer constitutes self-defence when the opponent cannot attack back.

Dropping elbow strike

A downwards elbow strike can be delivered to the head or body of an opponent who is bent over. A good target on the body is just under the shoulder blade. Anywhere on the head will get a result; precision is not really necessary. If necessary, this move could also be followed up with a knee to the head.

Uppercut

Generally aimed at the jaw, the uppercut can be a damaging shot. For maximum power, the attacker places his left hip forwards and to the opponent's right before he strikes, slightly bending at the knees so that he is just below the target. Jabbing his left fist upwards, he simultaneously pushes upwards from the slight crouch position for maximum force with the impact. Note that the right hand is in place to continue the attack with a punch to the abdomen.

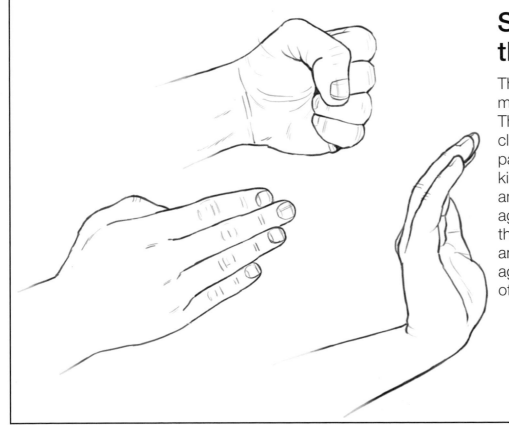

Striking with the hands

The hands and arms are the most accessible striking tools. The primary striking tools are closed fists against softer parts of the body, such as the kidney area or solar plexus, and the heel of the palm against harder parts such as the jaw. The edge of the hand and stiff fingers can be used against the eyes, throat or side of the neck.

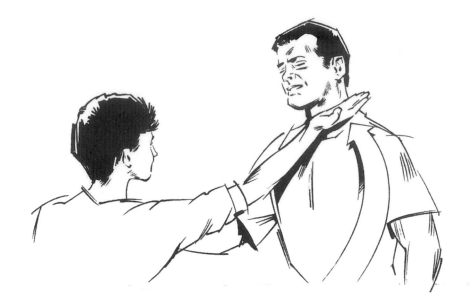

Edge of hand strike

The edge of the hand can be used to strike the carotid area (shown left), which can cause unconsciousness. This strike can slip between the shoulder and the rim of a helmet. The base of the skull (the medulla oblongata) is another area that can be effectively attacked with this strike in a downwards blow.

Chin jab

The chin jab is a rising strike under the tip of the chin, which not only transmits force to the brain but also snaps the opponent's head violently back and disrupts his posture. It can be followed through with an aggressive forward movement, turning into an opportunistic takedown against a somewhat dazed opponent.

There is a persistent myth that this strike can be delivered to the nose as a killing blow, but that simply does not work, although the blow may be hard enough to fracture the skull. It is, however, tremendously painful, so even a shot that misses the jaw and thus does not cause a knockout will still gain the soldier some advantage. The chin jab is also one of the few strikes that is effective against a helmeted opponent, as the area struck remains uncovered.

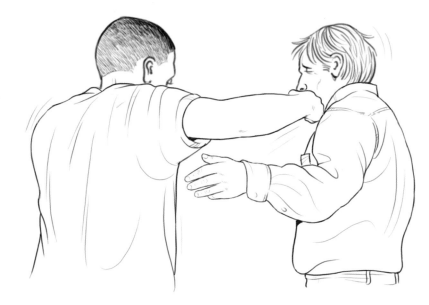

Hooked punch

A closed fist can be used to strike the head, though there are some risks of hand damage. A hook should be tight, not swung wildly, and will ideally connect close to the tip of the jaw. This jerks the head around and causes 'brain shake', which will disorient and possibly knock out the opponent. It will also unbalance him, allowing for a follow-up attack.

Cupped-hand strike

The cupped-hand strike (below) follows a similar path to the hook but is more extended. The aim point is just below the ear, striking with the fleshy 'L' at the base of the palm, opposite the thumb. The aim is to deliver maximum blunt force trauma to the opponent's head.

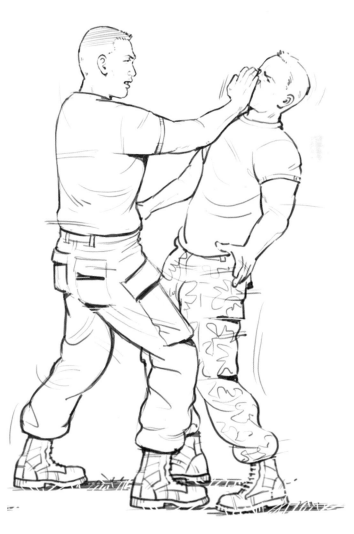

Palm strike

The palm strike can be delivered as a cross, or the attacker can step in and turn his strike into a takedown by driving the opponent's head up and back. The palm strike works when delivered to the chin or whatever part of the head is available, and can be delivered from the lead or rear hand.

Kicking techniques

Kicking is a difficult talent to learn, requiring balance and flexibility. If accurately delivered, it can be extremely effective, but beware that you could put yourself in a vulnerable position.

Flying kick (1)

Flying kicks are a good example of making yourself vulnerable during an attack. While the weight of the attacker's body is fully behind the powerful kick, there is little margin for error and even a slight mistake can result in the attacker hurting himself far more than his opponent. Note the position of the foot with the heel making contact.

Flying kick (2)

The flying kick straight ahead when delivered from a leap is extremely successful if executed accurately and with sufficient determination to succeed. The kick effectively pushes the opponent backwards, knocking the air out of their lungs and making them land in a vulnerable prone position.

Low kicks

Feet may be used to attack from the front, side or back to any part of the opponent's anatomy. They are especially useful for attacking the opponent's lower region, with lower kicks generally more forceful. Low kicks also make it easier for the attacker to keep their balance, as they do not have to hit a high target such as the side of the head. The best targets are the lower abdominal region, groin and knee.

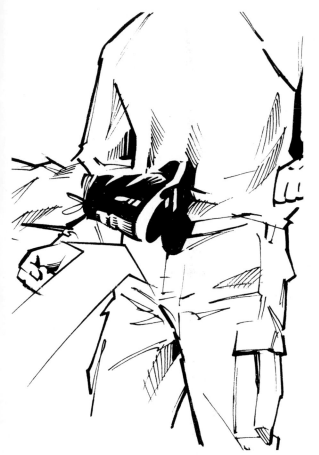

Kick defence (1)

When defending against a roundhouse kick to the body, the soldier above covers his ribs with his arm and allows his body to flex, absorbing the kick. It will still hurt, but the soldier will now be well positioned to attack the opponent while he is still regaining his balance after the failed kick. From here, you could attack the opponent's right knee.

Kick defence (2)

Another defence against a roundhouse kick is to weaken the attack by moving closer to the attacker or sideways, away from the strike. If you have enough time to do this, the evasion puts you in a position of attack while the opponent is still regaining balance from the missed kick. Take full advantage of this, and the open guard of your opponent, to launch your own attack to the groin or solar plexus.

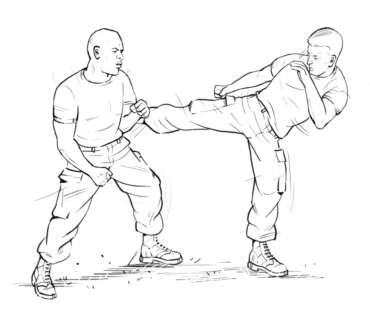

Chokes and headlocks

There is no set situation in which to use a choke or headlock. It is a case of looking for openings for these formidable methods, which, when used correctly, can quickly end an attack.

Scissor choke

Sitting astride your opponent, cross your hands with palms down and grab his lapels as deeply to the back of the neck as possible. Pushing your elbows downwards and forcing your wrists into either side of the neck will apply pressure and leave your opponent struggling for air.

Upwards choke

This upwards choke is done with an arm around the throat and your opponent's head being pushed into your underarm with a quick, upward pressure. You could also squeeze or twist the head from left to right. The best way to escape from a frontal attack is to respond by grabbing the enemy's testicles. If you are trapped in a hold, look for any unguarded areas, or take out the legs, if you are able.

Standing forearm choke (1)

As a basic technique for attacking from behind, the soldier wraps his right arm around the opponent's neck, his elbow under the opponent's chin. The soldier puts his upper left arm on the opponent's left shoulder and lays the straightened fingers of his right hand in the crook of his left elbow.

Standing forearm choke (2)

Tightening the choke shown above, here the soldier puts his left forearm and hand to the back of the opponent's neck and chokes by squeezing his arms towards each other. This secure choke means that the likelihood of the opponent dropping to escape the hold is minimal.

Forearm choke

This choke assumes that the opponent has been knocked to the ground. From this position, pin your opponent by falling on him. Using your forearm, press down heavily on the throat. The combination of your weight and pressure on the throat means that submission is likely, especially if you can immobilize the arms.

Multiple assailants

Success in fighting is often about being the first to make a move. This is especially true in dealing with multiple attackers. Take control of the fight from the word go by making the initial attack.

Three-on-one situation

Facing multiple assailants is as dangerous as it gets in the world of unarmed combat. Here, the single attacker must initiate the attack. He needs to manoeuvre the situation so that one of the attackers is distracted.

Never assume that the attackers will come at you in succession. They will aim to keep the upper hand by attacking all at once, leaving the soldier with very little chance of fighting back once the blows land.

Strategy

The soldier should first attack the opponent in front, before moving on to the next closest attacker. He needs to land the best shot he can, at vulnerable areas such as the eyes, throat, groin or jaw. The aim is to ensure that the number of threats is reduced, so you want to disable the opponents with one blow.

Tactics

Note how the first attacker has been temporarily disabled and placed in the way of the third attacker, while the soldier moves on to make his next attack. Using one attacker as a shield buys you valuable seconds to attack another opponent one-on-one. Going to ground can be fatal, so if you are knocked down, get up quickly.

Improvisation

To have any hope of surviving a fight with a group, a soldier needs to have practised techniques that can somehow bring order to chaos. However, with these tactics, improvization is key, as you never know who will attack next or how they will make this attack. Take the first available opportunity to make your getaway.

Defending yourself

Group-on-group

If you are fighting group-on-group, utilize the team advantage and work together. Members of your team should aim to occupy the attentions of a greater number of hostiles then their comrades. This should, in theory, mean that more of the enemy group are disabled than your side, gaining an advantage that you should use to end the fight.

Always attack

The lone fighter must attack. He cannot afford to be grabbed or taken to the ground. Nor can he be defensive against one opponent while there is another lining up an attack. Each movement must gain some advantage, such as pushing one opponent into another.

Reducing the odds (1)

The odds can be temporarily evened by moving so the opponents get in one another's way, or by pushing them into one another. This is sometimes referred to as 'stringing the fish', i.e. getting the opponents lined up rather than surrounding the soldier. It is relatively easy to do with two hostiles, becoming more difficult as numbers increase. Obstacles can also be used to prevent some members of a group closing in.

Reducing the odds (2)

Few people will walk right over a friend to attack an enemy. By putting one opponent down and using him as a barrier, the attacking man can keep his comrades at a distance while he makes his next move. Alternatively, taking this action (as shown below) you can gain the advantage of surprise. Remember that the sooner the fight is over, the sooner you can assist wounded comrades.

What it's like

There is a lot of back-and-forth in movie fights and sporting bouts. That tends not to happen in real, serious combat. It's more like someone being hit by a car – one side has the advantage and keeps it unless they yield it by doing something stupid. The opponent isn't given a chance to even get into the fight, let alone win it. The key is to be the car, not the pedestrian, in any fight you might encounter.

231

Blocks and counters

While pure defence does not win fights, good use of blocks and counters can be used to set up a devastating counterattack. If you do have to fight, an offensive-defence is often your best chance.

Double-handed block

This block (shown left) not only prevents a blow from landing, it enables you to use your opponent's strength against him by disabling the attacking arm as well as pulling him down so that he is doubled over, exposed to attack at the back of his head, groin or knee joint.

Smother block

If the soldier can read his opponent's intentions early enough, he can 'smother' the attack, preventing it landing at all. The smother is defence and counterattack in one. The defender moves in and drives his forearms into the attacker's shoulder and the crook of his arm, causing intense pain and possibly sending the attacker staggering backwards.

Punch defence

Against a swinging punch to the head, the defender covers by raising his arm as if trying to grab the back of his own head. As soon as the deflected attack lands, the defender wraps the striking arm and grips it firmly, winning the advantage. As the attacker struggles to pull his arm free, the defender launches his own counterattack.

Ducks and weaves

Do not forget that avoiding blows altogether can work in your favour. This ducking action not only moves you from harm's way, but it brings you in closer to the attacker's body, making it easier for you to launch a counterattack to the groin, abdomen or solar plexus. From this position, an uppercut strike to the jaw is also possible.

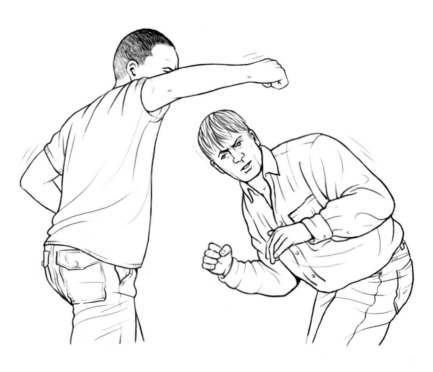

Elbow block and strike

The elbow block is a powerful defensive tool if used effectively, as it provides a block against attack as well as delivering what can be a painful blow from the sharp elbow. Additionally, it is relatively painless to deliver and can also be used as an attack in its own right. The elbow strike shown in the bottom image will land hard against the jaw, knocking the attacker's head backwards. It is also effective delivered from a side-on position into the solar plexus.

Deflection (1)

Attacks that are coming straight in, such as a knife thrust (left) or a front kick (below), can be deflected to the side with a sweeping motion. This motion may be enough to knock the weapon out of the attacker's hand. If not, it still opens him up to a strong counterattack.

Deflection (2)

Meeting the force of any straight attack head-on is a bad idea; instead the soldier moves down one arm of the tactical 'Y' (see page 238) and sweeps the attack to the other side. This combines deflection with an element of evasion. It also allows you to strike with more power as you have your body weight behind the attack.

Essential skills

Never forget in armed combat that while weapons are often described as dangerous, they can be used for good or ill. It is the person whose hands the weapon is in where the true danger might lie.

Focus point

It is not wise to focus your attention on any one part of the opponent, but instead to rest your eyes roughly on the spot marked 'X'. Peripheral awareness picks up movement better than direct vision, so you will actually be more aware for what the opponent is doing by focusing on the 'X', as opposed to staring him directly in the face.

Hidden weapons

Always watch an assailant's hands, as they might contain a hidden weapon, such as this knife held in the palm.

Legitimate use of weapons

If you carry a weapon that is legally permitted, then the only question is whether the use of that weapon constitutes reasonable force under self-defence law. However, weapons are forbidden by law in some localities. Taking a weapon into such an area 'just in case' would not be lawful and you might be prosecuted, even in circumstances where you were justified in using the weapon. If, on the other hand, a confrontation turned nasty and you used a weapon that happened to be there (perhaps a kitchen knife or a tool that was present for a legitimate purpose), this would be an entirely different situation under the law from going armed into a confrontation you could have avoided. If violence is brought to you and you have no choice but to defend yourself, arming yourself may well be justified, even if weapons are not normally allowed in that locality. Train yourself to see the weapon potential of any object near your locality.

Restraining an assailant

'Control and restraint' techniques are the province of police and security personnel, who can follow the techniques with use of handcuffs to ensure that a restrained opponent stays that way. There is no point in using restraint methods unless they can bring the situation to a satisfactory, non-violent conclusion.

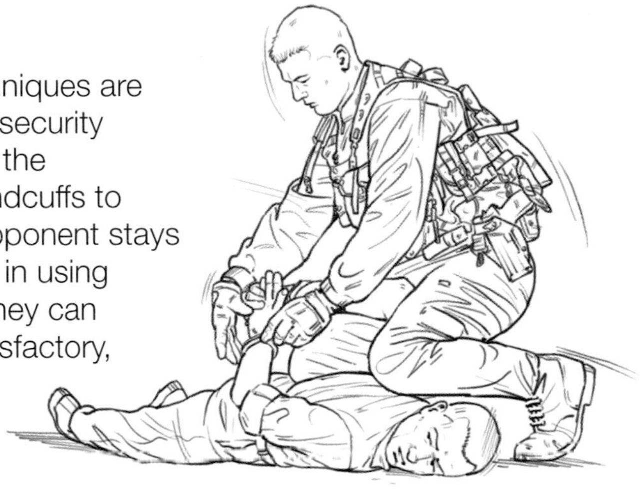

Groin hit

A blow to the groin is not necessarily an instant fight-ender, but a direct hit will almost always cause the opponent to react defensively. Often he will bend forward, breaking his posture and guard, and making himself vulnerable to further attack. From the position of attack shown here, when the opponent doubles over you would be well placed to deliver an uppercut to the chin, or to bring your knee up to make contact with the face.

What to attack and where to defend

Knowing your own strengths and an opponent's weak points is crucial if you want to win an armed fight. Attacking the right place can mean the difference between causing pain and total defeat.

Angles of attack

The US Army identifies nine broad angles of attack when using handheld weapons. Number five (the white circles) is a lunging attack, which can be either aimed high or low, at vital organs. Note that no matter which angle is used, the attack is likely to end in some sort of debilitating impact.

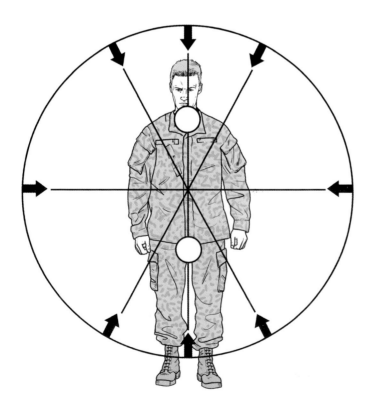

The tactical 'Y'

Wherever possible, the soldier will not stay in front of an attack, where it is most powerful. Facing a charging enemy with a bayonet is one of the worst places you can find yourself. Move out of the line of attack, positioning yourself on the opponent's flank to deliver a counterattacking blow.

The body: vulnerable areas

The dark-shaded areas here are extremely vulnerable to hard physical attack, particularly the head and neck. The genitals and limb joints are other points to target, which can distract or immobilize the opponent without the potentially lethal effects of hitting the other areas. While you should aim for the most vulnerable areas if you fear for your life, it is better to land a blow that causes relatively little harm, but that buys you some time, than not to land one at all.

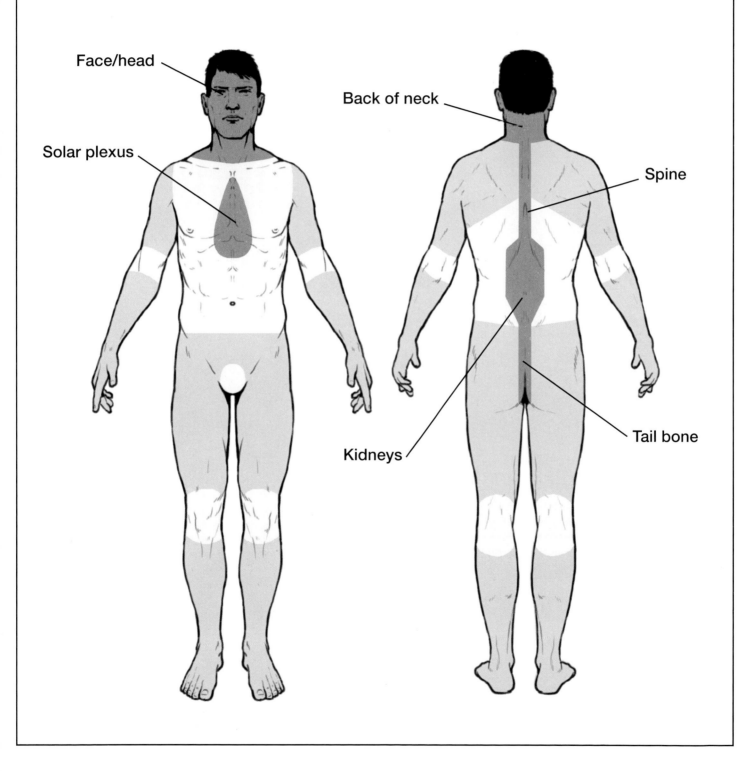

Face/head

Solar plexus

Back of neck

Spine

Kidneys

Tail bone

Weapon threat versus weapon use?

There are many situations where weapons are used as a threat rather than immediately being brought into action. Any armed confrontation should be defused without weapon discharge.

Weapon retention

Military and police personnel are trained to retain their weapons when under physical attack. This is an essential survival skill, but it is sadly not always successful. Every now and then a police officer is murdered with his or her own weapon, or that weapon is turned on fellow officers or innocent bystanders.

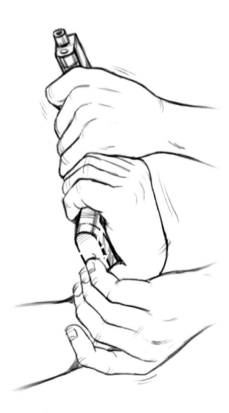

Handgun disarm

Twisting a weapon out of the hand is a common component of military disarming techniques. Once the wrist reaches the limit of its movement, the weapon can be levered free. In this case the weapon is gripped by the barrel, ensuring that it does not point in a dangerous direction.

No guarantees

There is no guarantee that giving up property will keep you from harm. Some criminals will cut or stab their victims even after getting what they want, so throwing down property (rather than handing over) and then quickly fleeing is a sensible option. Here, the attacker has a choice between picking up the loot and giving you a headstart, or coming after you immediately.
It is fair to assume that someone who tries to take you somewhere at weapon point intends something more serious than robbery.

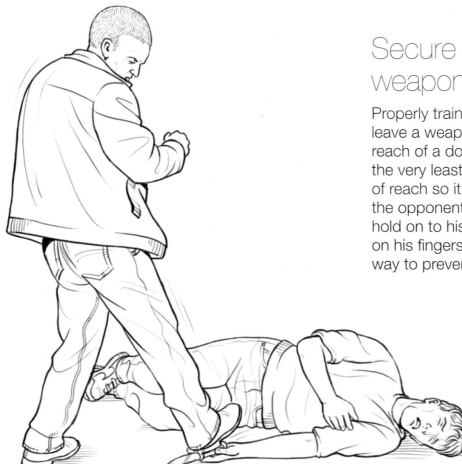

Secure the weapon

Properly trained personnel never leave a weapon within grasping reach of a downed opponent. At the very least they will kick it out of reach so it cannot be used. If the opponent is determined to hold on to his weapon, stamping on his fingers might be the only way to prevent him from using it.

Blunt weapons

Blunt weapons rely mainly on the delivery of kinetic energy, i.e., the amount of damage they can inflict is determined by mass and speed. Even a small blunt object can add impact to a blow.

Two-handed push strike

A push strike is used to deliver a sharp blow to the face or perhaps the throat. It will rarely end a fight on its own but will cause an opponent to recoil and open him up for additional strikes. This blow is often used from a two-handed neutral stance. Ensure that the maximum force is used by leaning forward onto one leg and pushing into the knee.

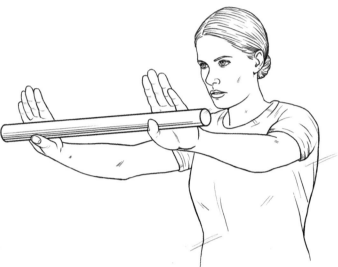

Blunt weapon one-handed ready stance

A blunt weapon is normally used from a weak side forward stance, which adds power to a blow as well as preventing an opponent from grabbing the weapon. Stances vary, but often the lead hand is used to fend off anyone closing in on the weapon user (shown left). Remember that the only reason for being within striking distance is to enable you to strike. If you are not intending to attack, get out of range.

Two-handed ready position

The commonest two-handed ready position is a weak side forward stance similar to that used with a one-handed weapon (left). A more square-on 'neutral' stance is sometimes used (far left), not least because it holds the weapon ready in a fairly non-threatening manner, while still ensuring that an attack could easily and quickly be launched. If you are positive that violence is about to be used on you, the ready position shows that you are willing and able to meet any aggression with confidence, which might in itself be enough to dissuade some attackers.

Backhand strike

A backhand strike comes from over the weak side shoulder and is made with a straightening action of the arm, with the wrist turning to accelerate the weapon as it nears the target point. This wrist action speeds up the attack and results in a more forceful blow.

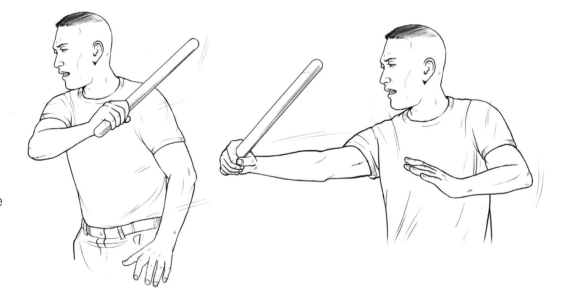

243

Defending yourself

Blunt weapons tip

Most people will make big, heavy swings with a blunt weapon, and tend to hit at a point about one-third of the way down the weapon. This shortens the reach of the weapon considerably. With lighter sticks, it is better to 'feed the tip' and use wrist motion to strike with the tip of the weapon. This increases both reach and impact, allowing you to strike while maintaining a safe distance.

Two-handed overhead strike

An overhead strike comes more or less straight down and with great force. Blocking such a strike is not usually the best option because of the force involved. Instead, moving slightly to the side will cause the blow to miss and expose the overcommitted attacker to a countermove.

Gaining advantage

Note that many strikes need to be delivered in such a way that they momentarily leave the body open to attack. This is due to the need to build up speed and momentum in the blow. Gain the advantage by watching for strike preparation and making a short, but powerful blow to a vulnerable area such as the eyes, nose or groin. Using the tip of the weapon means that more energy is transferred over a smaller area for a stronger blow.

Two-handed forehand blow

A two-handed swing (above) follows a similar path to a one-handed blow, but on a shorter arc. Putting the weak hand on the weapon reduces the reach but vastly increases the force that can be delivered.

Overhead strike

Delivering a two-handed overhead strike takes a relatively long time compared to many other blows, and it is a very committed movement. The descent of the weapon is normally accompanied by moving or leaning forward to put everything behind a crushing blow. Note that face and body are both exposed during the strike, so use it carefully.

Edged weapons

Knives and blades are some of the most common weapons, as they are easy to obtain and conceal. Such weapons can be used to cut or stab, although the mechanics of use are quite different.

Knife ready stance

A strong side forward stance presents the weapon towards the opponent and keeps the body well away from his weapon. A weak side forward stance allows better use of the 'off hand' to deflect attacks or grab the opponent, but requires the confidence to get close before attacking.

Knife fighter stance

Many knife-fighting stances conceal the weapon as much as possible, using the body and the unarmed hand. The unarmed or 'off hand' is actively used for defence and sometimes to grab or strike the opponent. Note that the position of the body in knife fighter stance makes it easy to lunge forwards quickly with a stabbing action, while protecting much of the body against attack.

Slashing attack

Slashing attacks cause significant bleeding. If an artery (for example in the neck or inner thigh) is hit, then death can occur quickly. A slash to the brow is rarely life-threatening but will blind the opponent with blood and probably intimidate him enough that he seeks escape rather than further combat. In most cases, a slash will cause pain and blood loss, but will not incapacitate.

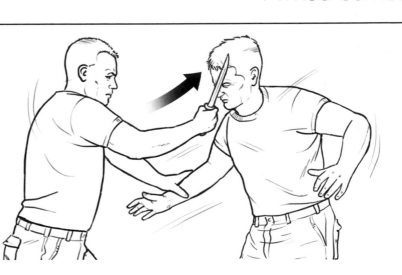

The forehand slash (above) is effective on the head, but also to the thigh as the low attack is often less anticipated and therefore unguarded.

The backhand slash (above) often follows a forehand cut. Remember that it is more likely to hit the outside of a limb.

The leg slash (right) can be fatal, so should only be used in extreme circumstances such as war zones.

Upward stab (1)

The most basic knife attack is the upward stab, delivered from a weak side forward position with the knife held quite low and thrust slightly upward towards the opponent's torso. Most such attacks are aimed to go in just under the ribs (shown left), with the upward strike assisting entry.

Upward stab (2)

When using an upward strike, the opponent will try to recoil away, which may prevent deep penetration. Grabbing his head and pulling him onto the weapon ensures the success of the strike. With the blade angled upward coupled with the force downwards, it may find the heart, lungs and associated large blood vessels. Only to be used in extreme situations, this is likely to result in a rapidly fatal injury.

Lunging stab

The soldier steps through from an out-of-range weak side forward stance into a lunging position, greatly increasing his reach. The danger of such a long, committed attack is obvious; an alert opponent could deflect the strike and counter. However, the attack may come as a surprise if the defender thinks he is safely out of reach.

Back stab

A stab to the kidneys will rapidly disable an opponent, who is likely to then bleed to death. Grabbing his head ensures that the knife penetrates deeply. It must be noted that this is in no way a 'fighting' technique – it is an assassination. Such a stab, as with the throat slash from behind, should only be used under the most extreme, life or death, circumstances.

Firearms for self-defence

Guns are undoubtedly dangerous tools, but they need training to use effectively, and shot placement must be precise to have a decisive effect on an assailant.

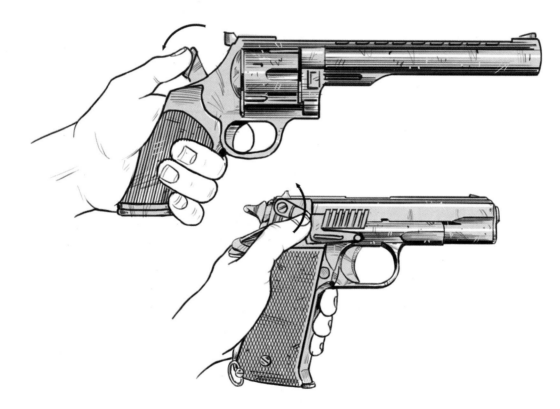

Many revolvers have no manual safety devices, but they do have a device that prevents the hammer from contacting the firing pin unless the weapon is cocked.

Most semi-automatic weapons have a manual safety device in place that prevents the gun firing until it is actively disengaged.

Handgun safety

Most firearms have some kind of safety device to prevent an accidental discharge. Always engage the safety when the gun is holstered or otherwise carried on the body. When the weapon is not in use, remove the ammunition from the gun and ensure that a round doesn't remain in the chamber (in automatic handguns).

Bolt-action rifle

Many sniper weapons and most civilian hunting weapons are bolt-action designs. After each shot the bolt is manually operated, ejecting the spent case and loading a new round. This results in a fairly low rate of fire. However, this is offset by the weapon's accuracy at longer ranges. If you are purchasing a firearm to use as defence for your home, you are unlikely to find that a bolt-action rifle meets your needs.

Double-barrelled shotgun

Many sporting shotguns are double-barrelled designs reloaded by breaking open the weapon and placing new cartridges into the breech. This is a much slower process than changing a magazine. The effective range is fairly short, but at close range their stopping power is unparalleled.

Gun safe

You should keep all your firearms in a purpose-built gun safe like the one shown here. If the safe is operated by keys, make sure you know where those keys are at all times, and always keep them hidden in a secure location. Also make sure your ammunition is stored securely, in a separate location to the weapons.

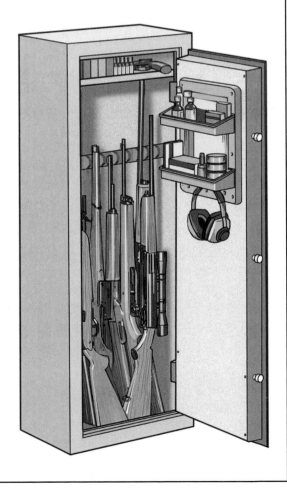

Shooting posture

The two-handed firing stance (right and below) is effective for accurate shooting. The hands create a push-pull lock on the weapon, which extends towards the target. As a general rule, the more contact there is with the ground and the lower the stance, the more accurate the shooter will be.

The draw

The handgun user first clears clothing out of the way, then draws his weapon. He pushes it out at the target as if trying to stab it with the muzzle, establishing a secure two-handed grip on the weapon as he does so. While fumbling with clothing can cost valuable seconds, it can be necessary to avoid the gun being visible.

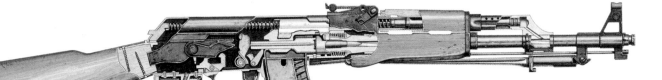

Assault rifles

The AK-47 and its many variants is a selective fire, gas-operated assault rifle capable of fully automatic or semi-automatic fire. It is effective at both long and short ranges. The simplicity of the weapon's design and operation has meant that it is the most widely produced and copied assault rifle in history.

Submachine guns

Submachine guns are small, full automatic firearms normally chambered for pistol-type ammunition. They are useful in similar situations to PDWs (below), and use detachable magazines, so they can be reloaded very quickly to deliver high firepower at short range. They lose accuracy over long distances.

Personal defence weapons

Personal defence weapons (PDWs) such as this FN P90 are ideal for close-range urban combat and defence. They deliver high firepower out to a modest effective range, which is enough for most purposes, but are outranged by rifles fired in open terrain.

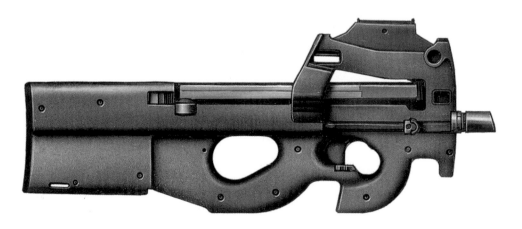

Improvised weapons

It is possible to spend a lifetime making a list of the perfect weapon to counter each possible scenario, but the reality is that when violence starts, you fight with whatever you have to hand.

Door key

Something as simple as a key can be employed as a weapon. The best use is to gouge at an assailant's flesh in order to secure release from a grab. This is unlikely to end a situation, but can be followed up with use on vulnerable areas or may be enough to facilitate escape.

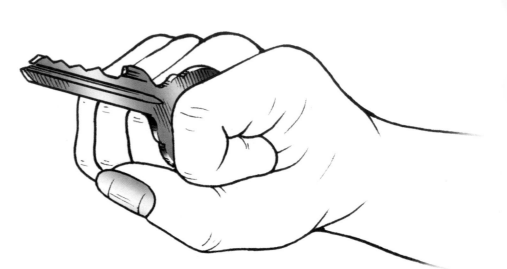

Household objects

Common sense will indicate which household and garden implements can be used as effective weapons. Small and light items are most useful in the same manner as keys – to gouge flesh, inflict pain and secure release from a grab. Larger implements can be used to block attacks as well as strike.

Fire extinguisher

A large fire extinguisher is an awkward and heavy weapon that can only be used with fairly large, obvious movements. If an object of this sort is the only weapon available, then you are probably better throwing it at an opponent's chest to send him staggering than trying to strike with it.

Wooden chair

The humble wooden chair is a common improvised weapon, lagely due to their ubiquity. Use it as a useful weapon/shield combination. Rather than swinging it, hold it by the seat with the legs pointed at the opponent and jab sharply. This keeps him at a distance, ensures that your torso is largely shielded and inflicts pain that might drive him off.

Hostile climate survival

Some climates seem almost designed to test human beings to the extreme. While the human body is an efficient system (if well maintained), a harsh climate and unforgiving terrain expose many potential weaknesses, from hypothermia to poisoning.

Survival in hostile climates, the subject of this chapter, begins with knowledge. You should study every aspect of the regions or countries you intend to visit, comprehending the culture, wildlife, terrain and weather. Alongside such knowledge, you also need to have a core body of survival skills. Remember the key elements of survival – water, food, shelter, rescue – and learn how to match the survival skills with the specific environment.

Allied to tenacity and resourcefulness, your knowledge and survival skills should keep you alive and get you to safety, even when the world is at its most hostile.

A climber tackles a sheer rock face.
Climbing develops an excellent
survival mentality, as it forces
the climber to think logically and
carefully even during physical stress.

The tools of prediction

Predicting the weather helps you to make more informed survival decisions. Being equipped with and prepared to use technology makes it possible to form highly accurate weather predictions.

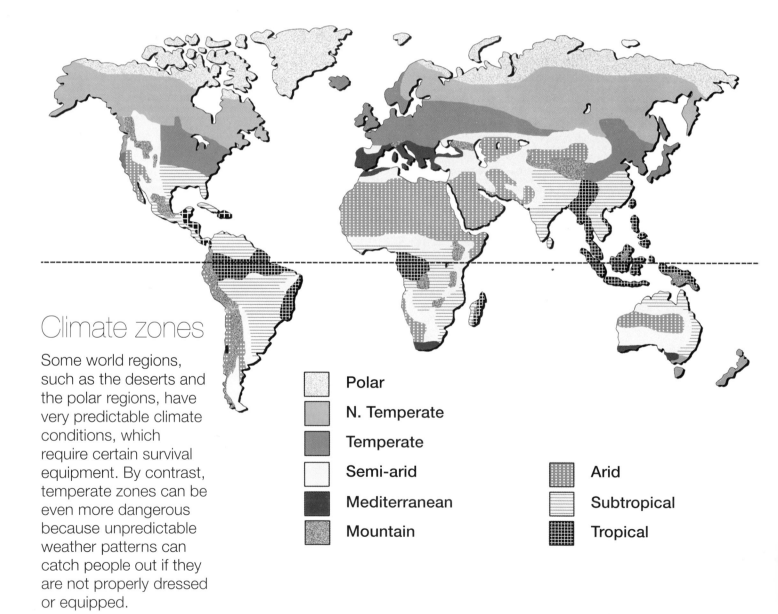

Climate zones

Some world regions, such as the deserts and the polar regions, have very predictable climate conditions, which require certain survival equipment. By contrast, temperate zones can be even more dangerous because unpredictable weather patterns can catch people out if they are not properly dressed or equipped.

Polar

N. Temperate

Temperate

Semi-arid

Mediterranean

Mountain

Arid

Subtropical

Tropical

Thermometers

The wet and dry bulb thermometer (left) can be used in tandem to determine relative humidity by comparing temperature differences.

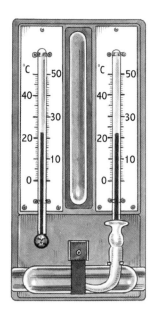

Aneroid barometer

The aneroid barometer functions via a vacuum-filled capsule which compresses when air pressure rises and expands when it falls. A dial provides readings (right).

Winds

The wind is an excellent indicator of changes in weather conditions. At low levels, winds flow around regions of relatively low pressure (cyclones) and high pressure (anticyclones). Winds flow anticlockwise around lows in the northern hemisphere, and clockwise in the southern hemisphere. Wind systems rotate in the opposite direction around the centres of high pressure.

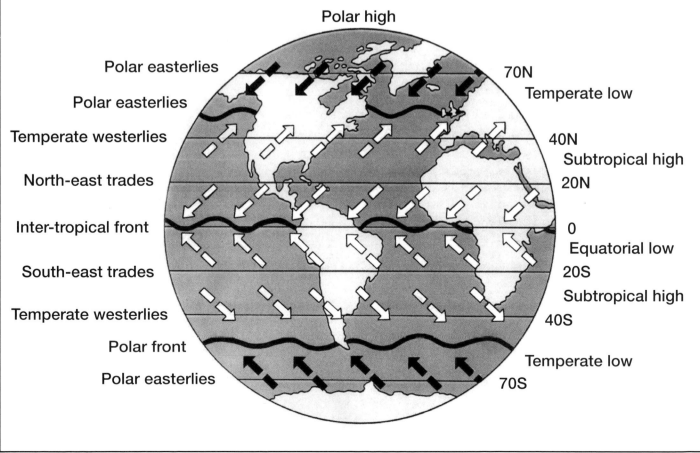

Polar high

Polar easterlies

Polar easterlies

Temperate westerlies

North-east trades

Inter-tropical front

South-east trades

Temperate westerlies

Polar front

Polar easterlies

70N
Temperate low
40N
Subtropical high
20N
0
Equatorial low
20S
Subtropical high
40S
Temperate low
70S

Natural indicators

As useful as they are, if technological systems of forecasting are not available, you will have to take your clues about future weather from the skies and the natural world around you.

High- and low-pressure areas

High-pressure weather systems are formed when air cools and sinks, and are usually associated with clear skies and fine weather. Low-pressure systems evolve as air warms and rises, this producing atmospheric instability, cloud formations and storms. Herding animals tend to respond to falling air pressure by huddling together lying down on the ground. This system is not foolproof, however.

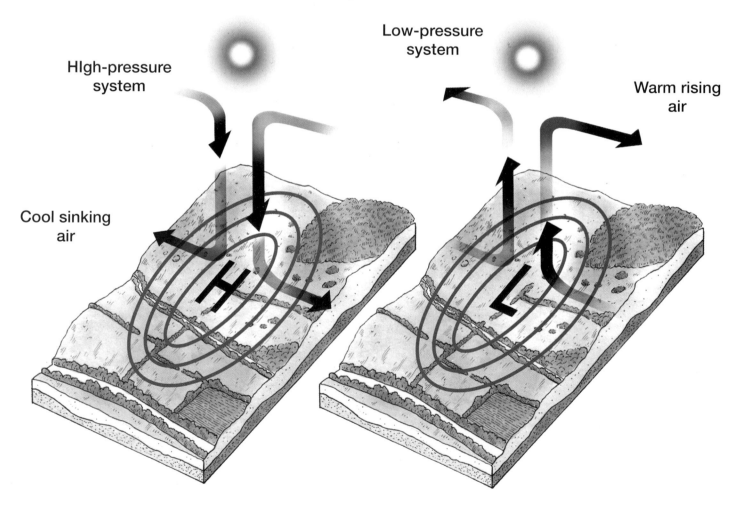

HIgh-pressure system

Low-pressure system

Warm rising air

Cool sinking air

Plant weather indicators

The illustrated plant types all respond to changes in the levels of air humidity, often folding up their petals or leaves in humid conditions to protect their seeds from possible rainfall. Each plant is shown in sunny conditions (left of image), and in rainy conditions (right of page).

In addition to the pictured plants, look out for pine cones, which close their scales as the air becomes more humid with the onset of wet weather, opening them on the approach of fine weather as the air dries out. The silver maple turns its leaves up in the expectation of wet weather.

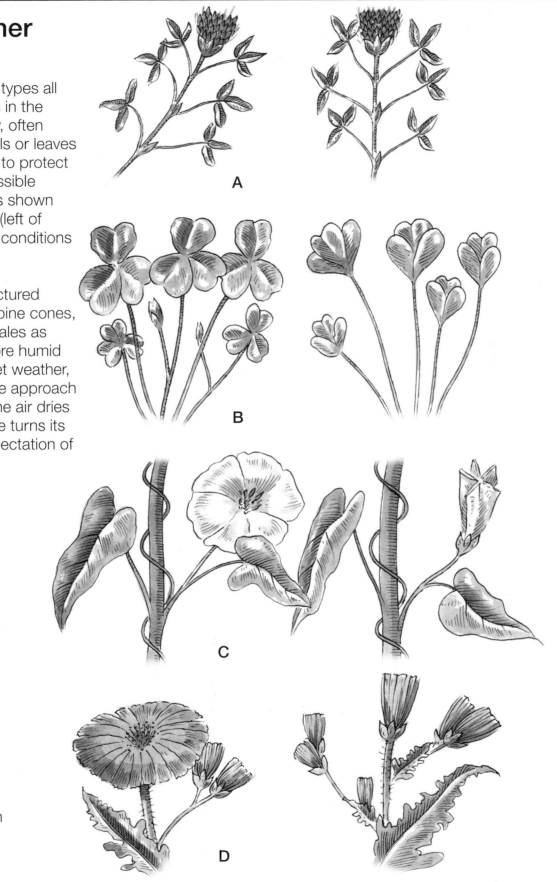

A. Clover in the sun
B. Shamrock
C. Morning glory
D. Chicory

Cloud types

Recognizing cloud types means you can judge the weather for the next 24 hours, making it an essential skill for survival activities. Each cloud type carries a varying probability of rain.

HIgh cloud: cirrocumulus; often associated with dry weather

High cloud: cirrus; generally indicates changing weather

High cloud: cirrostratus; generally indicates changing weather

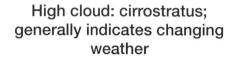

Mid cloud: altostratus; often indicates rain

Low cloud: stratus; similar to fog

Mid cloud: altocumulus; often indicates rain

Low clouds: cumulus; cotton-wool appearance

Reading the clouds

This introduction to cloud types can prepare you for taking shelter and enable you to get your collection equipment out in time, but they can often not be read alone. In the northern hemisphere, the surest sign of rain is cumulus approaching at low level and cirrus at high level.

Low cloud: stratocumulus; appear as an overcast sky

Low cloud: cumulonimbus; the biggest clouds, indicating showery rainfall

Low cloud: nimbostratus; classic rain cloud, often appears grey and dense

Cloud shapes

Clouds are the best elements to observe for predicting the weather. Generally, the lower, thicker and darker the cloud base, the greater the likelihood of poor weather, the towering anvil-headed cumulonimbus bringing the worst weather conditions. If you are unsure, it is probably safe to assume the worst weather and take the appropriate precautions for it.

A. Cirrus
B. Cirrocumulus
C. Cirrostratus
D. Altocumulus
E. Altostratus
F. Stratocumulus
G. Nimbostratus
H. Cumulus
I. Stratus
J. Anvil Head
K. Cumulonimbus
L. Rain, hail and squall winds

Desert conditions

Survival in the desert is, above all, concerned with finding water and making shelter as soon as you can. With temperatures reaching up to 55°C (131°F), death by dehydration can be rapid.

Points to note

- The temperature range in the desert can be as great as 30°C (86°F), with frosts possible during winter months.
- Flash floods may run off the high ground without warning, and thus be life-threatening. This is likely to happen in rocky plateau deserts such as the Golan Heights.
- Sand dunes can be up to 300m (1000ft) high and 24km (15 miles) long.
- Salt marshes should be avoided. They are flat areas where water has evaporated leaving an alkaline deposit.
- Rain erodes sand into canyons and wadis, which can be difficult to traverse.
- Sandstorms are frequent and, apart from being extremely uncomfortable, they can also cause you to lose your bearings.
- Mirages are refractions of light through heated air. The effect they have on objects makes it difficult to assess distances and identify objects.

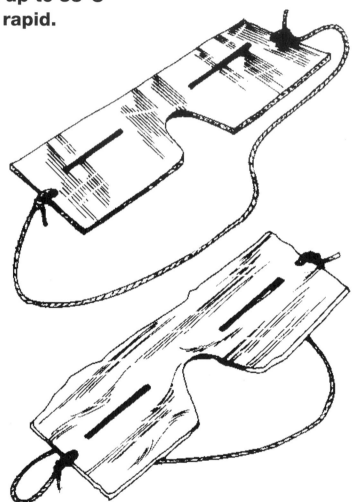

Improvised goggles

The sun can damage the eyes as much as the skin. If you do not have appropriate eyewear, improvise sunglasses by cutting slits in a piece of strong material (top image), or a cutout section of tree bark (below image), and use a cord to fit the 'glasses' securely around the head. Another option is to wrap a cloth (preferably white to reflect light) around your face, cutting two slits for vision.

Protective clothing

This Arab-style headdress is ideal for desert survival. It protects the skull and the back of the neck against the sun, while a face cloth prevents sand inhalation and a burnt nose and cheeks. If you are unused to desert conditions, follow the general rule of covering as much bare skin as possible with loose, white clothing. Wear a wide-brimmed hat and keep your boots on at all times during the day to prevent burned feet and animal bites or stings.

Desert regions

Desert regions mainly straddle the Equatorial lines, although some deserts are to be found as far south as Argentina. All are characterized by extreme aridity and high temperatures. Shade is likely to be rare, so construct a shelter as soon as you can, using natural features if suitable and safe.

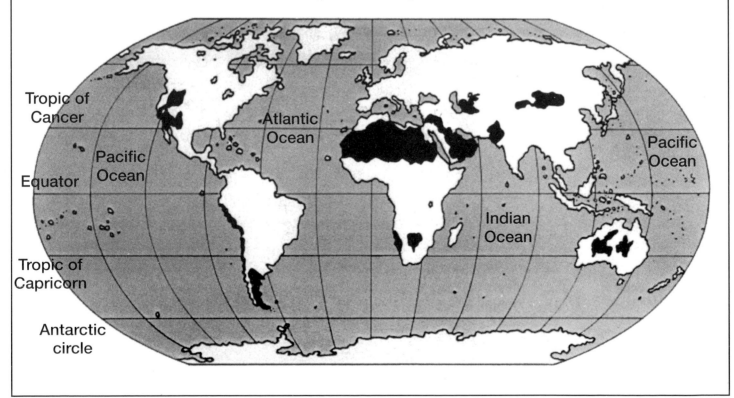

265

Water

Finding water is the primary consideration in the desert. Even if you rest in the shade, without water you will be dead in three days. Water is undeniably scarce, but can still be found.

Dry riverbed

Daily water intake in desert conditions should be a minimum of four litres (one gallon). If you are active, this should go up to nearer 12 litres (three gallons) per day. When digging for water in a dry riverbed, dig on the outside of the bends, as this is usually the last place the water evaporated from, and so is more likely to have water beneath the surface.

Dig here

Dig here

Water intake

Water intake required every 24 hours to maintain water balance during resting conditions:

°F	°C	US/UK pints	Litres required
95°	35°	8½/7	4
90°	32°	6½/5¼	3
80°	27°	2/¾	1

As a rule of thumb, if you have one litre (0.2 gallons) of water, at a maximum temperature of 43°C (110°F) in the shade, you should last for three and a half days, resting in the shade at all times. If you rest during the day and walk at night (travelling about 40km/25 miles), you should last two and a half days.

Water sources

Several key desert water sources are represented here: an oasis, a well and a dried-up riverbed. The palm trees are a good indicator of subterranean water. African bushmen are known to extract water from the ground by inserting a long hollow reed into the earth and sucking hard. After around ten minutes, water may begin to flow up the reed.

1. Cut off the top of a barrel cactus

Water from a barrel cactus

Any water collection in desert conditions is likely to take some time and effort, essential as it is to your survival. Cutting through the tough cactus plant can be difficult, so do this only if other water sources are unavailable, and then only in the cool of the evenings to reduce the amount of water lost through sweating.

3. Drink the contents through a straw

2. Mash up the pulp inside

Food

Just like water, food is admittedly scarce in the desert, but can be found in a select group of plants and desert wildlife. Remember to avoid eating unless you have a source of water.

Plant foods

The agave plant is common to deserts throughout the Americas and the Caribbean, and it provides edible flowers and flower buds, both of which must be cooked before consumption. The baobab, prickly pear and carob are common desert foods. They are good sources of vitamins and fibre, and the prickly pear and baobab trees can also both be tapped as useful sources of water.

Agave

Baobab

Prickly pear

Carob

Cooking and eating

Edible pulp can be extracted from carob seedpods. The fruit and seeds of the baobab can be eaten raw. Boil young leaves. Prickly pear fruit can be eaten raw and the young pods can be eaten when cooked. Cook and eat desert grass, and look for fruit trees such as fig and date.

Wild gourd

A useful desert survival plant that looks similar to a vine, wild gourd creeps along the ground and produces brown fruits, which are edible. Unripe fruit does need boiling prior to eating. Young leaves and seeds are edible when cooked. Stems and shoots contain water – chew them to access it.

Locusts as food

Locusts are a good source of protein in the desert. Attract insects at night with a small light and kill by striking them with a leafy branch. Remember to remove the legs and wings before cooking and eating them. Other viable desert animal foods include rabbits, rodents, snakes, lizards and birds.

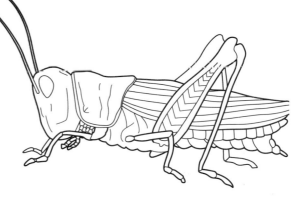

Drawing out a rabbit

Make a fire outside a rabbit warren, and waft the smoke into the entrance. When the smoke forces the rabbit to emerge, strike it with a stick. Alternatively, position a snare wire around the hole.

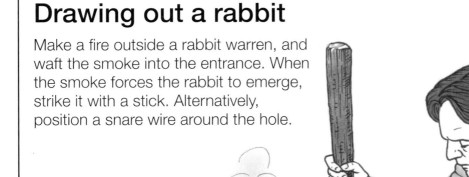

Jungle movement

Tropical regions offer the survivor many sources of food, water and shelter. Yet the hot climate, prevalence of disease and dangerous creatures mean the tropics remain a hostile environment.

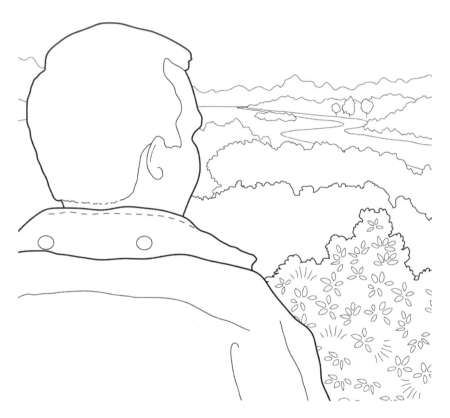

Collecting feature

A collecting feature or handrail is a linear feature in the landscape which provides a directional guide. For example, the walker here knows from the map that the river he can see to his north runs in an east-west direction; as long as he keeps it in view on his right-hand side, he will be travelling west. Such features can be especially useful in the dense jungle terrain.

The monsoon

Monsoons occur in India, Myanmar (Burma) and Southeast Asia. Monsoons are not only associated with heavy rainfall. Between November and April runs the 'dry monsoon', during which time northern winds from Central Asia produce sparse, intermittent rainfall and much fine weather. By contrast, between May and October the 'wet monsoon' is brought in on southern winds from the Bay of Bengal, resulting in heavy, often torrential rain that lasts for days or weeks at a time. It is the alternation of high rainfall and intense sunlight that gives the tropics its lush vegetation. If you are travelling to such areas, avoid the 'wet monsoon'.

Log raft

Log rafts are a good means of travel down relatively calm rivers with manageable currents. Note here how the cross-members that secure the log platform sit in groups cut into the main platform logs, and squeeze them tightly together by a self-tightening knot.

Crossing a river

Streams and waterways are obstacles in almost all wilderness environments. If at any point you need to cross a waterway, first choose an entry point away from rapid, rocky or deep waters, and a place where the current is at its least threatening. Using a loop of rope to make a river crossing ensures that the person in the water is fully enclosed by the line for both the initial and subsequent crossings.

Quicksand

Quicksand is commonly found along tropical rivers and on flat shores. Should you find yourself sinking into quicksand, it is vital that you try not to struggle because this will only make you sink more quickly. Smoothly adopt a spread-eagled position on your back. This helps to disperse your body weight and stop you from sinking. Now make swimming actions to move yourself out of the quicksand, or get companions to throw you a lifeline. Spread out, and swim or pull along the surface to reach firm ground.

Camps and shelters

Safe camps and shelter are essential in jungle conditions. Do not forget that darkness falls quickly in the tropics so construct shelters during the day. Never sleep on the ground.

Building and positioning

The jungle will provide you with all the materials you need to build a shelter. Bamboo shafts can be used to make any structural part of the shelter, and frames of sticks or bamboo can be thatched with large leaves or elephant grass. Look up and check for any dead wood, coconuts or insect nests that might come crashing down on you.

Hammock

With limited protection needed for covering, a hammock can be simple to construct as well as comfortable. You will need a length of fabric wider and longer than your body – anything too narrow and you will be in danger of falling out every time you move – securely attached to a pole at either end, with rope for hanging your hammock.

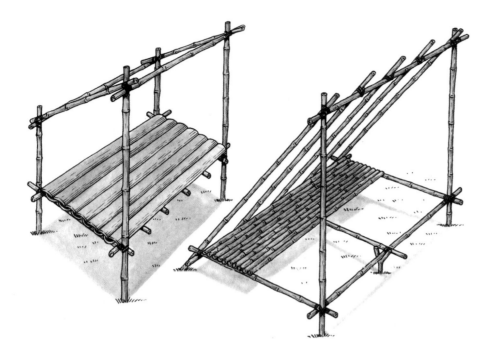

Platform shelters

The tropics have plentiful materials for shelter building. In jungle areas, always ensure the main platform of the shelter is built above the jungle floor. Clear away as much underbrush and dead vegetation as possible around your campsite to reduce insects and remove hiding places for snakes. Ensure that rivers or streams nearby will not endanger you if they flood owing to a sudden downpour.

Seashore shelter

Less ambitious than the platform shelter shown above, this seashore lean-to shelter uses natural supports as the sides and adds planks of wood to provide sides and a roof. Covering your shelter ensures that minimal water or sunshine can find its way through the roof, and a door can be added with heavy fabric or tarpaulin. This creates an enclosed shelter that is cool as well as breezy.

Finding water

The tropics usually contain plentiful supplies of surface water such as streams, ponds and rivers, although these must be purified. Additionally, many tropical plants are good sources of water.

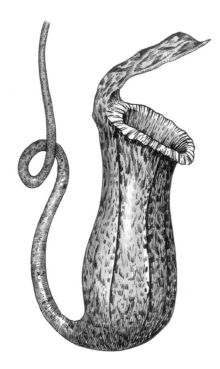

Pitcher plant

Pitcher plants are structurally designed to capture water, and some of the larger specimens can hold up to four litres (one gallon) of fluid. However, always filter and purify any water taken from this plant, as insects often fall into the pitcher, are trapped, then slowly digested by the plant.

Bamboo

Bamboo sections will often contain water suitable for drinking. Tap the bamboo and listen for water, then cut out a section and drink from the open end if the water appears clean. You can leave sections of bamboo positioned to drip into containers for later use, which can be also purified to ensure its safety for drinking.

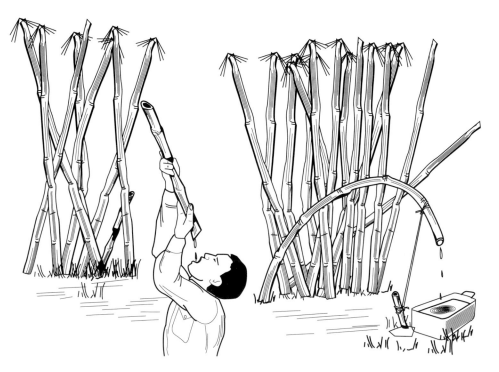

Water from a vine

Chop off a section of vine about 1.5m (5ft) long, then chop off a few inches from the bottom of the section. Water will begin to drip out of the bottom, which can then be caught in a container.

Water purification

The best ways of purifying suspect water are:

- Boil it for at least three minutes.
- Use water-sterilizing tablets.
- Use two or three drops of iodine to one litre (two US pints/1¾ UK pints) of water, allowing it to stand for 30 minutes.
- Use a few grains of permanganate of potash (a form of salt derived from permanganic acid) to one litre (0.2 gallons) of water and allow it to stand for 30 minutes.

If you are taking water from a stream, don't drink it directly from the surface but use a receptacle so as to check that the water is free from such things as leeches. Muddy water can be strained through a sand-filled cloth or a bamboo pipe filled with leaves and/or grass.

The following sources of water will most probably require purification:

- Stagnant water, such as small pools or water in tree trunks.
- Water holes and large rivers. The water should be strained, allowed to stand for a few hours, strained again, and then purified by boiling or dissolving sterilizing tablets.
- Water gained from digging. You can dig into sand a few yards up from the seashore and stop digging as soon as water starts collecting. This water should be fairly clean and free from salt, but must be purified.

Jungle food – plants to eat and to avoid

Tropical areas are full of plant food, several of which are familiar and easily identifiable. However, there are some highly poisonous varieties, so be sure about your identification process.

Bamboo

Bamboo is easy to recognize and is often readily available in the moist soil of jungle climates. As well as being a useful source of water, bamboo shoots up to around 0.3m (1ft) can be eaten raw or cooked. Take care to remove the fine, black hairs that can be found along the edge of the leaves. Boil bamboo seeds before eating.

Taro

The taro plant grows to about 0.5–1m (2–3ft) and can be identified by its heart-shaped leaves. Eat these young leaves, roots and stalks, which can be cooked by either boiling or roasting. If boiling them, change the water several times to get rid of any extracted poisons.

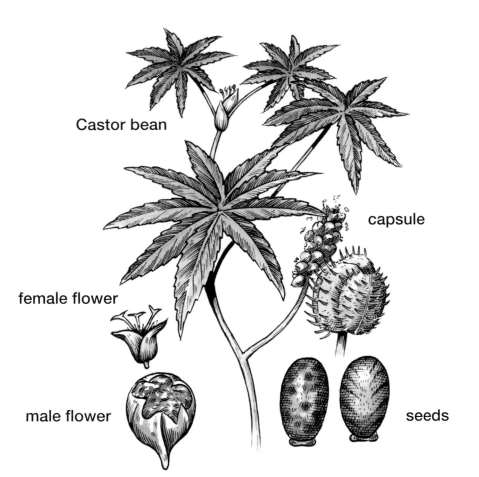

Castor bean

capsule

female flower

male flower

seeds

Poisonous tropical plants

Research the following plant types and avoid them. Apply the Universal Edibility Test (see page 141) to any plant you cannot positively identify.

- nettle trees
- strychnine tree
- physic nut
- cowhage
- duchesnia
- pangi
- castor bean
- white mangrove
- water hemlock
- lantana
- manchineel
- poison sumacs
- rosary pea

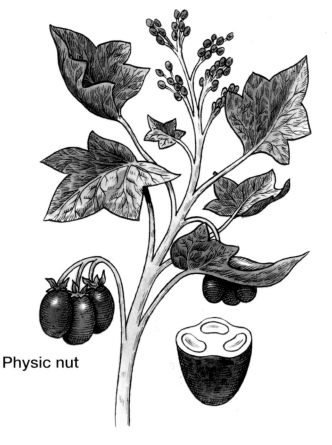

Physic nut

Poisonous tropical plants and fruits

The tropics is replete with highly poisonous plant types. Do not eat anything which you cannot positively identify or which you have not proven as safe through the Universal Edibility Test. Castor beans (shown above) contain ricin, which is used as a poison, with the lethal dose thought to be four to eight seeds. The physic nut contains an oil that can be poisonous in large quantities.

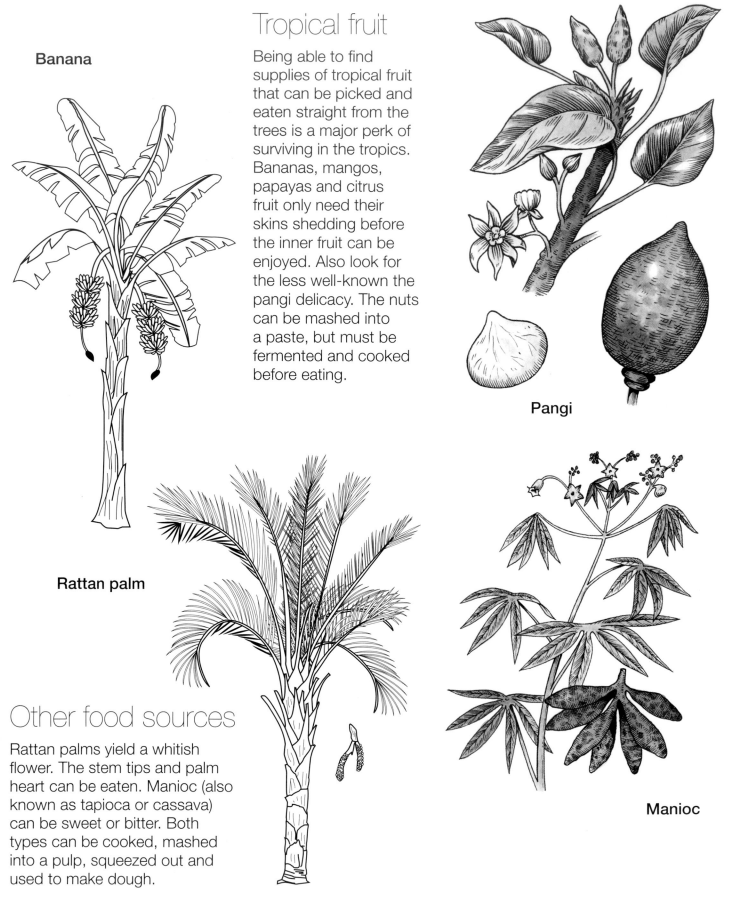

Banana

Tropical fruit

Being able to find supplies of tropical fruit that can be picked and eaten straight from the trees is a major perk of surviving in the tropics. Bananas, mangos, papayas and citrus fruit only need their skins shedding before the inner fruit can be enjoyed. Also look for the less well-known the pangi delicacy. The nuts can be mashed into a paste, but must be fermented and cooked before eating.

Pangi

Rattan palm

Other food sources

Rattan palms yield a whitish flower. The stem tips and palm heart can be eaten. Manioc (also known as tapioca or cassava) can be sweet or bitter. Both types can be cooked, mashed into a pulp, squeezed out and used to make dough.

Manioc

Coconut

Easily recognizable, the coconut tree is an excellent source of food. The meat is high in protein and vitamins and the milk is very nutritious. Young coconuts are an excellent source of coconut water, which is an useful source of electrolytes. The seeds can be used to extract oil, and even the left-over husks and leaves can be used for making shelters.

Coconut palm

Coconut fruit, cut in half

Breadfruit

cross-section of breadfruit

Breadfruit

Another widely used and plentiful crop is the breadfruit. The trees produce yields of up to 200 fruit per year. The large, green fruit can be baked, boiled or fried and the taste is said to resemble freshly baked bread or potatoes. The fruit does not last long, so pick only when needed.

Abundant crop

Many tropical plants grow abundantly, such as wild rice, sugar palms, taro and the wild yams shown here, identified by the heart-shaped leaves growing on opposite sides of the vine. The yam is a ground creeper, and its tuberous root can be boiled and eaten like a vegetable. Do not eat them raw, as they need to be cooked in order to rid them of poison. If your survival experience is likely to be of long duration, collect plentiful supplies of wild rice, which can be boiled or roasted to be eaten, or ground into flour.

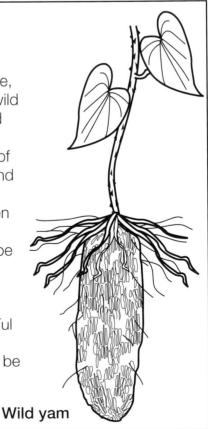

Wild yam

279

Preventing injury and illness

Tropical climates are perfect for the incubation and proliferation of serious diseases. Ensure that you have received all vaccinations and take great care to protect yourself from parasites or injury.

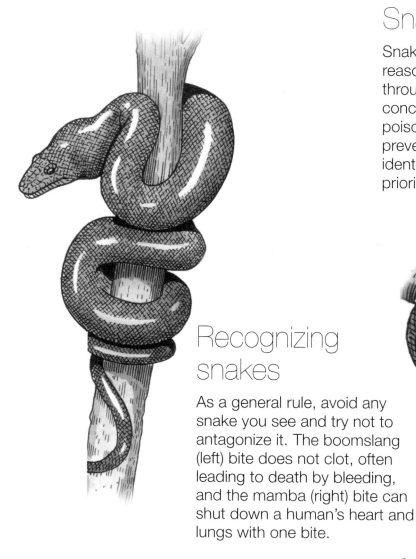

Snakebites

Snakes – as well as insects – are one of the many reasons you should wear boots when moving through the jungle. Tropical areas contain high concentrations of snakes, many of which are poisonous or even lethal. Snakebites are best prevented rather than cured. If someone is bitten, identify the snake before cleaning the wound. Your priority is to get medical help as soon as possible.

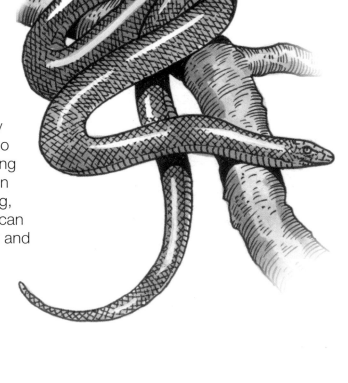

Recognizing snakes

As a general rule, avoid any snake you see and try not to antagonize it. The boomslang (left) bite does not clot, often leading to death by bleeding, and the mamba (right) bite can shut down a human's heart and lungs with one bite.

Tropical diseases

These are typical tropical diseases, listed with symptoms, method of transmission and basic treatment, including prescribed drugs. When dealing with any tropical disease, you should get the victim to a hospital rather than attempt self-treatment.

- **Bilharzia**
  Disease of bowel or bladder. Transmitted by microscopic fluke or worm, passing into the body through infected drinking water or broken skin. Treatment: fluids, rest, niridazole.
- **Amoebic dysentery**
  Chronic illness producing fatigue, general illness, and bloody stools. Transmitted by ingesting contaminated water and uncooked food. Treatment: fluids, rest, flagyl.
- **Malaria**
  Potentially fatal febrile illness transmitted by mosquitoes. Treatment: quinine, paludrine and darapryn.
- **Dengue fever**
  Transmitted by insects. Produces headaches, joint pain and rashes for up to seven days, then abates leaving the casualty with immunity.
- **Yellow fever**
  Insect-borne disease producing vomiting, pains, fever and constipation. Treatment: rest and general care.
- **Typhus**
  Transmitted by lice or rat fleas, it is potentially fatal. Symptoms include vomiting, headache, nausea, rash, fever and coma. Treatment: professional medical attention.

Protective clothing

When collecting insects, particularly of the flying and stinging variety, cover the entire head with netting, wear gloves and place elastic bands around the trouser ankles. Insects are actually the most dangerous creatures in the tropics, carrying diseases that cause widespread illness and death. Take preventative measures at all times.

Escaping a bite

If confronted by a snake, move slowly away from it, giving it plenty of room to escape. If the snake is coiled and erect, it may be preparing to strike. If you have to kill one, chop at its head with a club or machete, or drop a large rock on it. The North American rattlesnake (above) is not fatal, but a bite can lead to swelling, internal bleeding and even paralysis.

Coral snake

Coral snakes are amongst the most lethal snakes in the world. Just 3–5mg (0.0002 ounces) of their venom can be fatal to an adult human. Take care not to step on a snake when walking, particularly when stepping over logs and stones, and watch that a snake is not coiled around a branch when you go through foliage. Check bedding, clothes and backpacks carefully.

Scorpions

Scorpion stings range from merely painful through to lethal. US Army tropical survival courses actually include eating scorpions for food, as only 25 out of about 1000 scorpion species are dangerous to humans. Scorpions like to sleep in dark, protected spaces, so look for them each morning in dark corners of boots, clothing or equipment.

Hornet

Hornets deliver the most excruciating sting, likened to the feeling of a red-hot rivet being driven into the skin. Don't kill a hornet, as its distress signals can encourage the others in its nest to attack you. Never camp near a nest and avoid antagonizing the creatures. If you are allergic to the stings, administer an epinephrine injection and seek medical help as soon as possible.

Climate and terrain

Mountains are truly dangerous places for the unwary and inexperienced and should be avoided in survival situations. Terrain, climate and gradient can hamper even simple movements.

Rain-shadow effect

The windward slope of a mountain tends to attract higher levels of preticipation as moist air rises up the mountain side to form rain clouds. The leeward side of the mountain subsequently suffers from a rain-shadow effect, the descending air being drier and less prone to severe winds.

Moist air

Windward side

Dry air

Significant mountains of the world

Mountains usually exist in ranges which consist of peaks, ridges and intermontane valleys. Mountain climates can vary widely, with mountains in temperate zones having strongly marked seasons. The opposite is the case in desert regions, where equatorial mountains have often indistinguishable summers and winters. There can be rapid changes in temperatures no matter where you are, so ensure that you are prepared for any eventuality, no matter where you are going in the world.

Asia	Feet	Metres
Everest (China-Nepal)	29,028	8848
K2 (Kashmir-Sinkiang)	28,250	8611
Nanda Devi (India)	25,643	7816
Ararat (Turkey)	16,808	5123
Jaya (Indonesia)	16,503	5030
Kinabalu (Malaysia)	13,431	4094
Fuji (Japan)	12,388	3776
North & Central America		
Mckinley (USA)	20,320	6194
Logan (Canada)	19,551	5959
Citlaltepetl (Mexico)	14,688	4477
South America		
Aconcagua (Argentina)	22,834	6960
Huascaran (Peru)	22,205	6768
Sajama (Bolivia)	21,463	6542
Chimborazo (Ecuador)	20,702	6310

Europe	Feet	Metres
El'brus (Russian Federation)	18,510	5642
Mont Blanc (France-Italy)	15,744	4808
Matterhorn (Italy-Switzerland)	14,688	4477
Etna (Sicily)	10,902	3323
Africa		
Kilimanjaro (Tanzania)	19,340	5895
Kirinyaga (Kenya)	17,057	5199
Stanley (Zaire)	16,763	5110
Toubkal (Morocco)	13,664	4165
Australasia		
Cook (New Zealand)	12,316	3754
Antarctica		
Vinson Massif	16,066	4897
Erebus	12,447	3794

Avalanches

While an avalanche can occur wherever snow lies, it is influenced by certain conditions. If the snow is well bound together, then the risk of avalanche is reduced. If there are marked differences in the hardness of layers of snow, then the risk of avalanche starts to increase.

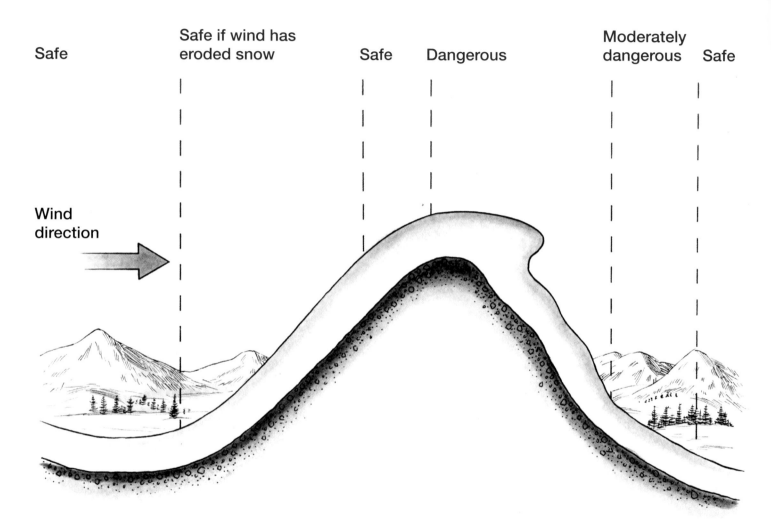

There are many different types of avalanche structure, but you should be especially cautious about overhanging slabs of wet snow which have the wind behind them.

If you are in an area in which you fear an avalanche is likely, take the following precautions. Cross the danger zone one at a time, connected by a rope, taking advantage of any available protection such as rock outcrops. If you are caught in an avalanche, try to maintain your present position, which will allow dangerous snow to pass safely below you.

If you find yourself falling in an avalanche, try to move across to the side of the fall by rolling sideways. Use swimming motions to try to remain near the surface.

If you are buried, try to clear a breathing space. Remain silent to conserve oxygen. Once the movement stops, try to punch an air hole and dig your way to the surface. Let dribble slide from your mouth to help you determine which way is upright (the dribble will slide downwards).

Atmospheric pressure change

The chart below shows how swiftly atmospheric pressure drops with the increase in altitude. Altitude sickness tends to begin occurring at altitudes above 2400m (8000ft).

With any movement around mountains requiring conscious effort and technique, preventing altitude sickness is vital for safe passage. The drop in air pressure combined with physical exertion can result in headachy, flu-like symptoms, which can develop into dizziness, fatigue and, in extreme cases, pulmonary edemas (fluid in the lungs) or cerebral edemas (swelling in the brain). Slowing the ascent can prevent altitude sickness, but be aware of the symptoms and stop your ascent if any present themselves. This will allow your body to acclimatize to the lower pressure.

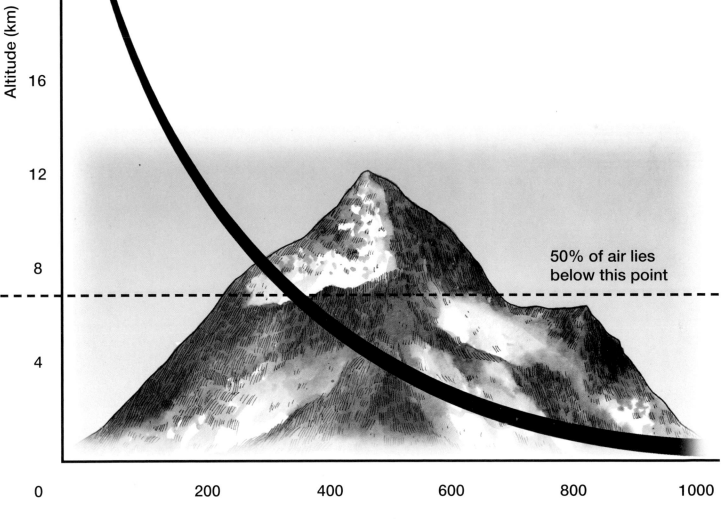

50% of air lies below this point

Altitude (km)

Pressure (mb)

Mountain movement

Inefficient movement in the mountains results in wasted energy, fatigue and a greater likelihood of accidents. Mountain movement across snow and ice also brings its own challenges.

Breaking a fall

The braking procedure using an ice axe involves flipping onto your front, gripping the ice axe diagonally across your body. Dig the axe pick into snow, pushing down with full body weight.

Traversing

Do not walk straight up very steep gradients. The traversing technique is simply a zigzag movement up the slope that allows the legs to avoid the full stress of the incline. Turn at the end of each traverse by stepping off in a new direction with the uphill foot. This movement also eliminates the risk of losing your balance by preventing you having to cross your feet.

Braking positions

To brake yourself during a slide, either adopt a spread-eagled position, digging in with your heels (above), or push yourself off the slope as shown above right – this latter position drives all your weight onto your toes, which then act as brakes. If you are holding an ice axe, dig the shaft vertically into the slope. If the snow is hard, force the pick of the ice axe into the snow to slow your descent. Once you are moving more slowly, use the axe and your hands and feet to get further holds.

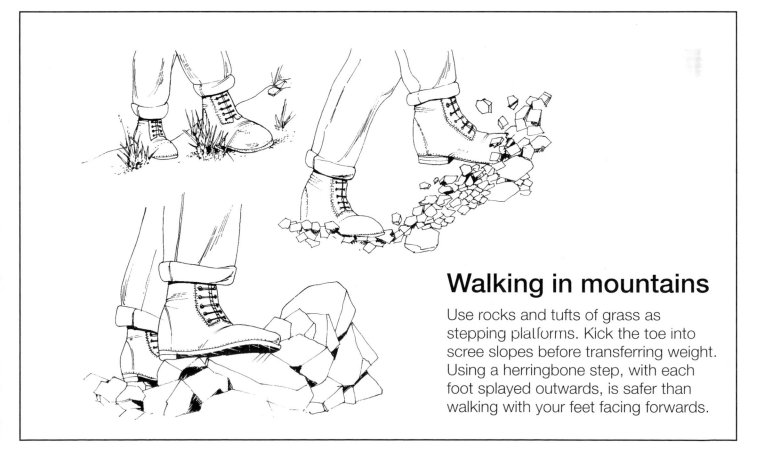

Walking in mountains

Use rocks and tufts of grass as stepping platforms. Kick the toe into scree slopes before transferring weight. Using a herringbone step, with each foot splayed outwards, is safer than walking with your feet facing forwards.

Climbing techniques

Climbing techniques cannot be learned from a book, but acquiring as much knowledge of the methods as you can will provide a clear advantage to survival in mountainous terrain.

Abseiling (1)

When abseiling, make sure you lean out from the rockface at a 45° angle and keep the legs spread shoulder width apart for stability. Brake by leaning back and facing straight into the rockface. Make sure that no bare skin is in contact with the rope, or friction burns will result. The rope will slide through your hands, so gloves are advisable.

Note how the rope is wrapped around the body

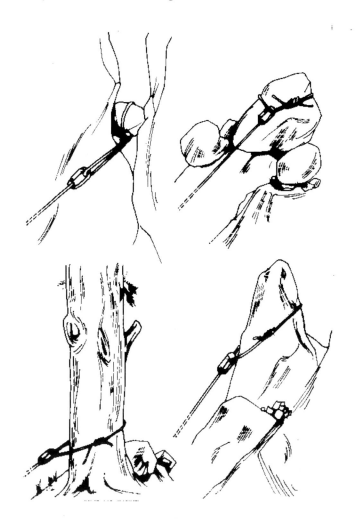

Walk backwards slowly to maintain a controlled descent

Anchor points

Select anchor points carefully. Test an anchor's strength prior to hanging your full weight on it, and ensure that the anchor has no sharp edges which will cut through the rope. As well as natural anchors such as rocks or trees, use artificial anchors such as chocks (metal wedges that fit into cracks) and pitons (metal spikes that can be driven into crevices).

Seat harness

With the midpoint on the hip, cross the ends of the tape in front of the body and tie three overhand wraps where they cross (A). From the front to the rear bring the ends of the tape between and around the legs and secure with a hitch (B). Bring both ends to the front, then to the opposite side and tie a square knot (C).

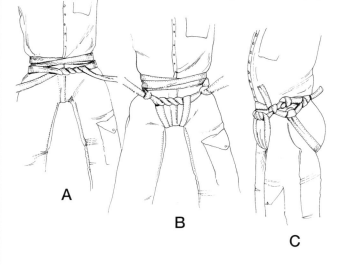

A

B

C

Abseiling (2)

Abseiling (above) is not an easy option and should only be attempted if you are experienced in the technique. Ensure that the anchor takes your weight and is securely fastened to the rope. Tie a knot at the end of the rope to prevent abseiling off the end, and check that it reaches the ground before descent.

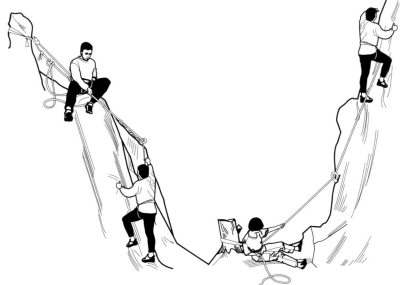

Belaying

Belaying is a way of climbing for two or more people using ropes. The belayer (the person who feeds out the rope) should be firmly anchored to a solid structure and must lay the rope out to run freely through the braking knot. The skill of belaying is to not let too much slack develop or take it up too quickly.

In an emergency

No matter how much care you take, mountains are dangerous, unpredictable places. An emergency can occur quickly, so prepare for this eventuality by knowing what to do if the worst happens.

Avalanche survival

When caught by an avalanche, if possible 'swim' to safety by thrashing the arms in a crawl stroke to stay on the surface. If you are submerged, thrash your arms and legs as the avalanche slows to create a breathing space for when movement stops, allowing room for air.

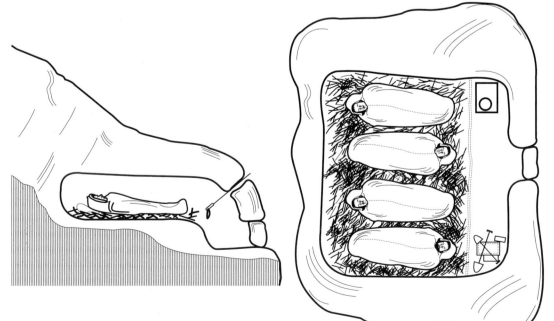

Snow cave

If you are stranded on a mountain, shelter is essential to survival. Snow caves can be built into ledges where snow drifts have formed. Cut deep into the snow to form a central chamber and, if there is any vegetation available, use it to make an insulating platform. Seal the door with a snow block or rucksack, but leave some ventilation.

Types of avalanche

Wet slab avalanches are the result of snow mixed with water. Hard slab avalanches are formed by huge chunks of snow which break off from a wind-compacted sheet. Soft slab avalanches consist of powdered snow. Wet snow is the most dangerous as it is denser and heavier.

Wet slab

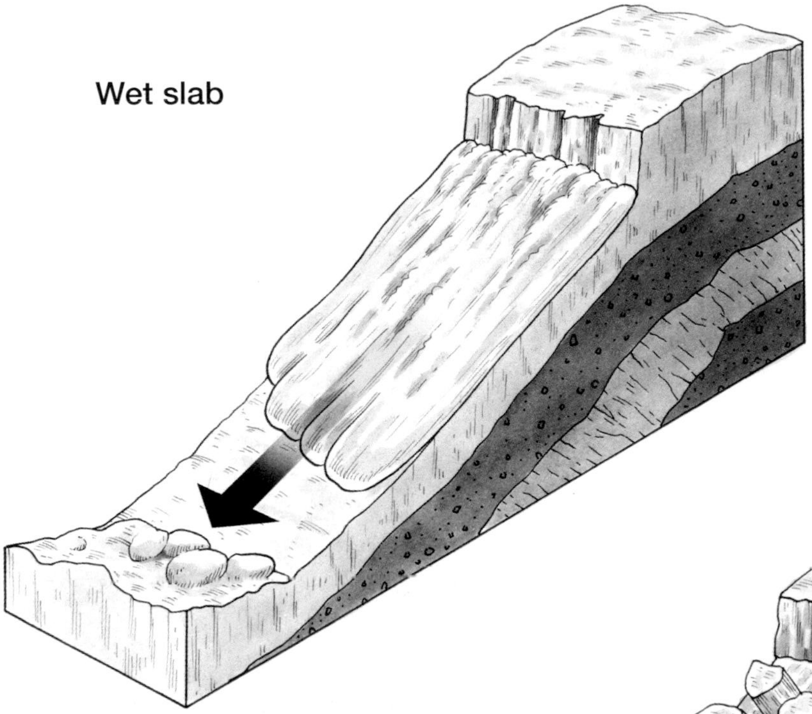

Hard slab

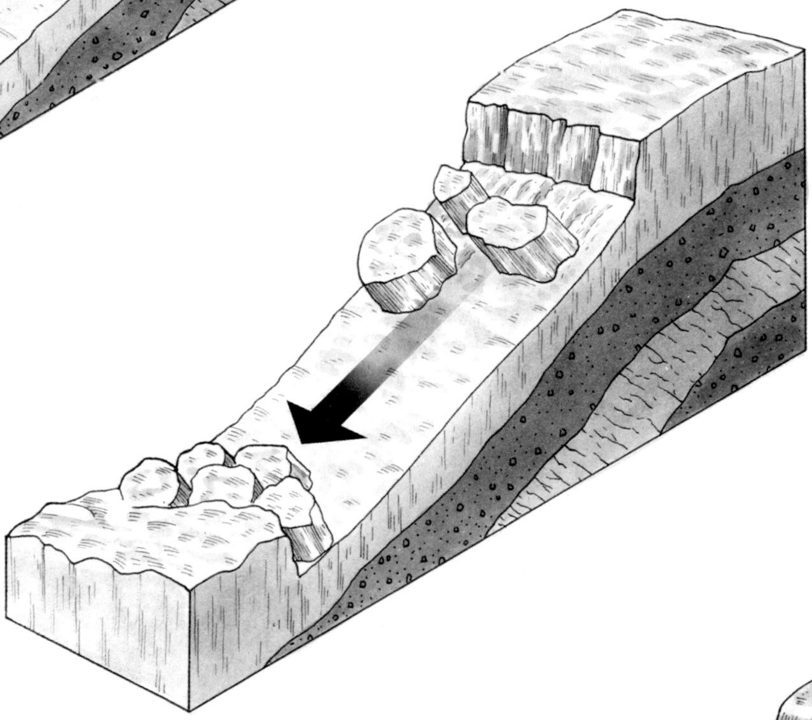

Soft slab

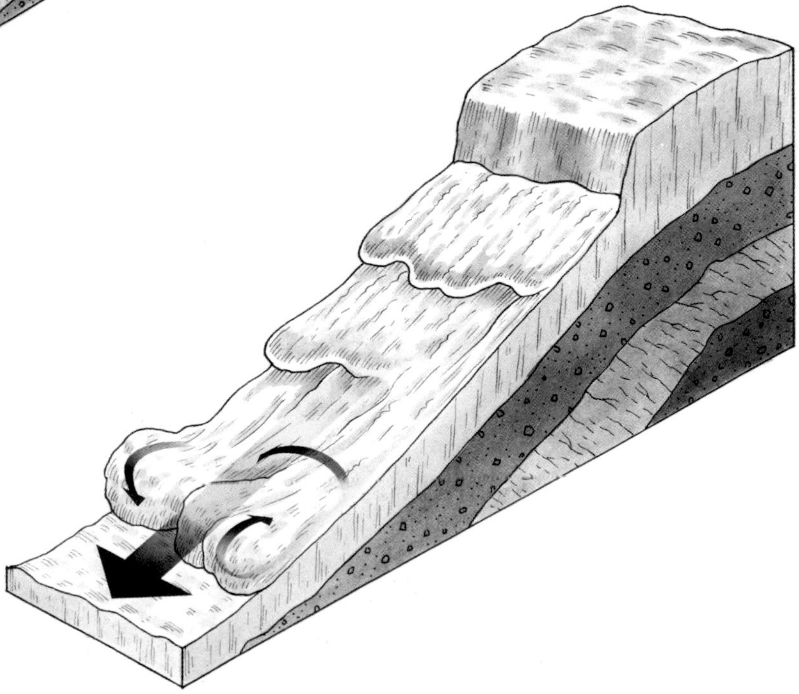

Last place
victim seen

Climbers' track

Most likely
burial area

Mountain rescue codes

The following codes are internationally recognized mountain rescue signals and can be transmitted by auditory (whistle or foghorn) or visual (flare, heliograph, flashlight) methods:

- **SOS signal**
  Auditory: three short blasts, three long blasts, three short blasts (repeat after a one-minute interval). Visual: three short flashes, three long flashes, three short flashes (repeat after a one-minute interval). A red flare also means SOS.
- **'Help needed' signal**
  Auditory: six blasts in quick succession (repeat after a one-minute interval). Visual: six flashes in quick succession (repeat after a one-minute interval). A red flare can also be used.
- **'Message understood' signal**
  Auditory: three blasts in quick succession (repeat after a one-minute interval). Visual: three flashes in quick succession (repeat after a one-minute interval). A white flare also means the message has been understood.
- **'Return to base' signal**
  Auditory: prolonged series of blasts. Visual: prolonged series of flashes. A green flare can also be used.

Rescue search

Searching for avalanche victims should follow a methodical procedure. Search downwards from the last position where the person was seen, using discarded pieces of equipment and clothing as further directional guidance. Speed the search up by using several people in an evenly-spread line.

Emergency procedures

In a mountain emergency, your priorities are simple: head downwards to reduce exposure to high-altitude weather conditions. Down in the valleys, you are also more likely to find civilization and rescue. Before moving off, look for viable routes down to the mountain floor.

Avalanche protection

Areas with a high avalanche risk often take precautions, which include avalanche walls to shore up snow accumulation, rakes, fences, wedges and forest to slow avalanche flow, avalanche gullies to channel an avalanche and deflectors to protect habitations if an avalanche occurs.

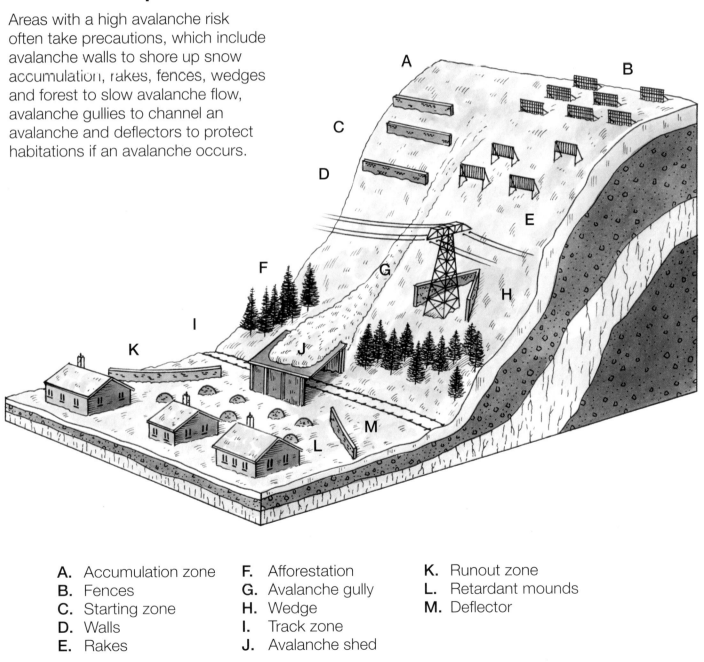

A. Accumulation zone	**F.** Afforestation	**K.** Runout zone
B. Fences	**G.** Avalanche gully	**L.** Retardant mounds
C. Starting zone	**H.** Wedge	**M.** Deflector
D. Walls	**I.** Track zone	
E. Rakes	**J.** Avalanche shed	

Safe movement

True polar environments are probably the most hostile climates on Earth. Food and shelter are scarce, subzero temperatures can kill in hours, and every movement is fraught with danger.

Falling through ice (1)

Walking on ice is always risky and should be avoided if at all possible. If you are alone and you fall through ice, try to claw your way out using knives, ice picks or ski poles to get adhesion on the slippery ice. Once out, strip off your wet clothes, and dry out as quickly as you can. If you stay in wet clothes you are likely to freeze.

Falling through ice (2)

If attempting to rescue someone who has fallen through ice, one person should lie flat across the ice to spread his weight while another person holds his ankles for safety. As the trapped person is pulled to safety, she should slide across the ice to safety without standing up. Spreading your body over a greater area of ice reduces weight.

Making snowshoes

A simple pair of snowshoes can make travelling in polar regions a much simpler task. They enable you to walk over deep snow with greater ease, as they spread your weight over a larger surface area. Modern snowshoes are made of materials such as lightweight plastic or metal, but some still use hardwood frames and rawhide. To make your own, you will need several lengths of pliable sapling (A) such as willow, and cord for lashing. Shape a length of sapling into a frame (B and C), with cross-members fitted (D) so that your feet have supports. Cord is used to tie the lengths of sapling together and then to tie the shoes over the boots (E).

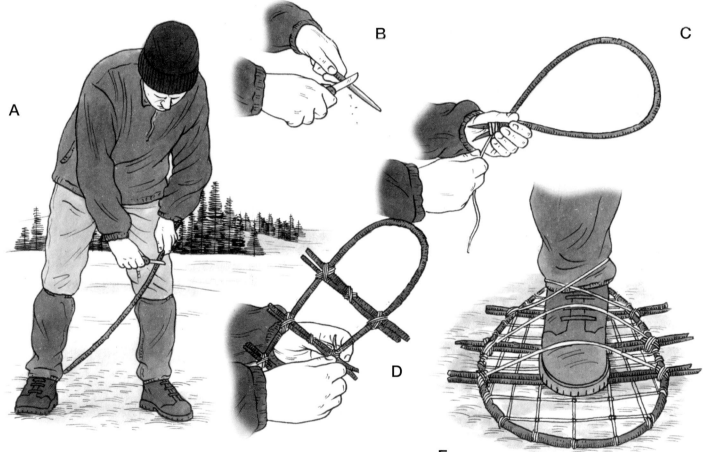

Snow signals

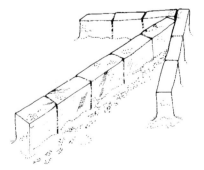

If you are socking shelter while awaiting rescue, rectangular blocks of snow can be used to build up snow signals on the ground for rescuers. Any rescue party will start looking in your last known position, so providing snow signals as close to this place as possible, and at regular intervals, will increase your chances of being found quickly.

Polar fire and shelter

With polar wind chill temperatures dropping down to –50°C (–58°F), having the knowledge and ability to build shelter and make a fire in a polar environment could save your life.

Polar fires (1)

Polar fires need special consideration, not least because they are surrounded by ice which will soon extinguish them. In snowy conditions, build fires on log platforms so that the snow does not make contact with the flames. Use resinous woods for fuel if they are available, as they will burn even when wet.

Polar fires (2)

The extreme polar winds of up to 32km/h (20mph) can quickly put paid to a fire you spent time and effort building. Enclose your fire against the wind to protect it, or build it in a pit. Use rocks as the enclosure if possible, as they will last and can be used as portable heat sources if wrapped. If you cannot find any, snow blocks will work temporarily.

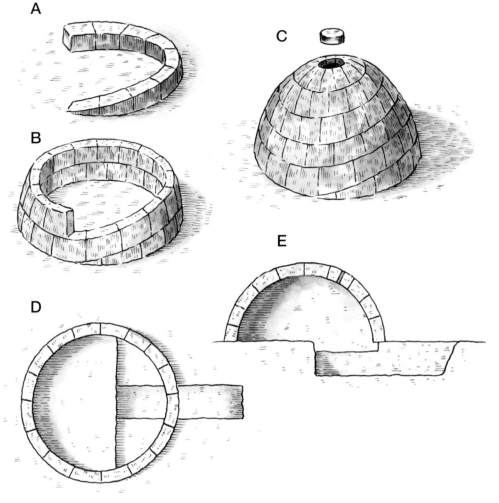

Igloo

Igloos are difficult constructions to make, so opt for more basic snow shelters if you do not have the skills. However, an igloo will provide a high degree of protection against polar climates and is an excellent option if you will be spending any length of time outdoors. Draw a circle about 2.5–3m (7–10ft) in diameter on the snow and stack snow blocks around the line (A). Build the igloo wall up, bevelling the tops of the blocks so that the igloo curves in towards the middle (B). A small hole should remain in the top of the roof, which should be enclosed with a disc of snow (C). Build a platform of snow for sleeping on (D), to which you can add layers of branches for insulation. The lower cold sink (E) acts as an entrance tunnel and ventilation.

Shelter rules

Whatever shelter you build in polar regions, observe the following rules.

- Always cover the floor of snow shelters with insulating material, such as boughs, dry grasses and moss.
- Build your shelter as near to sources of fire fuel as possible.
- Avoid building shelters on the lee side of cliffs – snowslides might bury your shelter.
- Limit the number of entrances you build; the more you have, the more heat is lost.
- Store firearms outside. Storing them inside encourages condensation to build up on the barrel and in the action, causing either rust or, if it freezes, weapon malfunction. (Always check the end of the barrel before use; a plug of ice could cause the gun to explode on firing.)
- Make a latrine area outside. If the weather is too extreme to venture out, either dig an additional latrine tunnel extending out from your snow cave, or urinate into tin cans and defecate onto snow blocks that are then thrown outside.
- If your sleeping bag gets wet, knock off any frost, then dry it near a fire.
- Check regularly that the shelter's ventilation holes are not blocked with snow, and chip off any coatings of ice – ice reduces your shelter's insulating properties.
- Do not allow excessive amounts of snow to build up on your shelter. The weight may cause the structure to collapse.

Finding water and food

Although vegetation is sparse in ice climates, edible plants can be found. However, these alone are unlikely to sustain you for long. It is probable that you will need to hunt for meat or fish.

Water maker

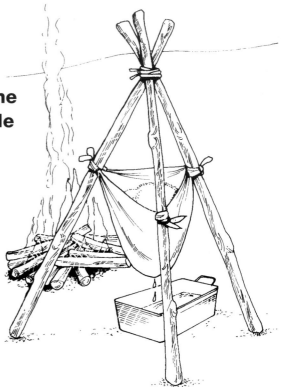

Eating snow or ice can accelerate hypothermia, cause tissue damage to the mouth and lips, and create stomach disorders. A basic device for melting snow and ice to water consists of a wooden tepee frame secured at the top with a bag of material tied between the struts. The bag is filled with snow and a fire built to one side; the melting water then drips through the cloth into a container.

Ice fishing

Fishing can yield good food supplies while leaving you free to hunt or build a shelter. To fish through frozen lakes, first cut a hole in the ice over deep water. Make a pennant from cloth or paper, and tie it to a light stick that is shorter than the diameter of the hole. Now tie another stick to the first. This stick should be longer than the diameter of the hole and must be secured at right angles to the first stick. Fasten the fishing line to the other end of the flagpole, and rest the long stick across the hole. When a fish takes the bait, the flagpole will be jerked upright.

Iceland moss

Rock tripe

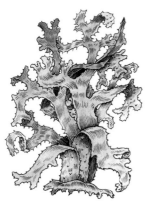

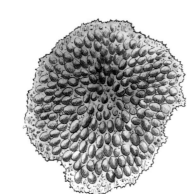

Edible plants

Iceland moss is a leathery plant with straplike branches. Rock tripe resemble greyish or brownish blisters and are found attached to rocks. With both plants, all parts are edible after several hours of soaking and then boiling. Other edible plants include bearberry, salmonberry, black or red spruce and labrador tea.

Shrew

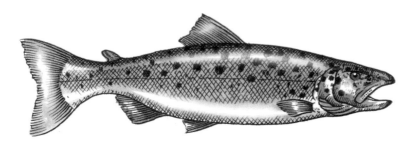

Mammals

Many polar mammals, especialy bears or seals, are large and dangerous, best killed with a hunting rifle of large calibre (7.62mm/0.3in plus) or spears. With both creatures, avoid eating the liver, as it contains lethal concentrations of vitamin A. Smaller mammals such as shrews, arctic hares, stoats and weasels can be caught with snares or deadfalls.

Fish

Arctic and subarctic rivers and seas are teeming with marine life, including salmon, arctic cod, grayling, trout and crayfish. Shellfish are also abundant, but both catching and eating them requires caution. Be careful of slipping along icy shorelines, and never eat already dead shellfish.

Salmon

Ptarmigan

Birds

Northern forests and tundra have many birds, especially water birds such as geese, swans and ducks. Ptarmigan and grouse are also plentiful and are relatively tame and easy to catch. Whatever animal you kill, do not waste a scrap of flesh or bone. Remove feathers and fur carefully and use for clothing and freeze meat to preserve it.

Abandoning ship

Water covers nearly three-quarters of the planet, yet humans are never more out of their element than when lost at sea. Surviving the initial emergency can expose you to many dangers.

Launching a life raft

On abandoning ship, first ensure that your life jacket is securely fastened. Throw the life raft canister overboard to leeward (downwind), having attached the static line to the toe rail. Throw the canister to a clear spot away from any debris.

Draw in the static line until it stops paying out, then give the line a sharp tug to initiate the CO_2 inflation mechanism. Now is also the time to grab any survival supplies to hand from the boat and take them with you on to the life raft (if it is safe to do so).

Allow the raft to inflate fully (it should take about 30 seconds), then load your survival gear inside before climbing aboard and casting off. If the sinking of your boat is likely to have been reported, keep your raft as close to the site as possible.

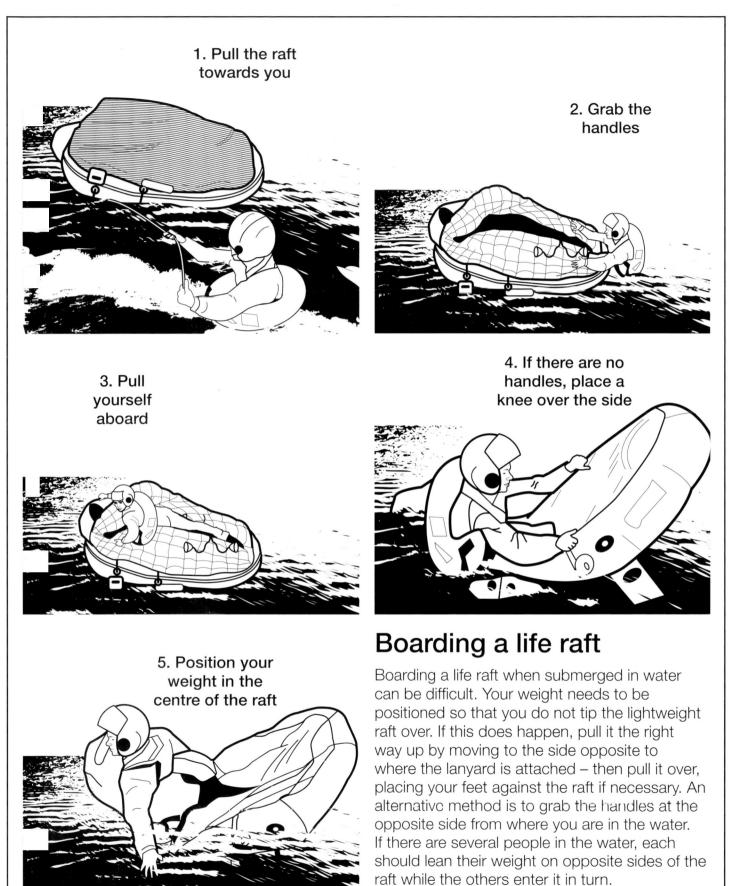

1. Pull the raft towards you

2. Grab the handles

3. Pull yourself aboard

4. If there are no handles, place a knee over the side

5. Position your weight in the centre of the raft

Boarding a life raft

Boarding a life raft when submerged in water can be difficult. Your weight needs to be positioned so that you do not tip the lightweight raft over. If this does happen, pull it the right way up by moving to the side opposite to where the lanyard is attached – then pull it over, placing your feet against the raft if necessary. An alternative method is to grab the handles at the opposite side from where you are in the water. If there are several people in the water, each should lean their weight on opposite sides of the raft while the others enter it in turn.

Survival in the water

If you are not in a life raft, your immediate dangers are drowning and hypothermia. Look for anything that will provide buoyancy or, ideally, get you out of the water altogether.

Crouching position

No matter how experienced a swimmer you are, the constant movement and use of muscles will quickly drain you of strength. The crouching position is a technique of energy conservation. Periodically, let the body and hands go limp in the water, and float in this position for as long as you can hold your breath, relaxing your muscles. Bring the arms upwards to return your body to the upright position. You could also float on the surface of the water with your arms and legs outstretched.

Floating together

When floating in a group, tie yourselves together so that you do not float apart. If you managed to retain your grab bag or any supplies, tie a link to it so that it does not get lost in heavy waves. Huddling together will also reduce heat loss.

Abandoning ship through fire

When jumping overboard into a sea covered with burning oil, jump into a clear patch of sea, then swim underwater to a safe spot. Do not inflate your life jacket before jumping in. Your priority is to get as far away from the sinking vessel as possible before it goes beneath the waves, as the powerful downward suction that is created will pull you under the water and drown you if you are still in the vicinity. If you have any time, put on warm wool clothing, waterproofs, hats and gloves for protection, and grab any supplies that are to hand.

Improvised float (1)

Tie the ankles of the trousers tight together then, holding the trousers by the waistband or belt, swipe them over your head to fill with air. Hook the tied ankles behind your neck to form a rudimentary flotation device.

No float

If you have no float, position yourself on your back with your arms out at your sides and your lungs fully inflated. However, this method is only useful in calm water.

Improvised float (2)

The improvised float enables you to expend far less energy in constant movement to just keep your head above the water. Use this energy to look for any debris, ideally something big enough for you to climb on. After fashioning a float, getting your body out of the water is paramount.

HELP posture

The Heat Escape Lessening Posture (HELP) reduces body heat loss by keeping as much of the torso as possible out of the water, pushing the arms against a flotation device to achieve lift. As well as the torso, aim to keep your head dry at all times, as much body heat is lost through it. This posture lessens the risk of hypothermia, although it should be your overriding goal to get fully out of the water into a raft or onto dry land as quickly as possible.

Avoiding reefs and rocks

If your life raft has disintegrated and you are attempting a floating landing, paddle towards the beach once the crests have passed, back-paddle when the next crest approaches (or turn and dive into it if it is large or breaking). Once in your approach, keep your feet below and ahead of you, paddling with your arms, so that your shoes hit the rock or reef first and your legs absorb the impact.

Survival in a life raft

If you are in a life raft and the sinking of your ship was reported, you are likely to be rescued quickly. If your position is unknown, you could be in danger of death by dehydration or starvation.

Landing in surf

Even with your sea anchor streamed for support, to prevent capsizing in the surf on your approach to land, you will need to back-paddle as wave crests approach. Everyone should be harnessed to the life raft and use the lanyards to prevent losing their paddles.

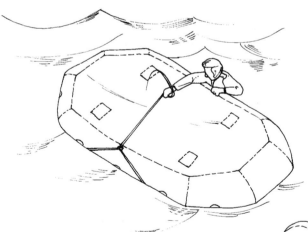

Righting a dinghy

To right a capsized dinghy, take a firm hold of the lanyard, place your feet on the side of the craft, then lean backwards while pulling to flip the dinghy over. Ensure that all supplies are safely stowed to prevent loss if the craft should be capsized. To prevent the life raft from floating away if a capsize occurs, attach one person to it with a line.

Landing a dinghy

Exercise caution when landing the raft on a shoreline. Avoid rocky, dangerous sections of coastline, coral reefs and areas where there are strong surface currents. If possible, choose shallow, sloping beaches for landing zones.

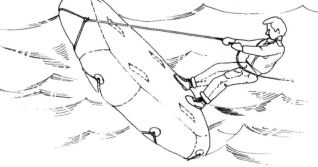

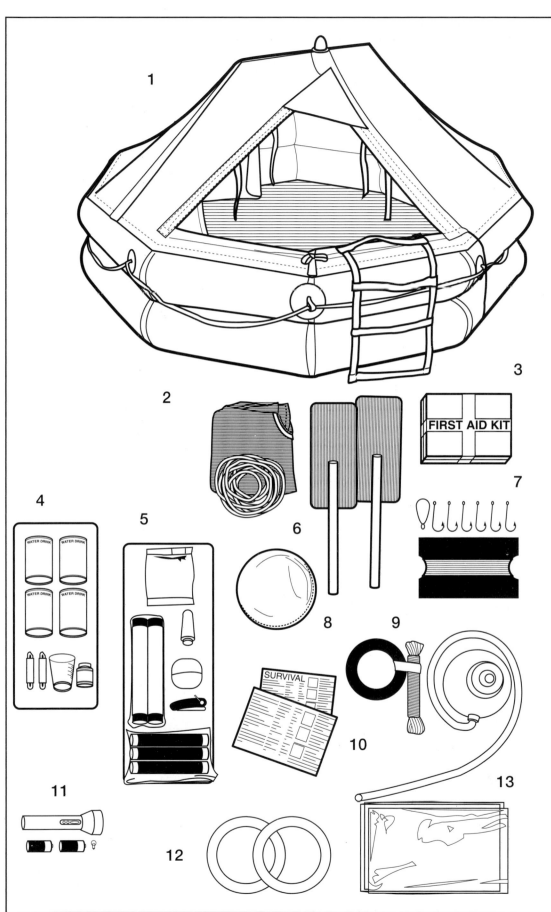

Life raft and contents

Aboard larger vessels, the contents of a life raft can easily be lost. Inspect the raft regularly, ticking off everything against a checklist and replacing missing items. Perishables such as bottles of water, medication and batteries have a shelf life, so also check and replace these items when necessary.

1. Life raft
2. Sea anchor
3. First aid kit
4. Water, can openers, cup and seasickness pills
5. Repair kit, flares, stopper, sponge, knife
6. Paddles
7. Fishing line and hooks
8. Bailer
9. Bellows
10. Survival leaflets
11. Torch (flashlight), batteries and bulb
12. Resealing lids
13. Quoit and line

Movement and signals

As a general rule, try to stay around the place where your ship sank for up to 72 hours, especially if you have sent an SOS. After several days, try to reach land yourself.

Using a VHF radio

A VHF radio will have ship-to-ship range of about 16–24km (10–15 miles). If you are able to make contact, remember to keep the radio on an agreed channel so that the rescuer can continue to communicate with you if and when required.

Smoke canisters

Smoke canisters are an excellent way of attracting rescue in daylight conditions, although only use a canister if there is a realistic chance of being spotted by a passing ship or aircraft. Flares or dye markers are also excellent signallers, as are reflective objects.

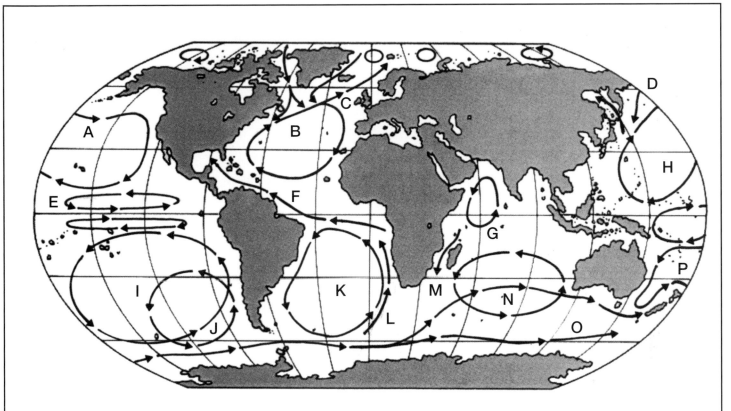

Ocean currents

Understanding ocean currents is an essential piece of research before embarking on any maritime trip. If lost at sea, knowledge of these currents will help you to make informed navigational decisions. You should also always inform someone of your intended route.

A. N. Equatorial
B. N. Equatorial
C. Gulf stream
D. Oyashio
E. Equatorial counter

F. Caribbean
G. N. Equatorial
H. Kuroshio
I. S. Equatorial
J. Peru
K. S. Equatorial

L. Benguela
M. Agulhas
N. S. Equatorial
O. Circumpolar
P. Eastern Australian

Using a sea anchor

Sea anchors are usually contained in most life rafts. Dragged behind the raft, they can prevent capsizing in rough seas and, conversely, can be used to catch currents and increase speed of travel. Unless you are in easy reach of land, use the sea anchor to keep you within the vicinity of the wreck for the following few days, as you will stand more chance of being rescued.

Drinking water

The key rule to survive at sea is simple: life means water, and water means life. Your stores of fresh water should be absolutely secure and no opportunity to add to them should be spurned.

Snow and ice

In colder climates, water can be obtained from ice and snow. Snow can be scooped off the canopy of the life raft directly using collecting vessels. Take care not to scoop snow too closely to the surface of the life raft canopy; you will risk contaminating the melted snow with salt encrusted on the canopy. Remember that snow is considerably less dense than water and a large amount of snow, even tightly compacted, will produce a significantly smaller volume of water.

Desalination kit

These kits use a chemical reaction to remove the salt from sea water. The production rate is about 560ml (1 pint) per hour and, although the results are not especially pleasant, the water produced is safe to drink. Use only when supplies are dangerously low.

Collecting rainwater

Rainwater collection equipment should be kept salt-free and ready for deployment at very short notice. Rain also offers survivor a chance to rinse encrusted salt from both body and clothes.

Reverse osmosis pump

After your life raft, personal flotation device (PFD), clothing, and distress beacon, the reverse osmosis pump is the most important part of your survival kit. It produces fresh water from sea water on demand provided it is well maintained. While there are other ways of collecting drinking water when at sea, these can never be solely relied upon.

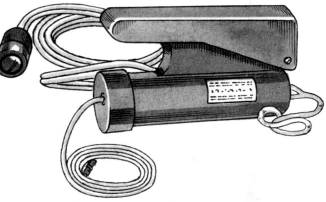

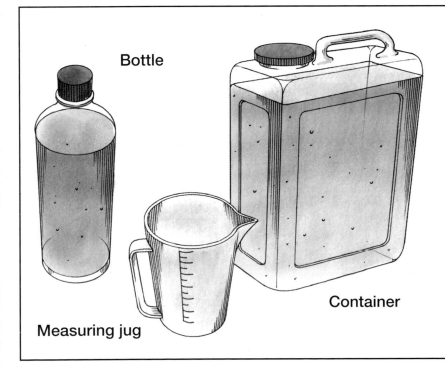

Bottle

Measuring jug

Container

Bottled water

Use every container available to store drinking water. Remember to leave an air gap in each bottle of water so they will float if dropped overboard during abandon ship. If you move quickly, you can catch supplies before they float away. A measuring jug or cup is useful as it means equal rations can be allocated to every crew member if the need arises. The storage equipment should be kept free from salt build-up, which could contaminate the drinking water.

Food

Once your fresh water supply is established, you can turn your attention to sources of nutrition. The body needs certain nutritional requirements to function, and the ocean can provide them all.

Dorado

Dorado are large fish that will provide decent quantities of meat. They are very strong, so ensure that your fishing equipment can handle the size. They feed on flying fish (shown left), which are also edible. Check the stomach contents of dorado for partially digested fish, which are easier for your own body to digest.

Food types

There is a chance that you will have some food supplies with you. Ration these out and begin to fish for food as soon as you have supplies of drinking water. Fish will act as your main source of protein, which is necessary for cell and tissue repair, digestion and healthy blood. Seaweed and plankton are excellent sources of nutrition and can be found floating in the ocean.

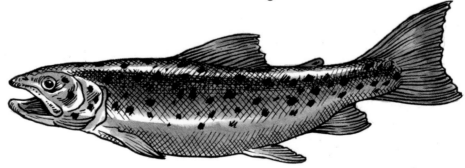

Landing a fish

A fighting fish, particularly one still on the spear, can cause devastating damage to your life raft. Once clear of the water, hold it by the gill and stun it with a blow to the head, then land it and kill it. The head contains some meat and the eyes are filled with salt-free fluid. The tail can be discarded, the intestines used for bait, and the rest can be eaten. Do not forget to dispose of waste carefully. Never throw innards or blood into the water in close vicinity of your raft.

Making rafts

A survivor must occasionally head out into water to improve chances of rescue, to transfer between land masses or to fish. Raft-making is an advanced skill and each should be well-tested before use.

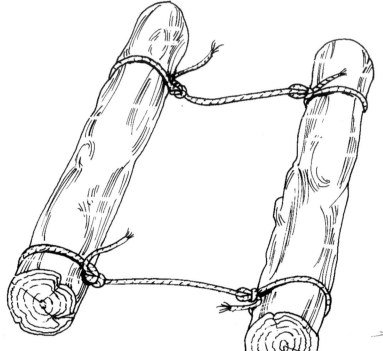

Log flotation (1)

One of the crudest one-person rafts is the log flotation raft. This consists of little more than two spaced logs tied parallel to each other with cord. Ensure that the knots are secure as movement could work them loose. Use collected vegetation stuffed into a bag as a buoyancy aid.

Log flotation (2)

The log flotation raft requires the 'pilot' to sit with his or her legs over one log and their back braced against the other. This raft is designed primarily to prevent drowning. It also keeps most of the body out of the water, which helps protect the survivor against hypothermia.

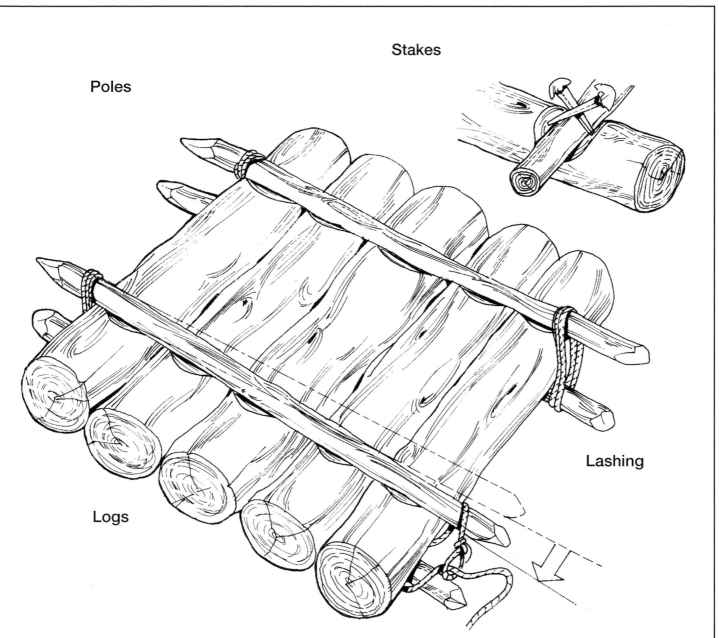

Poles

Stakes

Logs

Lashing

Lashed log raft

Rafts are constructed according to the availability of materials, tools and the skills of the raft-builder. The lashed log raft requires heavy logs, slimmer poles, rope and at least some engineering talent. Such log rafts are the most energy-intensive to make, but are also the most seaworthy when finished and are capable of holding more than one person.

First lay two long thick poles on the ground parallel with each other. Lay logs on top of these crossways, knocking them together tightly to form a square raft shape.

Now put two more thick poles over the top of the logs, mirroring the poles on the bottom of the craft. Tie each set of stakes to each other on both sides, so that the poles now grip the logs in a 'sandwich' structure.

Notch the ends of the gripper bars to stop the ropes from slipping. Construct a deck on top of the raft.

Brush raft

The brush raft requires two large sheets of material, large quantities of vegetation and rope. If properly made, it can support up to 105kg (250lb) of weight.

Spread a large poncho on the ground, and pile up fresh green vegetation (A) in the middle to a height of about 46cm (18in).

Now tie two strong branches together into an X shape and place on top of the brush stack.

Pull the poncho sides up around the brush and tie the ropes diagonally from corner to corner and from side to side (B).

Roll the bundle into the centre of a second large piece of material, so that it is facing downwards (C).

Now tie the second piece of material around the whole structure using ropes linked together and secured at each corner (D).

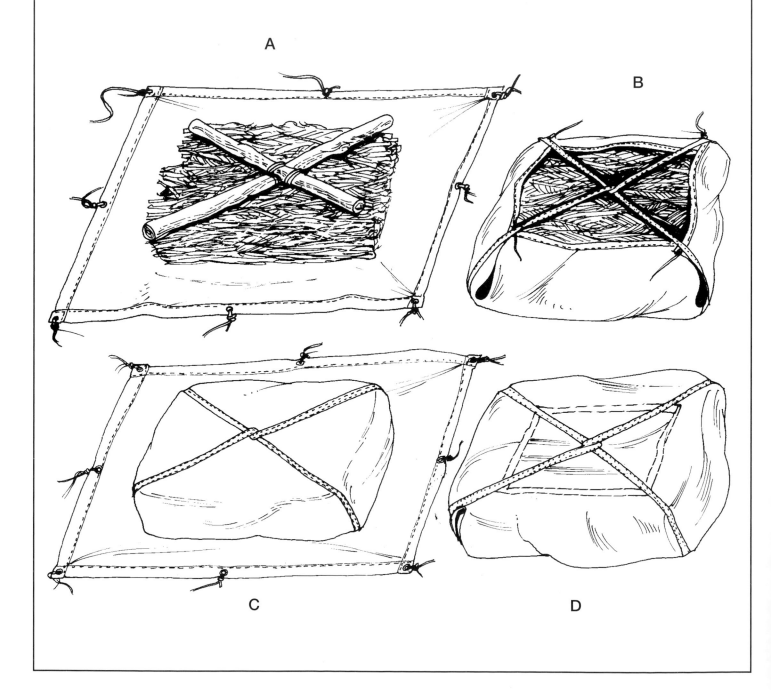

A

B

C

D

Improvising a mast

If they are not needed for rowing, the oars from your life raft can be fashioned into an improvised mast. Lash them together securely and attach a sail to the yardarm. Wrapping the blade of the oar in tough material and using a chopping board as a mast base will prevent damage to the life raft floor.

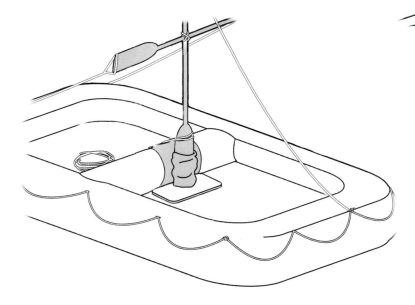

Improvised rigging

With the improvised mast in place, you will need any surplus rope you can muster to hang the rigging. This both supports the mast and yardarm, and allows a sail to be hung. A sail could be constructed from any fabric you managed to salvage. The raft's survival blanket is ideal for use as a sail, having the advantage of increasing visibility because of its reflective qualities.

Improvising a leeboard and rudder

The performance of your dinghy can be improved by adding a leeboard and rudder. The leeboard helps prevent the ship making leeway, while the rudder controls direction. Remember to guard against chafe wherever there is contact with the raft's buoyancy chambers.

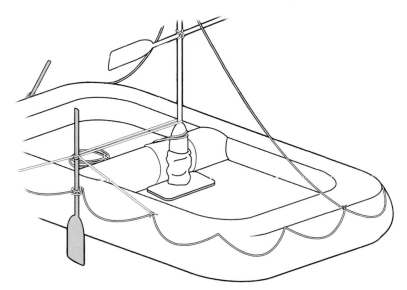

Dangers at sea

Surviving at sea is fraught with danger, even when you have basic water and food supplies. Being aware of many of the dangers you are likely to face can vastly increase your chances of survival.

Keeping cool

It is vital the survivor avoids fluid loss through sweating when at sea. Use the raft's canopy to shelter from the sun. If resting in the shade during the heat of the day does not prevent sweating, dampen your clothing in sea water and your body heat will be drawn away as the water evaporates.

Saltwater sores

These are an inevitable result of the prolonged exposure of skin to saltwater. Apply any protective oils or creams you have, otherwise leave them alone.

Jellyfish stings

Jellyfish stings vary considerably in their severity. While most common jellyfish deliver a sting roughly the same power as a bee sting, some of the large varieties, such as the sea wasp, can kill an adult in just 30 seconds (though three hours is more usual). Swim around any jellyfish in the water (this process is aided by wearing a snorkelling mask for visibility) and get ashore quickly. Do not touch dead jellyfish, as they are still capable of stinging. If you are stung, use a piece of clothing, the back of a knife or seaweed to clean off any stinging cells. Don't rub them, as this will spread the pain – use a scraping movement. Some of the stinging action can be counteracted by applying soap, lemon juice, baking powder or urine. Monitor a victim following a sting for signs of shock and systemic poisoning.

Venomous fish

Luckily, venomous fish are often easy to spot. As a general rule, if you are near coastline or reefs, avoid fish that are not easily identifiable. However, in mid-ocean, a wider variety of fish will probably be edible. If you have any doubts, try a small bite first, then wait for at least an hour, after which time you should have reacted to any poison.

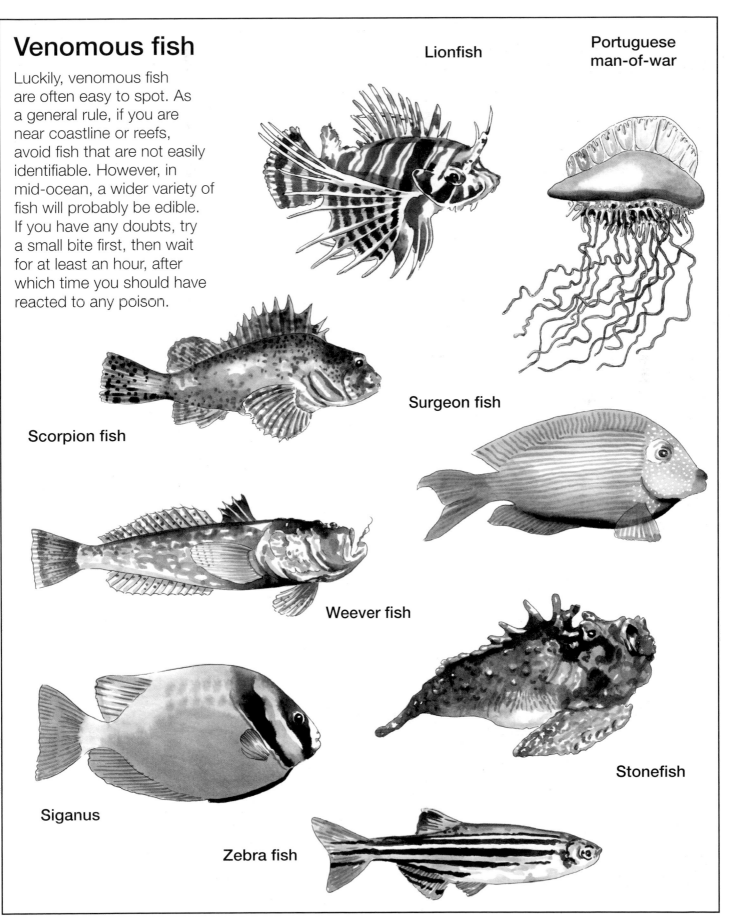

Lionfish

Portuguese man-of-war

Scorpion fish

Surgeon fish

Weever fish

Siganus

Stonefish

Zebra fish

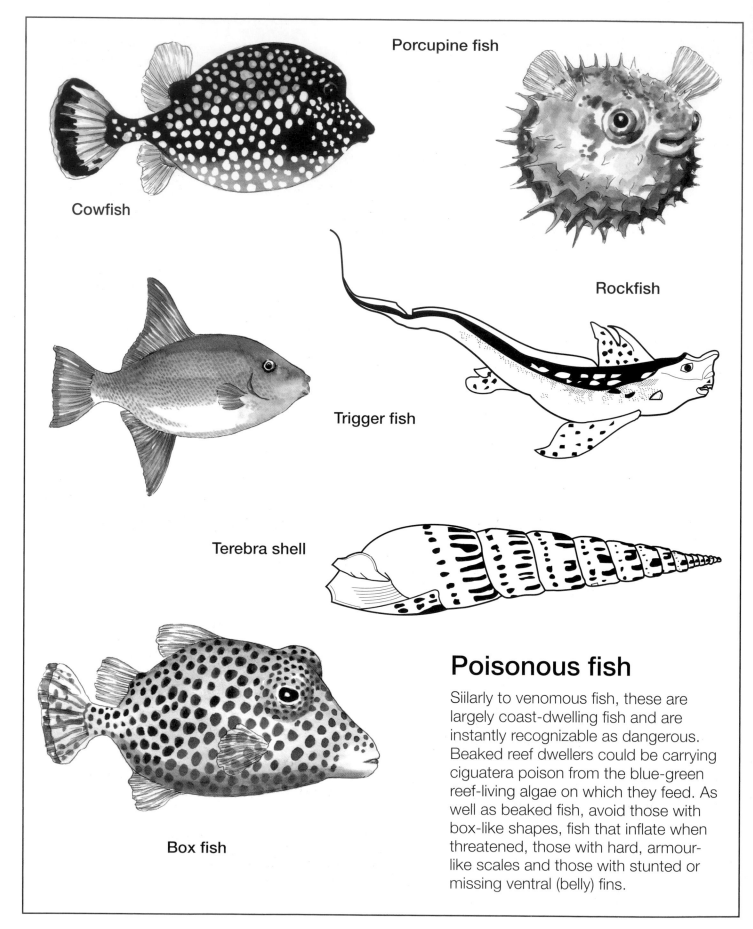

Porcupine fish

Cowfish

Rockfish

Trigger fish

Terebra shell

Poisonous fish

Siilarly to venomous fish, these are largely coast-dwelling fish and are instantly recognizable as dangerous. Beaked reef dwellers could be carrying ciguatera poison from the blue-green reef-living algae on which they feed. As well as beaked fish, avoid those with box-like shapes, fish that inflate when threatened, those with hard, armour-like scales and those with stunted or missing ventral (belly) fins.

Box fish

Dangerous sea creatures

Attacks by octopus and swordfish (top and middle) can occur but are not widely reported. The barracuda (bottom), particularly the Australian sub-species, have been known to attack people or steal catches. If caught, larger ones 1.2–1m (4–6ft) should be cut free but smaller ones can be landed. Watch out for the razor-sharp teeth.

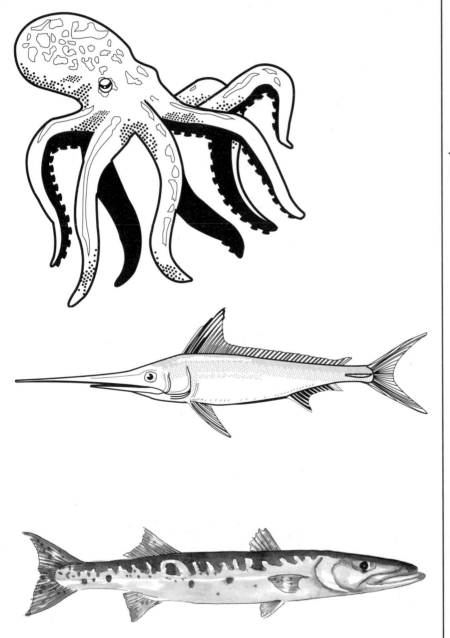

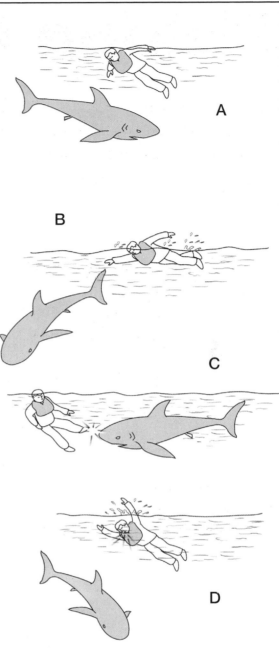

Defending against shark attack

Watch a circling shark constantly (A). If it circles in tightening patterns, swim away with strong motions (B), turning towards it if it makes an attack approach. Attempt to kick its nose (C) to ward it off, or scream and slap the water to scare the shark (D).

Making landfall

Sooner or later, you will find land, and land means safety. But coasts are killers, and to avoid falling at this final stage of the ordeal, you need to know when, where and how to land safely.

Finding a safe landing zone

Avoid the windward side of the island, as the surf will be at its most violent here. Around headlands, there will be back eddies that could sweep you inshore and shelter you from the surf, allowing you to paddle ashore safely. Try to make your way around the sides of the island so you can look for the best landing sites rather than risk a landing on the windward site. Areas sheltered from surf and wind make the best landing sites.

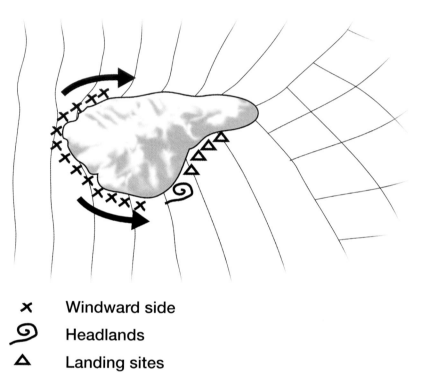

✕	**Windward side**
୭	**Headlands**
△	**Landing sites**
➡	**Look for a different site**

Finding a passage

Many islands, particularly in the South Pacific, are in shallow lagoons sheltered by a surrounding reef. If the island is inhabited, there will be a navigable path through the reef into the lagoon and this will be indicated by a gap, possibly marked with posts, in the ring of surf breaking over the reef. Look for this on the leeward side of the island.

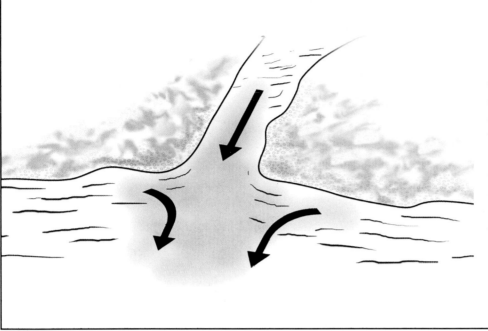

Landing in a river mouth

Smaller rivers will always be outward-flowing and coral doesn't grow in fresh water so the area will be free of reefs. Don't try to fight against the current: paddle your raft to one side and approach the shore. Larger, estuarine river mouths will be tidal, so if you are swept in, make your way to the bank before the tide changes or you may be swept back out again.

Orographic cloud

Mountainous islands are often capped with orographic clouds. These occur when warm, moist air from the sea is driven upwards by the mountainous coastal topography, cooling with altitude and condensing the moisture. Other clouds move with the wind but these appear to be stationary.

Wave interference

Ocean swell is very regular and changes will be noticeable by the survivor. When the swell hits an island, waves are reflected from the windward side and refract around the island to produce a particular pattern of interference in its lee. These wave patterns are reliable signals of land.

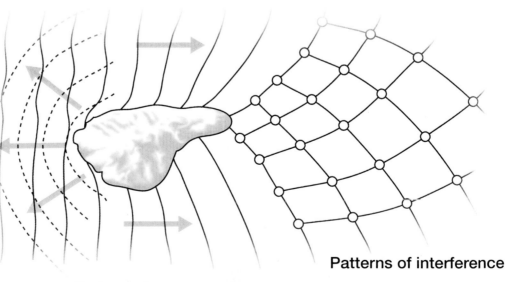

Refracted waves

Patterns of interference

Making a bad situation better

There are days when everything will seem to go wrong. In a survival setting, however, those days can be fatal.

One of the most serious situations you can face is dealing with an injured person in a wilderness setting. With no hospital within easy reach, you will have to draw upon first aid knowledge to keep that person's condition from deteriorating.

Anyone who intends to go on wilderness adventures should acquire a good working understanding of first aid. The range of conditions you might face are varied, from blisters to heart attacks, but with a basic understanding of anatomy and core treatment techniques you can make the difference between a person living or dying in front of you.

A soldier pushes himself hard through an assault course. Survival situations place the body under extreme stress, and injury is an ever-present threat.

Signalling equipment

In an emergency, your initial focus should be on attracting rescue. Knowing how to use signalling equipment can mean that your survival experience is blessedly brief.

Improvised signals

Large pieces of coloured material are ideal for attracting attention at sea or on land. The life raft is likely to have a survival blanket, which could be used for this task. If not, use your foul weather clothing; the brighter and less natural the colour, the better it will attract attention.

Signalling with a mirror

Mirror signalling projects bursts of vivid light over many miles, and can be performed with materials ranging from polished metal to DVDs/CDs or even belt buckles. At the first sight of a nearby ship or aircraft, begin signalling so that the craft will spot your signal and inform the authorities of your position.

Radio

A simple VHF radio will give you good short-range communications and will operate where cell phones lose their connection with satellites. Keep a supply of batteries with your signalling equipment.

Flashlight

Flashlight signalling is highly visible at night, but if you are low on batteries don't burn through them in a couple of hours. Ration out your signalling times sensibly.

Whistle

Easy to carry and simple to use, needing no further source of power, a whistle is one of the most useful tools for short-range contact and signalling.

Hold your flare at arms length, and keep the flare downwind so that the smoke and flame do not blow across you.

Signal fires

Learn these special forces tips about where to build signal fires if you wash up on land. You must get it right the first time—you may not get a second chance.

- Keep green boughs, oil, or rubber close by to create smoke.

- Build earth walls around fires if surrounded by vegetation or trees.
- Build fires in clearings. Do not build among trees: the canopy will block out the signal.
- If by a river or lake, build rafts to place fires on and anchor or tether them in position.

Communication

As a survivor, it is important that you are able to give signals which a rescue team, specifically an aircraft, will be able to see clearly. Plan and practise your signalling system in advance.

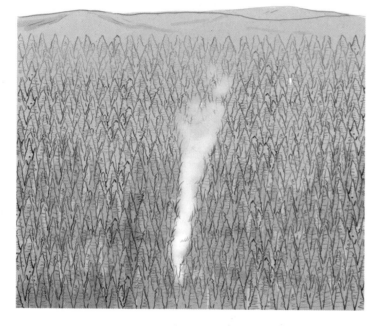

Smoke signals

Here. white smoke is highly visible against a green coniferous forest. Smoke and fire signals are excellent alternative means of signalling if you do not have flares. Use fires at night and smoke in the daytime. An important consideration with smoke signals is to generate smoke that contrasts with the background.

Body signals

Body signals should be performed in an expansive, staccato fashion to deliver the messages shown to the right:

A. Receiver is operating
B. Affirmative (yes)
C. Can proceed shortly, wait if possible
D. Need medical help or parts, long delay
E. Do not attempt to land here
F. Pick us up, aircraft abandoned
G. Use drop message
H. All okay, do not wait
I. Negative (no)
J. Land here (point in direction)
K. Need urgent medical help

— **Need doctor**

━━ ━━ **Need signal lamp**

═ **Need medical supplies**

K **Direction to proceed**

✕ **Unable to proceed**

➜ **Moving in this direction**

Ⅎ **Require food and water**

I> **Will try to take off**

⋁ **Need firearms**

L⅂ **Aircraft damaged**

▢ **Need map/ compass**

△ **Safe to land**

L **Need fuel/oil**

LL **All is well**

N **No**

Y **Yes**

⅃L **Not understood**

W **Require engineer**

Ground-to-air signals

Make these signals large, bold and with contrasting materials to provide information about your situation to overflying aircraft. If you find yourself in a survival situation and need rescuing, bear in mind that an aircraft flying overhead will not have time to read lengthy or unclear signals.

Signals using natural materials

If you become stranded in the wild, follow US Army advice and construct signals from the materials around you.

- Build brush or snow mounds that will cast shadows.
- In snow, tramp down the snow to form letters or symbols and fill in with contrasting materials: twigs or branches.
- In sand, use boulders, vegetation or seaweed to form a symbol.
- In brush-covered areas, cut out patterns in the vegetation.
- In tundra, dig trenches or turn the soil upside down.
- In any terrain, use contrasting materials so that the symbols are visible to aircraft.

A .—	M ——	Y —.——
B —...	N —.	Z ——.. —
C —.—.	O ———	1 .————
D —..	P .——.	2 ..———
E .	Q ——.—	3 ...——
F ..—.	R .—.	4 ....—
G ——.	S ...	5 .....
H	T —	6 —....
I ..	U ..—	7 ——...
J .———	V ...—	8 ———..
K —.—	W .——	9 ————.
L .—..	X —..—	0 —————

Morse code

Morse code can be delivered via light or sounds, and is internationally understood by the military or anyone working in rescue.

Map work

If you are lucky enough to have a map of the area you have found yourself in, ensure that you know how to interpret the wealth of information it can provide on terrain, distances and location points.

Three-dimensional terrain

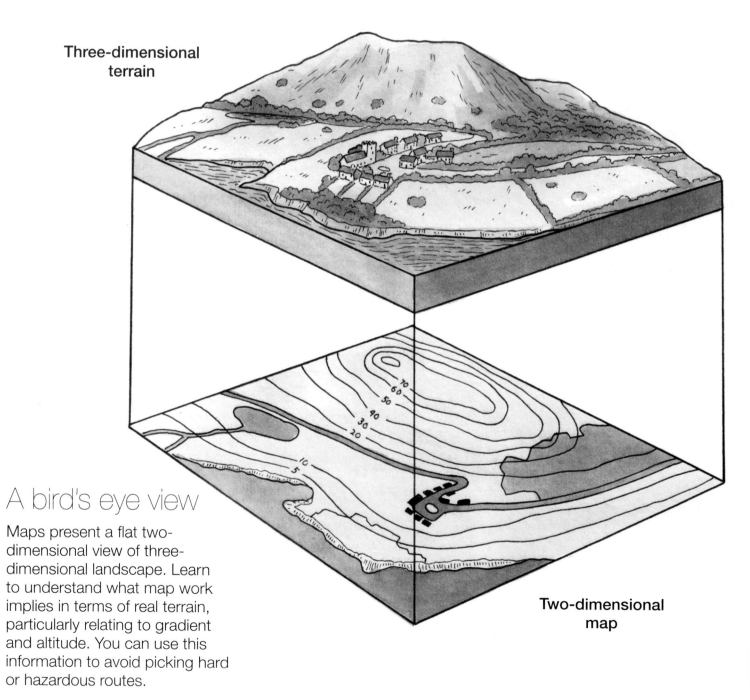

A bird's eye view

Maps present a flat two-dimensional view of three-dimensional landscape. Learn to understand what map work implies in terms of real terrain, particularly relating to gradient and altitude. You can use this information to avoid picking hard or hazardous routes.

Two-dimensional map

Map detail

Familiarize yourself with the map's symbols, and try to plot your route of travel to allow you accessible passage to civilization if you get into trouble at any point in your journey. Use a series of the symbols to triangulate your position, noting the objects that you should pass on your journey.

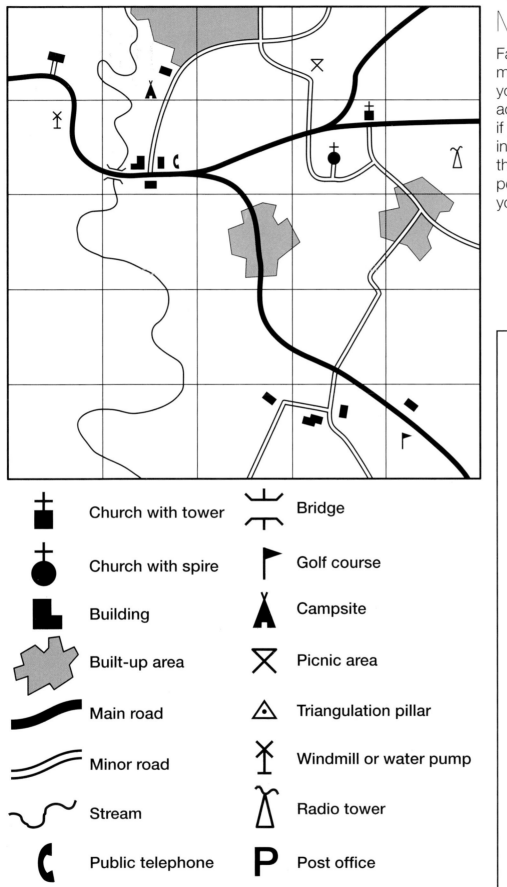

Symbol	Name	Symbol	Name
	Church with tower		Bridge
	Church with spire		Golf course
	Building		Campsite
	Built-up area		Picnic area
	Main road		Triangulation pillar
	Minor road		Windmill or water pump
	Stream		Radio tower
	Public telephone		Post office

Map grid

When giving a six-digit map reading, take your first reading from the top or bottom margin, and your second reading from the left- or right-hand margin. As an example, the map reference here is 20.4 x 55.8.

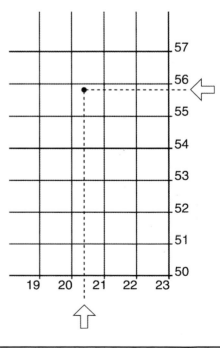

333

Making a bad situation better

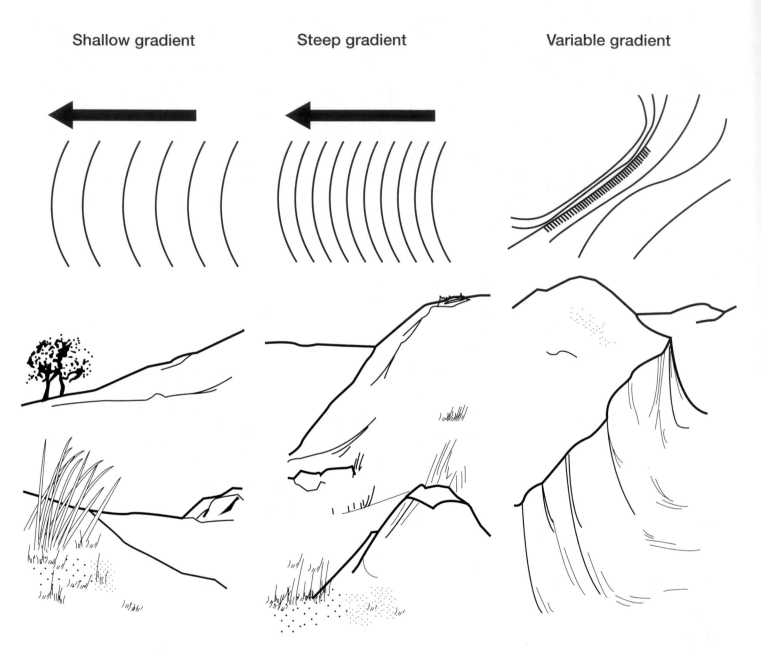

Shallow gradient

Steep gradient

Variable gradient

Contour lines

Contour lines on a map represent the gradient of the terrain. Contour lines usually appear as brown or orange. They connect areas of the same height, and are set at regular distances apart from one another, such as 30m (98ft). However, they will not be evenly spaced on the map. The more closely packed the contour lines, the steeper the gradient will be; if the lines are widely spaced, they indicate land of shallow gradient. A mixture of contour lines shows a rise with variable gradient. Check the gradients involved in your journey before you set off.

Map scale

A typical outdoor map scale is 1:50,000. This means that one unit of measurement on the map is equivalent to 50,000 of the same unit on the ground. Maps will also provide a scale guide so that you can measure out distances in useful increments such as 1km (0.6 miles).

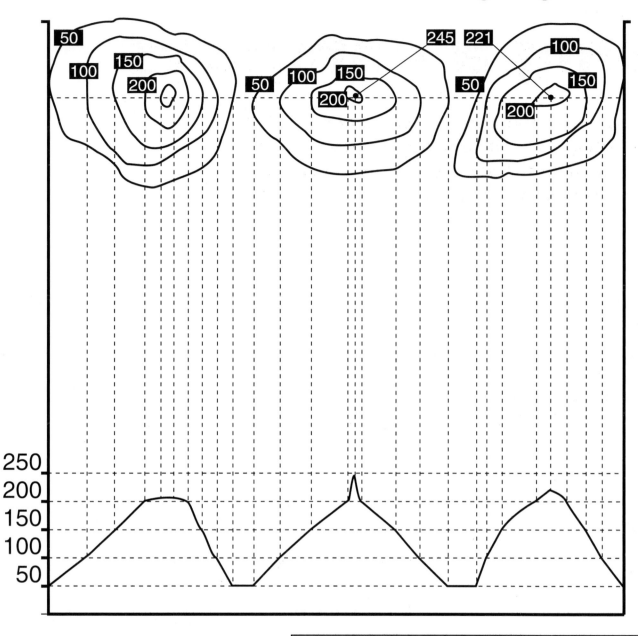

Cross-section

Map contour lines essentially give a cross-section of landscape features. Pay close attention to the altitude figures which straddle each contour line, and make sure you can operate at that altitude. If you cannot, plot an alternative route that takes you around the high-altitude.

Reading contour lines

- If contour lines are widely spaced, the slope is gentle. If narrow, the slope is steep.
- An absence of contour lines means that the ground is level.
- If several contour lines gather together into a single line, this means that there is a vertical cliff.
- Concentric contour lines with increasing height imply a hill or mountain.
- V-shaped contour lines imply a sharp spur of land or a V-shaped valley. U-shaped contour lines imply the same, albeit with more rounded shape.

Using a compass

Compasses are a fundamental piece of all soldiers' equipment and should be present in any survival expedition. They point to magnetic north, allowing you to plot your direction of travel.

Compass markings

Early compasses (right) were marked with the 'points' of the compass: north (N), north-northeast (NNE), northeast (NE) and so on. Modern compasses (far right) usually have a graduated scale divided into 360 degrees, with the value marked every 10, 20 or 30 degrees.

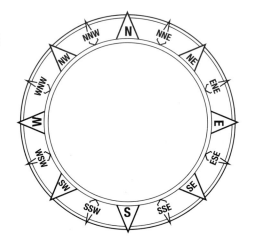

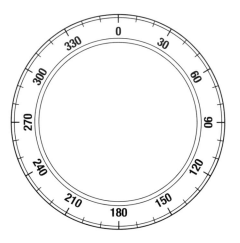

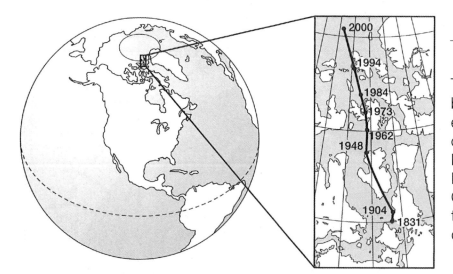

The wandering pole

The earth's magnetic poles are not fixed, but move slowly with time. A scientific expedition determined that the location of the north magnetic pole in 2000 was Lat 79° 19' N, Long 105° 26' W, on the Isachsen Peninsula in the far north of Canada. This illustration shows how far the magnetic pole has drifted northward during the twentieth century.

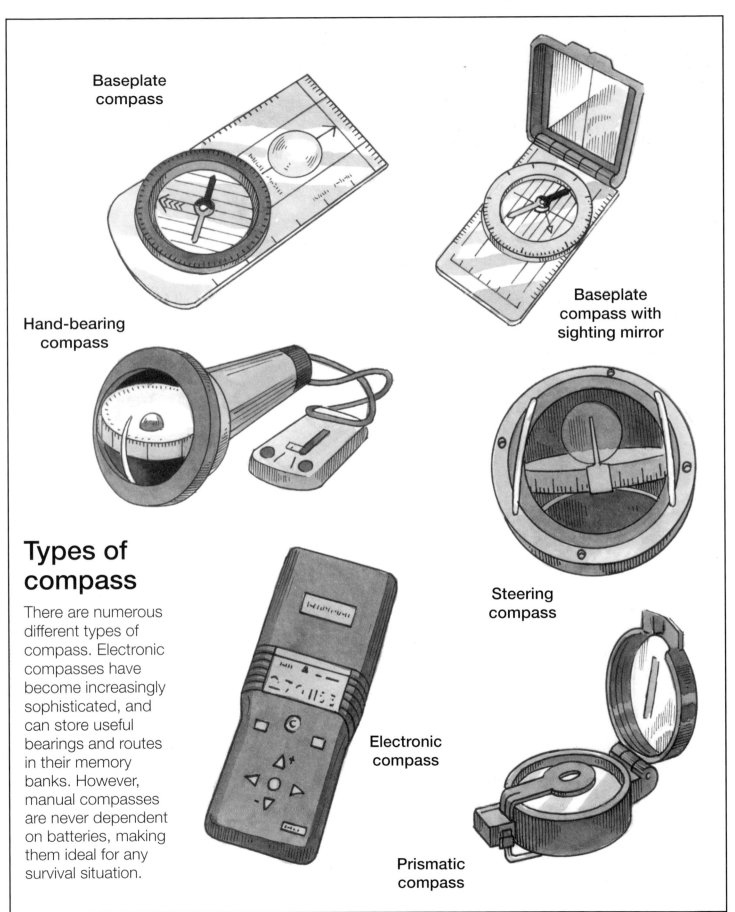

Baseplate
compass

Baseplate
compass with
sighting mirror

Hand-bearing
compass

Steering
compass

Types of compass

There are numerous different types of compass. Electronic compasses have become increasingly sophisticated, and can store useful bearings and routes in their memory banks. However, manual compasses are never dependent on batteries, making them ideal for any survival situation.

Electronic
compass

Prismatic
compass

Improvised compass

This improvised compass consists of nothing more than a magnetized needle (see page 339) balanced on a cork floating in water. Note that the water must be absolutely still, as tiny currents can affect the compass reading. For this reason, it is better to use a container on a flat surface. Fill it with water, insert the cork and the magnetized needle, then leave to settle.

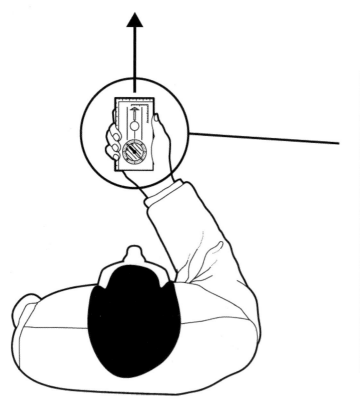

Following a compass course

When following a compass course, hold the compass in front of you and rotate your whole body to left or right until the direction-of-travel needle is correctly aligned with the orienting arrow. Similarly to the improvised compass above, try not to let your own movements affect the compass readings.

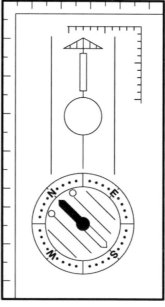

Magnetizing a needle

The US Army *Survival* manual notes that 'You can magnetize or polarize [a needle] by slowly stroking it in one direction on a piece of silk or carefully through your hair using deliberate strokes.' You can also achieve the same effect with another magnet or a piece of leather.

Stroke the needle slowly across fabric such as silk

Rub the needle across a piece of leather or with another magnet

Navigation using the sky

If you find yourself outdoors with no navigation equipment to help you find your way, there are many other methods at your disposal, some of which have been in use for centuries.

The night sky

Navigating by the stars has its limitations, especially when cloud cover prevents a clear view of the night sky. Yet when conditions allow, certain stars give very accurate navigational guidance. All survivors should familiarize themselves with the star information provided here. The Southern Cross (right) consists of four primary stars plus two 'trailing stars' out to the east. A dark nebula colours the sky just off to the side of the cross.

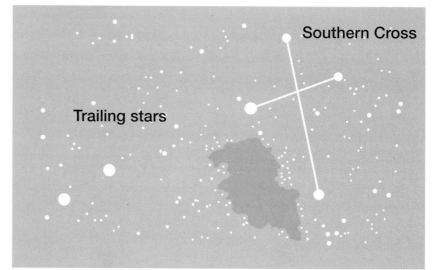

Southern Cross

Trailing stars

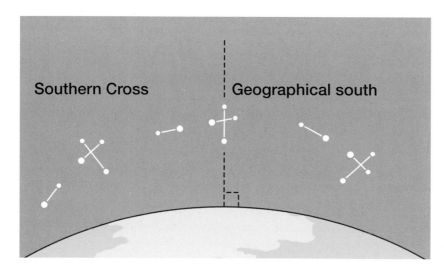

Southern Cross   Geographical south

Navigating by the stars

The Southern Cross is useful for finding south, but it is not as easy to find as the Pole Star. When the Southern Cross sits directly upright over the horizon as shown, the main axis of the group points at the geographical south. Other useful star patterns include the Big Dipper, which is very close to the North Celestial Pole (NCP). Orion rises above the equator and can be seen in both hemispheres. It rises due east, regardless of the observer's position, and sets due west.

Determining direction by shadow

The United States Marine Corps has a tried-and-tested method for determining location using just a stick and the shadow of the sun.

- Place a stick or branch in the ground at a level spot. Mark the shadow tip with a stone.
- Wait 10–20 minutes until the shadow tip moves a couple of inches. Mark the new position of the shadow tip with a stone.
- Draw a straight line through the two marks to obtain an approximate east–west line (the sun rises in the east and sets in the west—the shadow tip moves in the opposite direction).
- Draw a line at right angles to the east–west line to get an approximate north–south line.
- Inclining the stick does not impair the accuracy of the shadow-tip method, which means you can use it on sloping ground.

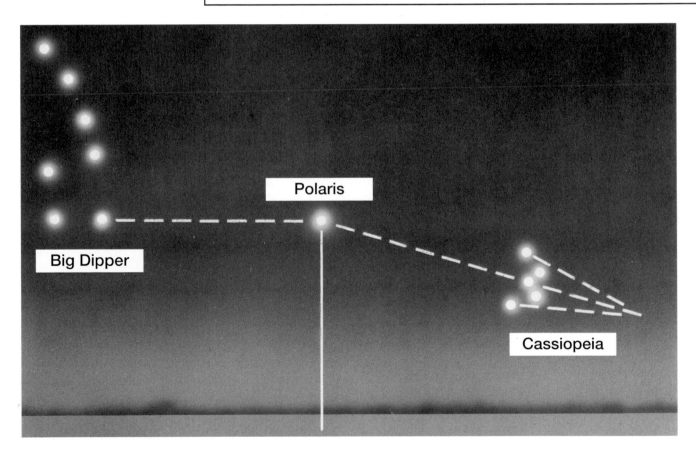

Polaris

Big Dipper

Cassiopeia

Star guide

The Pole Star, North Star or Polaris (to use its three most popular names) is a sure indicator of north. Extending lines out from the Big Dipper (the collection of stars on the left) or from Cassiopeia (the collection of stars on the right, which resemble the head of an arrow), will help you correctly identify the North Star, which sits in a relatively isolated aspect in the night sky. From there, you can plot your position.

Making a bad situation better

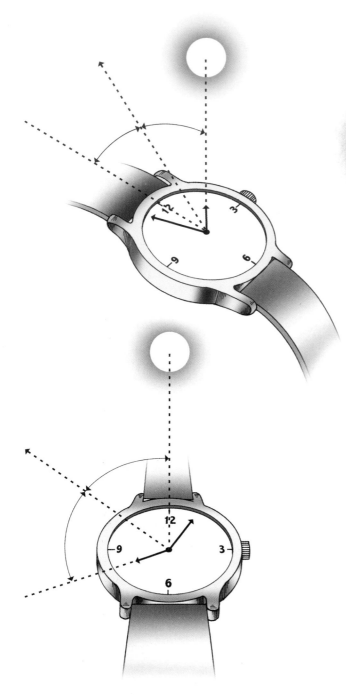

Watch navigation (1)

To navigate by watch in the Northern Hemisphere (above right), point the hour hand at the sun and bisect the angle between it and 12 o'clock to find south. In the Southern Hemisphere (above left), point the 12 o'clock mark at the sun and bisect the angle between the mark and hour hand to find north. No matter where you are, it is important to set your watch to true local time.

Watch navigation (2)

It is important to note that the watch navigation method is more accurate the further away you are from the equator. In middle latitudes it can produce an error of up to 20°. An useful trick is you only have a digital watch is to draw a clock face on a piece of paper, or scratch one on the ground, draw in a 12 o'clock mark and the hour hand showing the correct local time, and orient it as already described.

Navigation and the moon

Plotting your location from the moon can be a very handy technique. If the moon rises before the sun sets, the illuminated side will be on the west. However, if the moon rises after the sun sets, the illuminated side will be on the east. If the moon rises at the same time as the sun sets, it will be full and its position in the sky will be east at 18:00 hours, southeast at 21:00 hours, south at 23:59 hours, southwest at 03:00 hours and west at 06:00 hours.

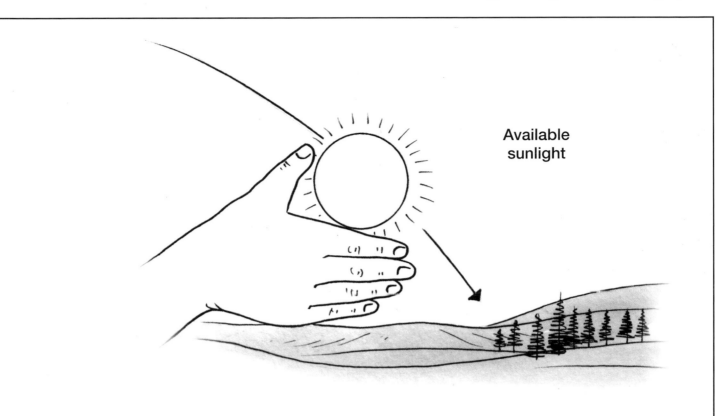

**Available
sunlight**

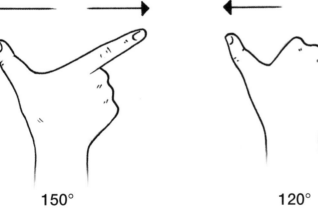

150°   120°

Estimating angles

Estimating angles can be a useful skill
for helping calculate distances and
also for computing bearings. Some
simple hand configurations, examples
of which are shown on the left, provide
rough guidelines to useful angles. It is
also useful to note that every finger's
width between the sun and horizon
represents about 15 minutes of
available sunlight (below).

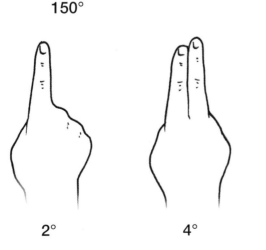

2°   4°   6°

Natural navigation and searching

If you cannot see the sun, stars or moon due to weather conditions, you can still determine direction by using natural signposts. However, they are not always accurate, so treat them cautiously.

Navigation techniques

A transit line is useful for keeping a sense of direction when travelling in the wilderness. Plot a straight line on your map between two visible and easily identifiable features (below image). Your relationship to this line against the terrain you are crossing (above image) will give you constant feedback about whether you are still on the right course to travel. Physically drawing the transit line on your map, accurately connecting your present position with the place you want to be, can be an useful reference guide. Naturally occuring transits provide excellent positiion lines.

The dead reckoning technique can be used effectively with transit lines. You will need some sort of writing implement and paper. The method consists of plotting and recording a series of courses before you set out, each one being measured in terms of distance and direction between two points. These courses lead from the starting point to your destination, and enable you to determine your position at any time, either by following your plan or by comparing your actual position on the ground in relation to your plotted course.

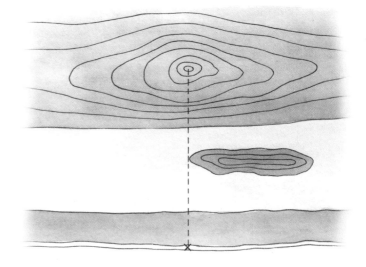

This is the road

Turn left

Turn right

Danger

Marking a trail

If you have to move from one position to another unexpectedly, leave trail signs to give search parties or other people information about where you have gone, or to provide details about what lies ahead. The trail signs above are useful as guidance markers or to provide information about potentially dangerous situations that people might otherwise stumble into unawares.

Making a bad situation better

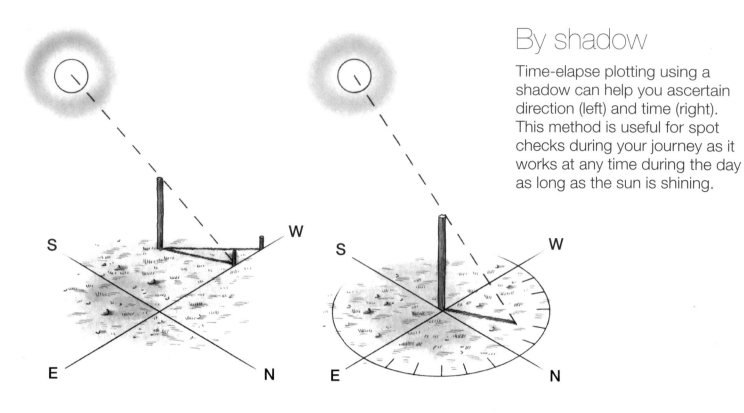

By shadow

Time-elapse plotting using a shadow can help you ascertain direction (left) and time (right). This method is useful for spot checks during your journey as it works at any time during the day as long as the sun is shining.

Natural signs

A very rough navigational aid is patterns of moss growth on trees and rocks. Generally, moss likes the darker, cooler, north-facing side of objects rather than the hotter, drier south side. However, this sign alone is not a reliable indicator of direction, so use the method with care. Consider its use with other supporting signs, such as the direction of wind from the angle of nearby trees or bushes.

Searching techniques

If you are lost in the wilderness, be aware of how search parties might be looking for you. They will generally use one of the two techniques shown below if searching on foot, while search helicopters will typically describe an ever-widening circle out from your last-seen position.

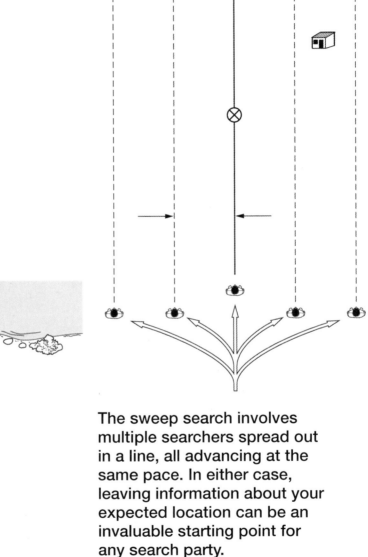

The square-search technique starts from a central position and then works outward systematically, turning at right angles and progressively lengthening the distance of travel to methodically cover an area of ground.

The sweep search involves multiple searchers spread out in a line, all advancing at the same pace. In either case, leaving information about your expected location can be an invaluable starting point for any search party.

Using GPS

The handheld Global Positioning System (GPS) has revolutionized navigation. A GPS receiver the size and cost of a mobile phone can tell you exactly where you are, anywhere in the world.

Handheld GPS receiver

Modern handheld GPS receivers are extremely powerful navigational devices, yet small and light enough to be carried in your pocket, such as the ones shown to the right and below. All have certain basic features in common, including an antenna, a small LCD display screen and a data input keypad. The systems can fail, however, so make sure that you are also comfortable with other, more traditional methods of navigation.

What to look for

There are some useful guidelines to observe when buying a GPS receiver for wilderness use. Make sure that it is sturdy, waterproof and will function in both extremely low and high temperatures. A transreflective screen will be easier to read in direct sunlight. Look for one with a good battery life, that utilizes automatic power-saving modes.

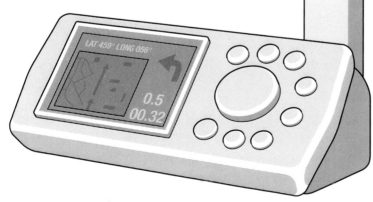

GPS signal reception

While they work anywhere in the world, in certain places a GPS receiver may not be able to get a clear satellite and will therefore provide an inaccurate position. Such places include cities with tall buildings, dense forest or jungle, and deep gorges. It may be necessary to stop and climb to a higher location in order to get enough satellite signals to fix your position accurately.

The human body

The human physique is both incredibly strong and intensely vulnerable. Knowing how life is sustained forms the basis of much of your emergency survival first aid treatment.

Circulatory system

The circulatory system works in a cycle, with its centre being the human heart. This immensely durable muscle pumps oxygenated blood throughout the complex network of blood vessels in the body.

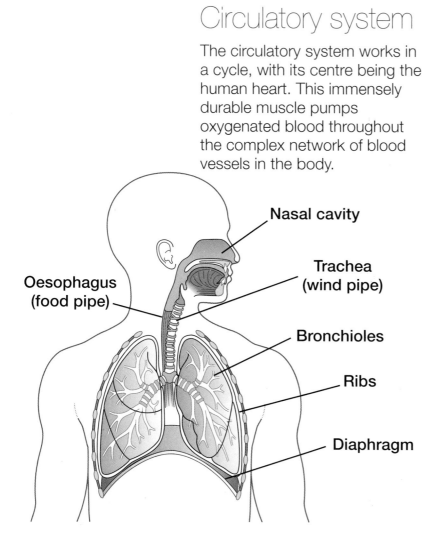

Nasal cavity

Trachea (wind pipe)

Oesophagus (food pipe)

Bronchioles

Ribs

Diaphragm

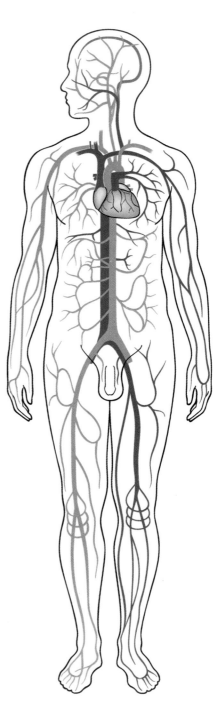

Respiratory system

The respiratory system consists of the mouth, nose, trachea and lungs, and includes the pulmonary arteries that take oxygen from lungs to bloodstream.

Nervous system

The nervous system consists of the central nervous system, peripheral nervous system and autonomic nervous system. Put simply, it consists of the brain, spinal cord and spinal nerves, controlling conscious action and unconscious bodily functions.

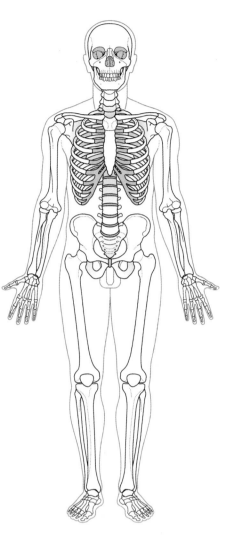

Skeleton

The skeleton (above) acts as the framework of the body. Of its many functions, it enables movement and protects and body's internal organs. It also enables blood cell production, calcium and iron stores and hormone regulation.

Lymph-node system

Lymph nodes make up the lymphatic system. They ensure that the immune system is regulated and defends the body against infection. Nodes are clustered around the head and neck, thorax, arms and groin.

Emergency diagnosis

When first confronted with a casualty – or worse, several casualties – your initial reaction may be one of mental paralysis. Learning to diagnose and grade emergencies can help you save lives.

A: vital systems

B: entire body

Main areas for diagnosis

Any first aid assessment should follow a methodical process of examination from top to toe. The immediate priority should be to assess the main vital systems (A) before going on to examine the entire body surface (B).

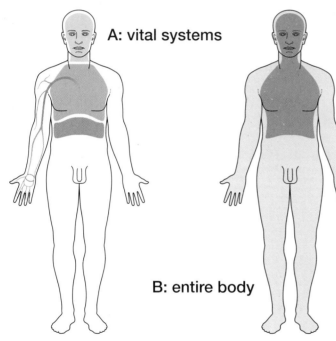

Airway and breathing

If a person is unconscious, the loss of muscular control in the tongue means that it can drop back and form a soft, but effective, plug at the entrance to the airway and prohibit respiration. Clear the airway for blockages and check the breathing by placing your cheek right next to the casualty's mouth and nose while keeping an eye on the casualty's chest.

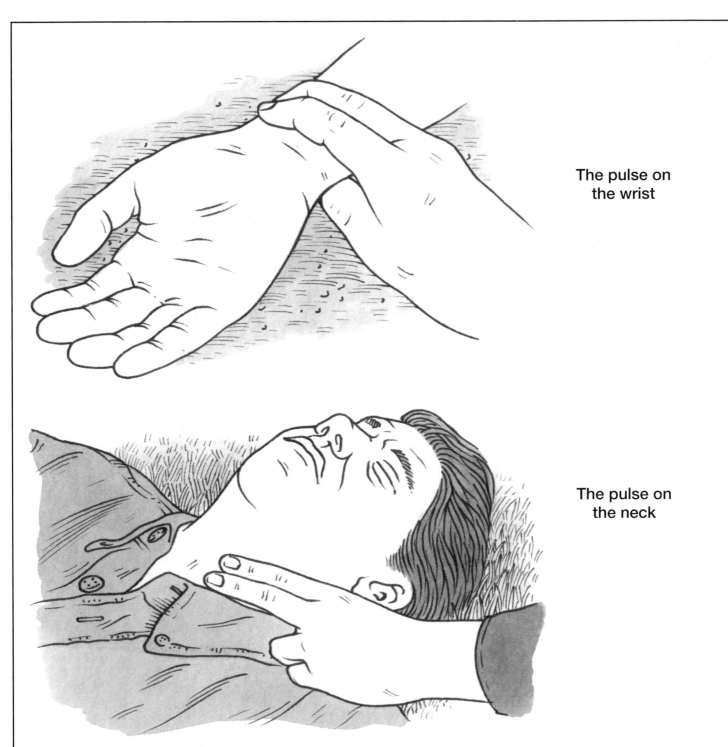

The pulse on the wrist

The pulse on the neck

Finding the pulse

When checking the pulse, take three fingers and place them over the artery situated on the inside of the wrist (top image), about 1cm (0.5in) in from the thumb side. For the neck, run your fingers down into the groove along the side of the throat (bottom image). To gauge the beats per minute, count for 30 seconds, then multiply by two. If you do not detect a heartbeat, then you need to deliver heart compressions (see below for details).

Tests and treatment

If there are no emergency issues, being able to check the casualty for signs of illness or injury, or making them calmer and more comfortable are the first steps of treatment.

Temperature

The body has a great capacity to regulate its own temperature, generally remaining at or close to the core temperature of 36–38°C (97.8–100.4°F). Yet this temperature control system is vulnerable, and never more so than in outdoor survival situations, where climate and environment are stacked against anyone trying to stay warm or release heat.

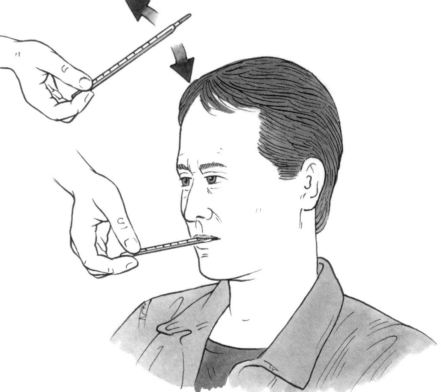

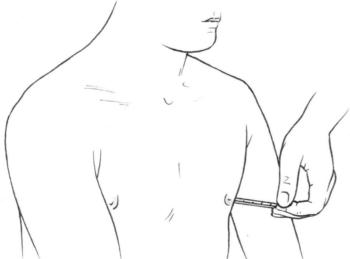

Taking a temperature

Temperatures can be taken orally, or by using the armpit or rectum. Using a clean, preferably sterilized, thermometer, place it under the tongue or in the armpit with the arm down. Hold it in place for 40 seconds or until the gauge stops increasing, then take a reading. Note that a raised temperature can indicate infection.

Using a blood pressure cuff

In an emergency, a systolic blood pressure reading is important and can be gained using a blood pressure cuff. Wrap the cuff tightly around the upper arm, and pump it tight until arterial blood flow to the arm is stopped (the pulse in the wrist stops). Slowly deflate the cuff while feeling for the return of the pulse. As soon as you feel it, take a reading from the gauge.

Pinch test

The pinch test checks for signs of dehydration. If someone is dehydrated, their skin is not as elastic as normal as the body uses water for the running of vital organs. Pinch a fold of skin. If it does not spring back into place immediately, the casualty is likely to be dehydrated.

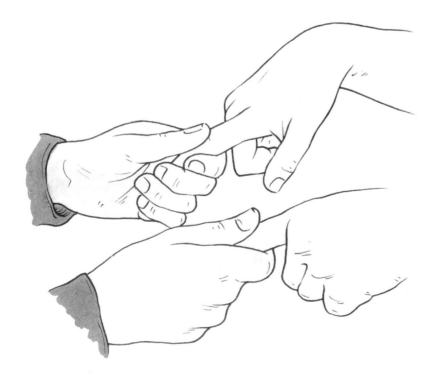

Two-finger grip test

Using your two forefingers, have the casualty squeeze your fingers, and note any dissimilarity in grip strength between the two hands. This could indicate a brain impairment such as a stroke or physical damage to the limb and will warrant further testing or observation.

Removing a helmet

If your patient is unconscious, there may be spinal or neck injuries that you are not aware of. Any movement to the head could exacerbate these injuries, so do not make these movements unless absolutely necessary. If you suspect an injury beneath a helmet, ensure that one person holds the back of the neck and chin securely, while you slowly remove the helmet.

Recovery position

Almost all casualties who are unconscious or semi-conscious should be placed in the recovery position if the treatment and injuries allow this. To place in the recovery position facing to the right, put the person on their front with their right arm and leg bent out to the side at right angles to the body, knee and elbow themselves bent. The other arm should extend outwards, perpendicular to the body.

Controlling shock

Shock is the circulatory system's loss of ability to deliver an effective blood supply around the body, meaning that first the limbs and muscles, then the vital organs, are deprived of oxygen supply. Lay the casualty down with his legs elevated to keep the blood concentrated more in the core organs. Loosen any clothing that might constrict blood flow.

Treatment for hyperventilation

Hyperventilation is a condition relevant to the survival first aider who has to deal with a panicked group member unable to cope with a dangerous or potentially life-threatening situation. It occurs when too much carbon dioxide is expelled from the body, producing symptoms of dizziness, fainting and muscle cramps. While reassuring the casualty and encouraging her to relax, get her to breathe into a paper bag or similar container, thereby raising the body's levels of carbon dioxide back to normal.

Artificial respiration and CPR

Any problems with breathing and heartbeat take priority in a first aid emergency. Without the respiratory system to take air in and oxygenate the blood, severe organ failure and death will ultimately result.

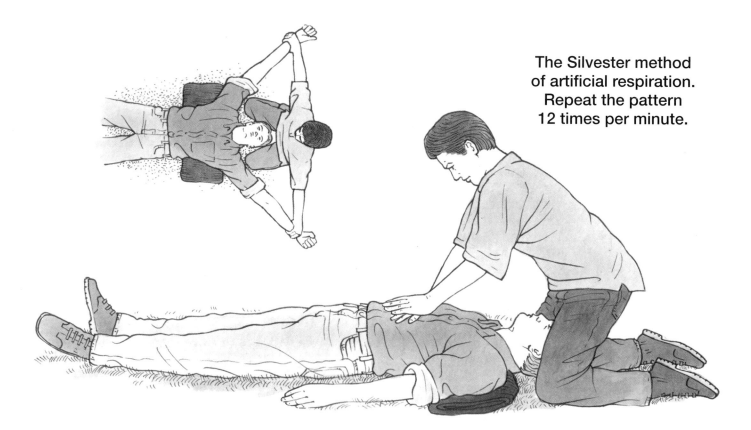

The Silvester method of artificial respiration. Repeat the pattern 12 times per minute.

Artificial respiration

Artificial respiration (AR) is the practice of externally supplying a casualty with enough air to keep their blood oxygenated. The Silvester method involves kneeling astride the casualty's head and placing your outstretched hands on their lower ribs. Then rock forward to apply pressure over the area before drawing their arms outwards in a wide 'Y' shape to complete the cycle.

Locating the heart for CPR

If you perform mouth-to-mouth with cardiac massage, this is a technique known as cardio-pulmonary resuscitation (CPR). To find the heart, run a finger up one of the lowest ribs until it meets the breastbone. Place the heel of your hand about one finger's width above this point, then bring the other hand on top and interlock the fingers.

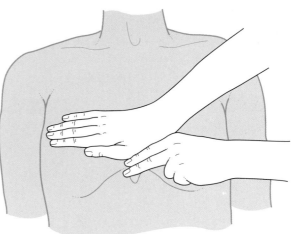

Holger Nielson method

This method should be used if the casualty is in, or must remain, in a face-down position. Two seconds of pressure are applied to the back between the shoulder blades (top) then the arms are raised by pulling them under the elbows, but not hard enough to lift the face off the hands. Repeat 12 times per minute.

Administering AR

Mouth-to-mouth ventilation is when we breathe into the casualty's lungs and supply the necessary oxygen for survival. Tilt the casualty's head back if you are sure there are no spinal injuries involved. Tilting the head allows for free passage of air down to the lungs. Pinch the casualty's nostrils, seal your mouth around the open mouth, and blow. Establish a pattern of six immediate breaths as fast as you can, then 12 breaths per minute until spontaneous respiration begins.

When you have located the heart, lean directly over the sternum.

Cardiac massage

When you have located the heart, lean right over the casualty with the arms straight and press the breastbone down by about 4–5cm (1.5–2in). Then release the pressure, but keep your hands ready on the spot, then follow with another compression. Maintain the compressions at a rate of about 100 pushes a minute.

Apply pressure in a steady rhythm. Counting the number of compressions out loud will help.

Interlock your fingers to provide a cushioning effect.

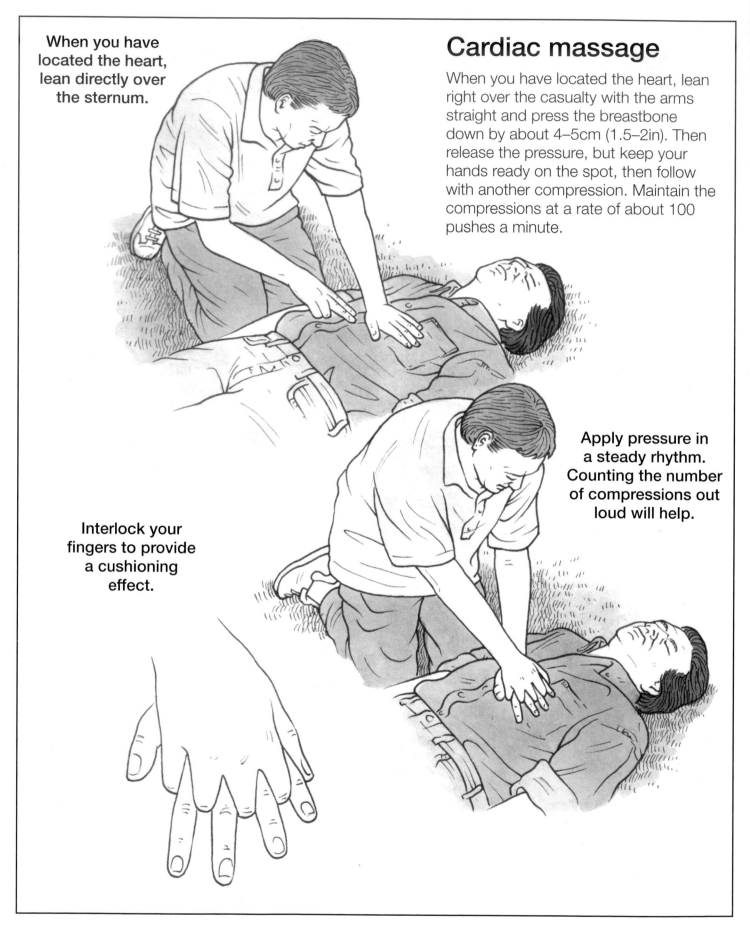

CPR on a baby

The main difference here is the pressure involved in the cardiac massage. For a baby, use a single hand or even just two fingers for the massage. Too much pressure could crack the rib bones. You do not need to pinch the nostrils as your mouth can fit over the baby's nose and mouth. Ensure that your mouth is sealed over their face so that no air is lost.

CPR on a small child

The technique here is more similar to CPR on an adult, but bear in mind that the bones on a growing child are not as strong as adult bones. You might only use one hand for the massage, as shown in the image on the left.

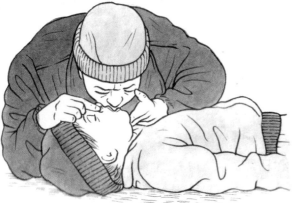

Face protector

Using a face protector is advisable in a survival situation. If there is a chance of mass epidemic, any first aiders need to take every care not to get infected. A face protector shields the casualty's face, while providing a nozzle through which you can blow. Note that while every chance to administer CPR should be taken, be realistic about your chances, especially if there are other victims who need medical attention.

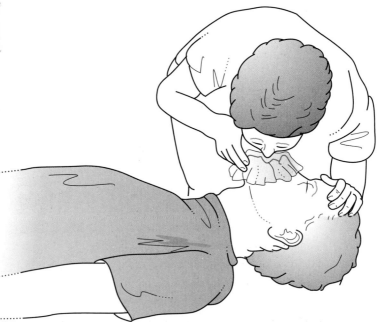

Carrying methods

Moving the injured is a sensitive procedure requiring judgement and, if possible, plenty of help. No further injuries should occur, but in a survival situation staying put can be deadly.

'Head back' technique

The 'head back' carrying technique is the best position for carrying a drowning victim. The position of the head lower than the torso encourages any water in the lungs to flow out.

Safe carrying

With any improvised stretcher, you will not have the safety features of a professional stretcher built in. Any jolts or spills could further injure the casualty, so take every care to carry them safely. Tying the casualty on to the stretcher means they can be carried more securely.

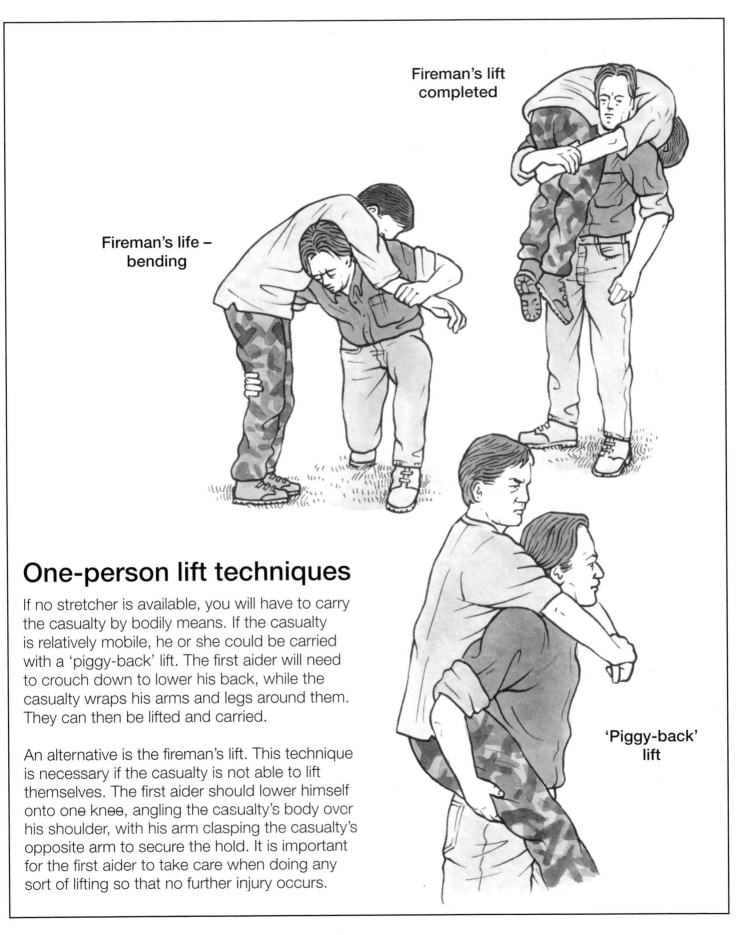

Fireman's lift
completed

Fireman's life –
bending

'Piggy-back'
lift

One-person lift techniques

If no stretcher is available, you will have to carry
the casualty by bodily means. If the casualty
is relatively mobile, he or she could be carried
with a 'piggy-back' lift. The first aider will need
to crouch down to lower his back, while the
casualty wraps his arms and legs around them.
They can then be lifted and carried.

An alternative is the fireman's lift. This technique
is necessary if the casualty is not able to lift
themselves. The first aider should lower himself
onto one knee, angling the casualty's body over
his shoulder, with his arm clasping the casualty's
opposite arm to secure the hold. It is important
for the first aider to take care when doing any
sort of lifting so that no further injury occurs.

Making a bad situation better

Stretchers

If you do need to carry someone, a stretcher is naturally the best mechanism. A professional stretcher is tailor-made to provide the safest and most secure carrying method. Note the handles, safety bars and wheels on the stretchers to the right, providing a smooth, safe journey.

Improvised stretchers

If you do not have a professional survival stretcher with you, one can be improvised from any pieces of strong material and two poles. If no poles are to hand, roll the edges of the carrying material to create a makeshift handle. Alternatively, use a hard, flat surface, but take care that the casualty does not roll off.

Two-person lift technique

Take up position on either side of the casualty. Cross your arms under the casualty's legs and lock hands, grasping tightly. Slowly lift the casualty, carrying him or her with their arms draped over your shoulders for security. This technique is safe and relatively easy. Take care not to jolt the casualty during the journey.

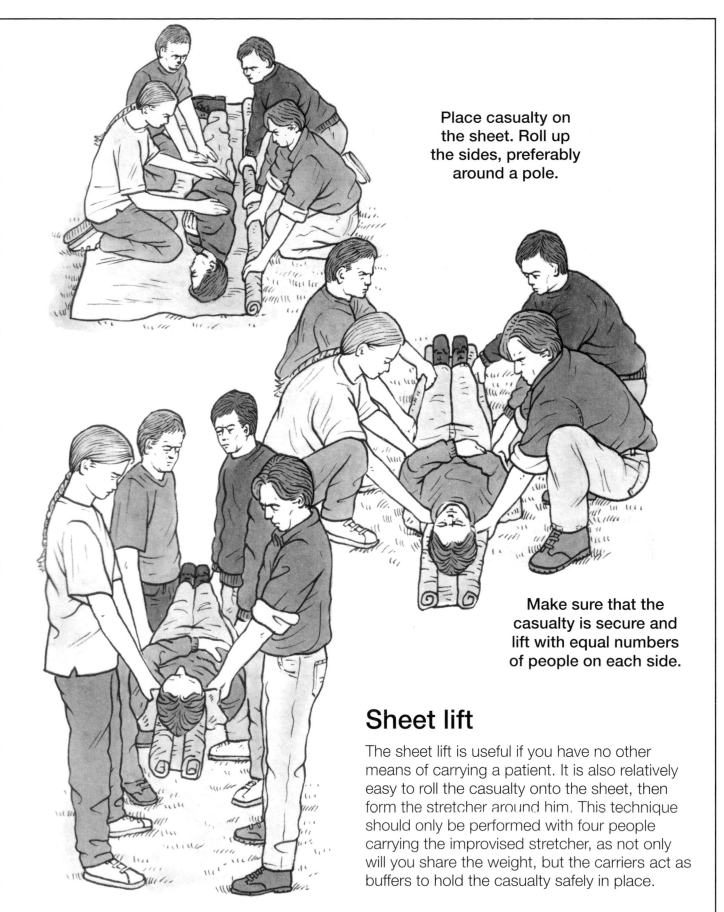

Place casualty on the sheet. Roll up the sides, preferably around a pole.

Make sure that the casualty is secure and lift with equal numbers of people on each side.

Sheet lift

The sheet lift is useful if you have no other means of carrying a patient. It is also relatively easy to roll the casualty onto the sheet, then form the stretcher around him. This technique should only be performed with four people carrying the improvised stretcher, as not only will you share the weight, but the carriers act as buffers to hold the casualty safely in place.

Choking and the Heimlich manoeuvre

A person suffering from a blocked airway is unable to breath and will send out clear distress signals. Knowing how to perform first aid for choking can immediately relieve many symptoms.

Self-treatment

If you are choking, perform the Heimlich manoeuvre on yourself. Sharp pressure to the sternum is required, so you will need a sturdy object that will not yield. Thrusting your body firmly forwards and downwards should force the obstacle out.

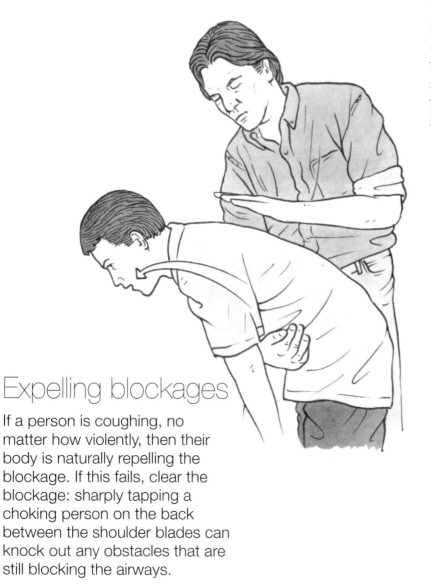

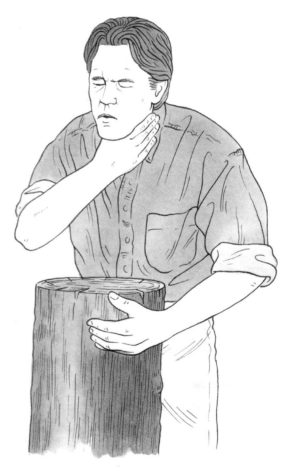

Expelling blockages

If a person is coughing, no matter how violently, then their body is naturally repelling the blockage. If this fails, clear the blockage: sharply tapping a choking person on the back between the shoulder blades can knock out any obstacles that are still blocking the airways.

First aid for choking

If sharply tapping the back does not work, perform the Heimlich manoeuvre.

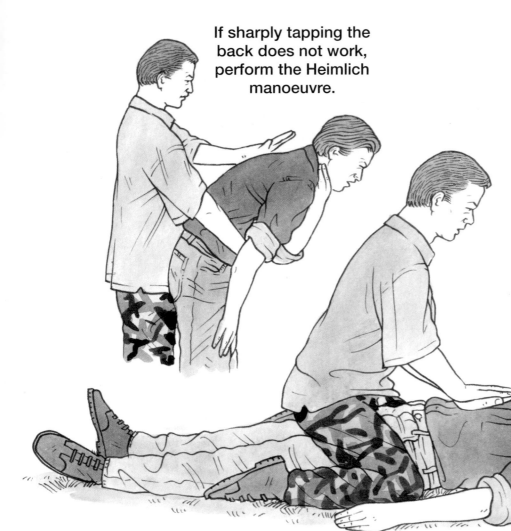

If the victim is conscious, perform the Heimlich manoeuvre. Standing behind the victim, wrap your arms around their waist. Make a fist and lodge it just beneath the casualty's breastbone (sternum) with the thumb side against the chest. Grip this fist with your other hand. Pull the fist sharply in and up. Repeat three times, then check the mouth. A similar manoeuvre can be performed on unconscious choking victims (left).

If the casualty is unconscious, press down on their breastbone and deliver five thrusts.

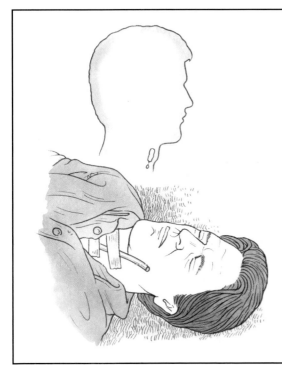

Crio-thyroid method

In some circumstances, a blockage in the windpipe just cannot be removed, and a more severe response is required to stop the casualty dying. It involves making an incision in the throat beneath the obstruction, into which a hollow tube is inserted and through which the casualty is able to breathe. This is an extremely dangerous procedure and should only be attempted by professionals if the casualty is in imminent danger of death.

Wounds and bleeding

When the body is wounded and bleeding, quick and effective responses from the first aider are needed to stop further damage or prevent potentially life-threatening developments.

Nose bleeds

Nose bleeds are a simple and common cause of blood loss which can be caused by a mild knock. Have the casualty sit with his head slightly forward and get them to pinch their nostrils while breathing through the mouth. Discourage any sniffing as this can allow blood to be swallowed and induce vomiting. Once bleeding has stopped, the area should be treated gently for several hours so the bleeding does not restart.

Abdominal wounds

With abdominal wounds, there is often the implication of damage to internal organs, and blood loss can be very severe. Place the injured person in a lying down position, with the knees raised slightly. This removes tension from the wound.

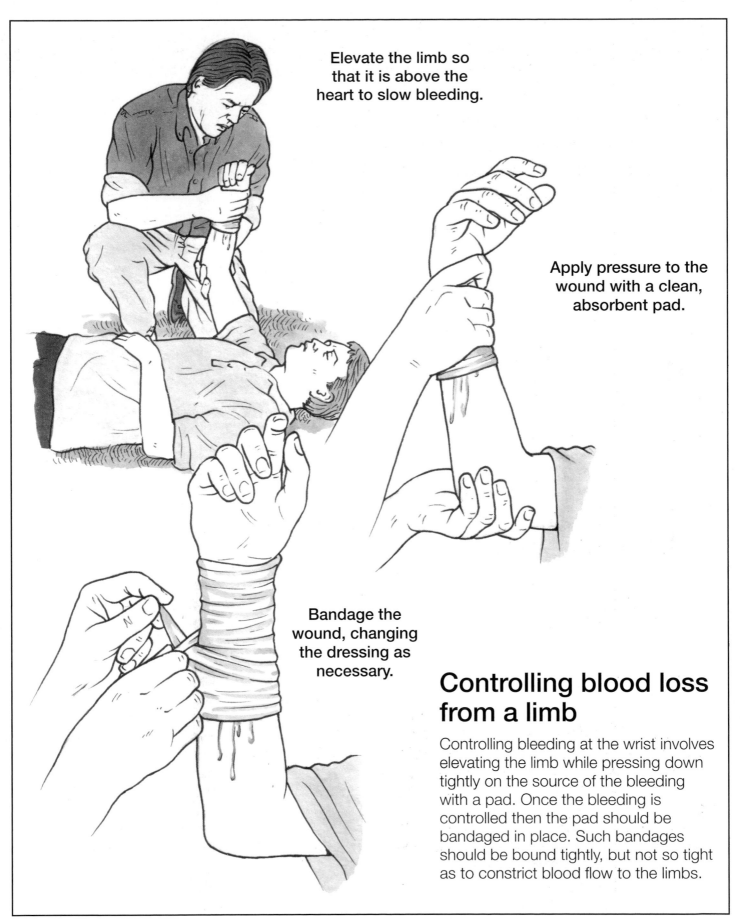

Elevate the limb so that it is above the heart to slow bleeding.

Apply pressure to the wound with a clean, absorbent pad.

Bandage the wound, changing the dressing as necessary.

Controlling blood loss from a limb

Controlling bleeding at the wrist involves elevating the limb while pressing down tightly on the source of the bleeding with a pad. Once the bleeding is controlled then the pad should be bandaged in place. Such bandages should be bound tightly, but not so tight as to constrict blood flow to the limbs.

Making a bad situation better

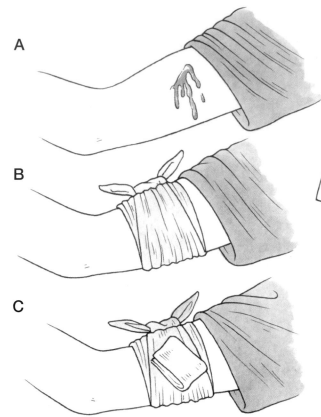

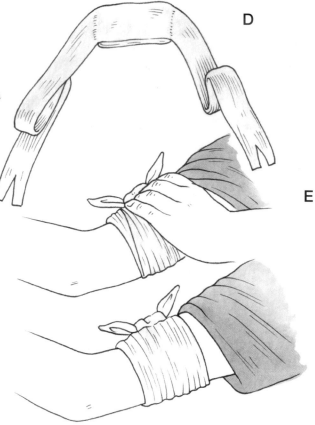

Controlling bleeding

In the series of images above, bleeding from the arm (A) is cleaned before being bandaged with the knot away from the bleeding site (B). Should blood begin to seep through the bandage, another pad (C and D) is bandaged into place (E and F) over the top. This should be enough to stem the flow. Change the pad if it becomes soaked in blood.

Applying a tourniquet

A bandage is looped over the limb (A) and tied (B). Then a stick is tied on top of the knot (C) and the pressure applied by winding until the bleeding is stopped, whereupon the stick can be bandaged in place (D). This technique should only be used as a last-ditch option to stem blood loss, as their use can cause tissue damage due to the lack of blood supply to the area. This can lead to infection and gangrene. Only use on the arm and thigh.

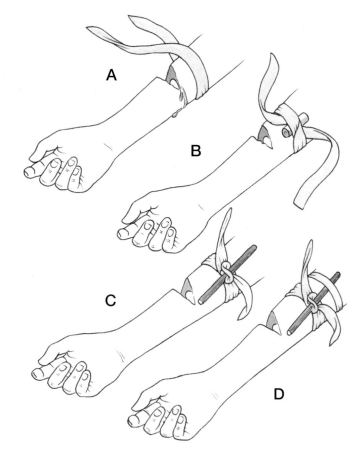

Types of wound

Wounds can vary in severity and generally fall into categories. The more serious wounds are those that are deep and those that involve damage to muscles, tendons and organs. Types are listed below:

A: Cut   **C:** Puncture
B: Avulsion   **D:** Graze

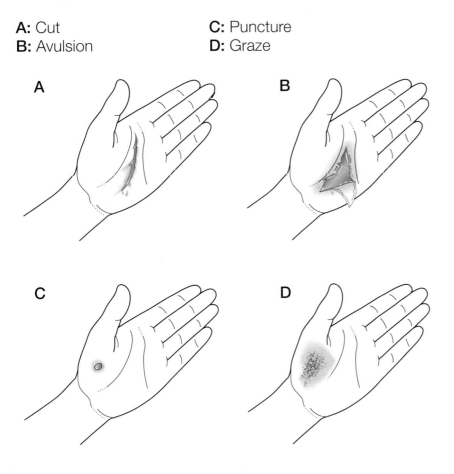

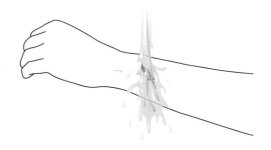

Cleaning wounds

Any wound should be thoroughly cleaned before dressing. If there is a wound to a limb, run water over the wound to wash out any debris. This is especially important if there is a chance that any splinters or fragments of glass are embedded in the wound. The water also washes away most of the blood. Check the wound and pick out any remaining debris with tweezers. If treating wounds, you should always wash your hands thoroughly and wear sterilized gloves when possible. When the wound is clean and dry, it is ready to be dressed. This prevents any bacteria entering the wound and causing an infection.

Human blood

The average human being has about 6 litres (1.3 gallons) of blood. Blood is composed of four different types of cell: red blood cells, platelets, lymphocytes and phagocytic cells. Red blood cells are the most significant to this chapter, as these contain haemoglobin, the molecule which enables blood to perform the vital function of carrying oxygen around the body.

The lymphocytes and phagocytic cells are types of white blood cell, and these are in effect the blood's guardians, fighting illnesses, infection, inflammation and the intrusion of foreign particles. Blood acts as an integral part of the immune system.

Finally, platelets assist in the process of forming blood clots, and are vital in the stopping of bleeding from wounds and healing. Finally, the blood cells are carried in plasma. This is a fluid which is approximately 90 per cent water and forms 60 per cent of the blood.

Stitching and bandaging

Bandaging can be an effective method of treating wounds. Occasionally, stitching is also required. While it is not recommended for the untrained, it can be warranted under certain circumstances.

Stitches

There are many modern adhesive stitches available on the market today, which should be included in any survival kit. They make closing wounds much more straightforward than stitching.

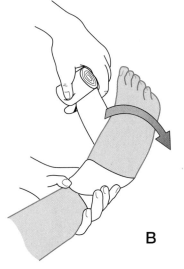

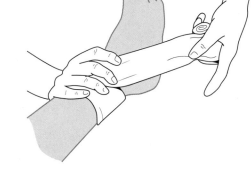

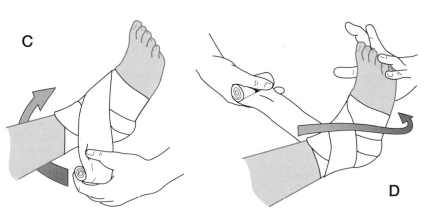

Bandaging a foot

The bandage is taken from the ankle (A) up to the middle of the foot (B), before being looped back to the ankle (C). Repeat so that the bandage crosses over each side of the foot. While such bandaging provides support, if the ankle has been twisted or broken, weight should be kept off the injury. If rest is not possible, improvise crutches.

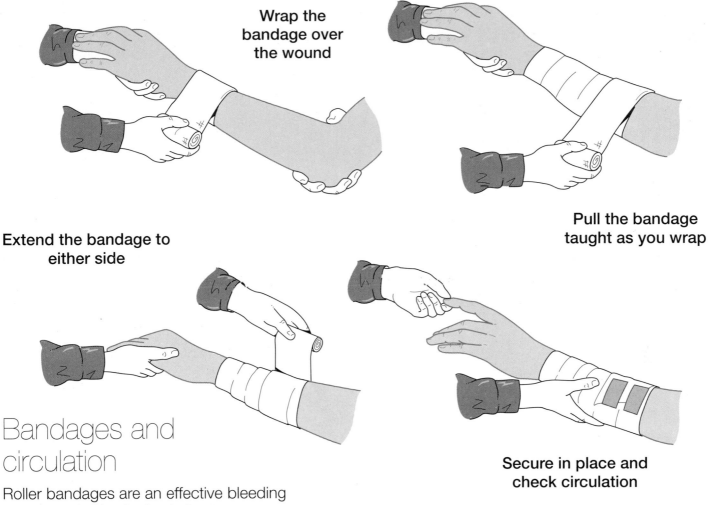

Wrap the bandage over the wound

Pull the bandage taught as you wrap

Extend the bandage to either side

Secure in place and check circulation

Bandages and circulation

Roller bandages are an effective bleeding control tool. Check circulation to ensure that the wrapping is not too tight.

Effects of blood loss

- *0.5 litre (1 pint)* If a person loses 0.5 litre (1 pint) of blood, the effects are not severe, perhaps just an inconsequential faintness that soon passes (assuming that the cause of the injury has not affected other vital functions).

- *1 litre (2 pints)* Beyond 1 litre (2 pints), the body starts to respond to a more serious challenge. 1 litre (2 pints) of blood loss starts the early stages of volume shock, when the casualty begins to lose the blood pressure necessary for the effective transfer of oxygen into the body tissue. They may become very faint, pale and unstable on their feet.

- *2 litres (4 pints)* With this much blood loss the casualty can collapse, their vital signs showing a rapid, weak pulse as adrenaline levels rise in response to the danger. The skin will also become clammy and pale as blood is diverted to major organs. The casualty may feel very sick and thirsty.

- *3 litres (6 pints)* With this much blood loss, the situation becomes life-threatening. The respiration and pulse signals will both be extremely poor, and the casualty will probably be unconscious. After this, cardiac arrest and respiratory failure can soon follow.

Making a bad situation better

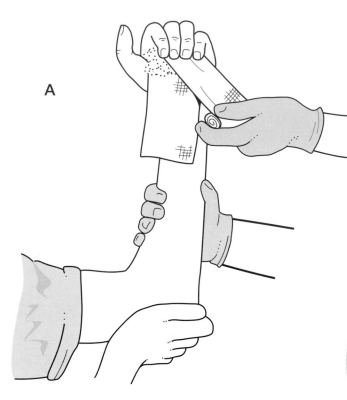

A

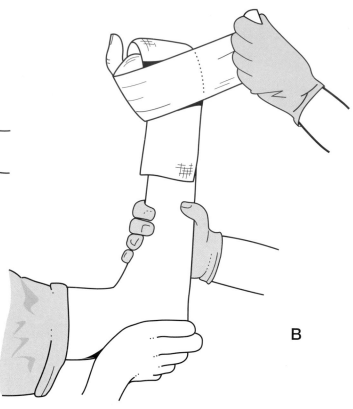

B

Palm bandage

Bandaging areas that are often in motion, such as the palm, can be tricky. Get the casualty to grip a thick sterile pad (A) and then bind the fingers in place with a roller bandage, leaving the thumb free (B). This provides an extra level of protection for the wound and should also stem the blood flow.

Bandaging an elbow joint

Wounds in the joint creases are awkward, both because of their location and also because the large blood vessels in the area can make the bleeding severe. Place a pad in the crook of the elbow and bend the limb so the pad is held in place. When bleeding has stopped, bandage securely.

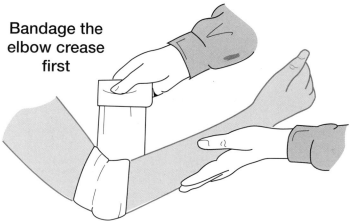

Bandage the elbow crease first

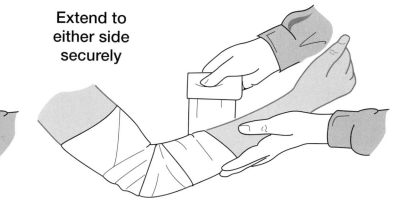

Extend to either side securely

Stitching a wound

Stitching is useful if the wound is a clean straight cut which is not too deep, and is in danger of infection through climatic influences. Do not close up a wound which is dirty or over 12 hours old.

Adhesive sutures are the easiest way to draw a wound together. Butterfly sutures can be bought, or made by cutting regular adhesive plasters to the corresponding shape. To use these, simply draw the edges of the wound together and stick across; try to get the edges of the wound as close as possible.

Stitching requires much more skill to apply, and also needs some confidence. Take a sterilized needle or thread (or sterilize both by boiling for 20 minutes), and make a stitch at the mid point of the wound, drawing the edges together. Then cut the thread and tie it, before making other individual stitches out from the centre until the wound is fully closed.

Leave the stitches in place for 5–14 days (for the face, five days; for the body, 10 days; and for the hand or foot, 14 days) before their removal. However, before that time, if an infection appears you should remove some or all of the stitches to allow drainage.

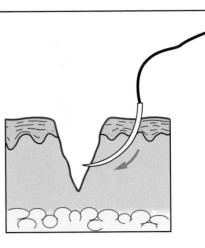

Ensure that needle and thread are sterilized

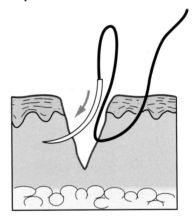

Make an initial insertion at the mid point of the wound

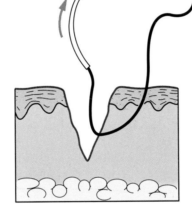

Pull the thread upwards

Stitch through the opposite side of the wound

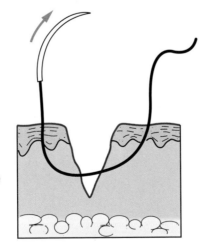

Pull the thread upwards

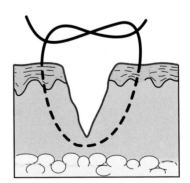

Draw the edges together and tie the thread

Consciousness and head injuries

Changes in consciousness, personality or behaviour can be some of your first indicators that a medical problem is developing or that life is in danger.

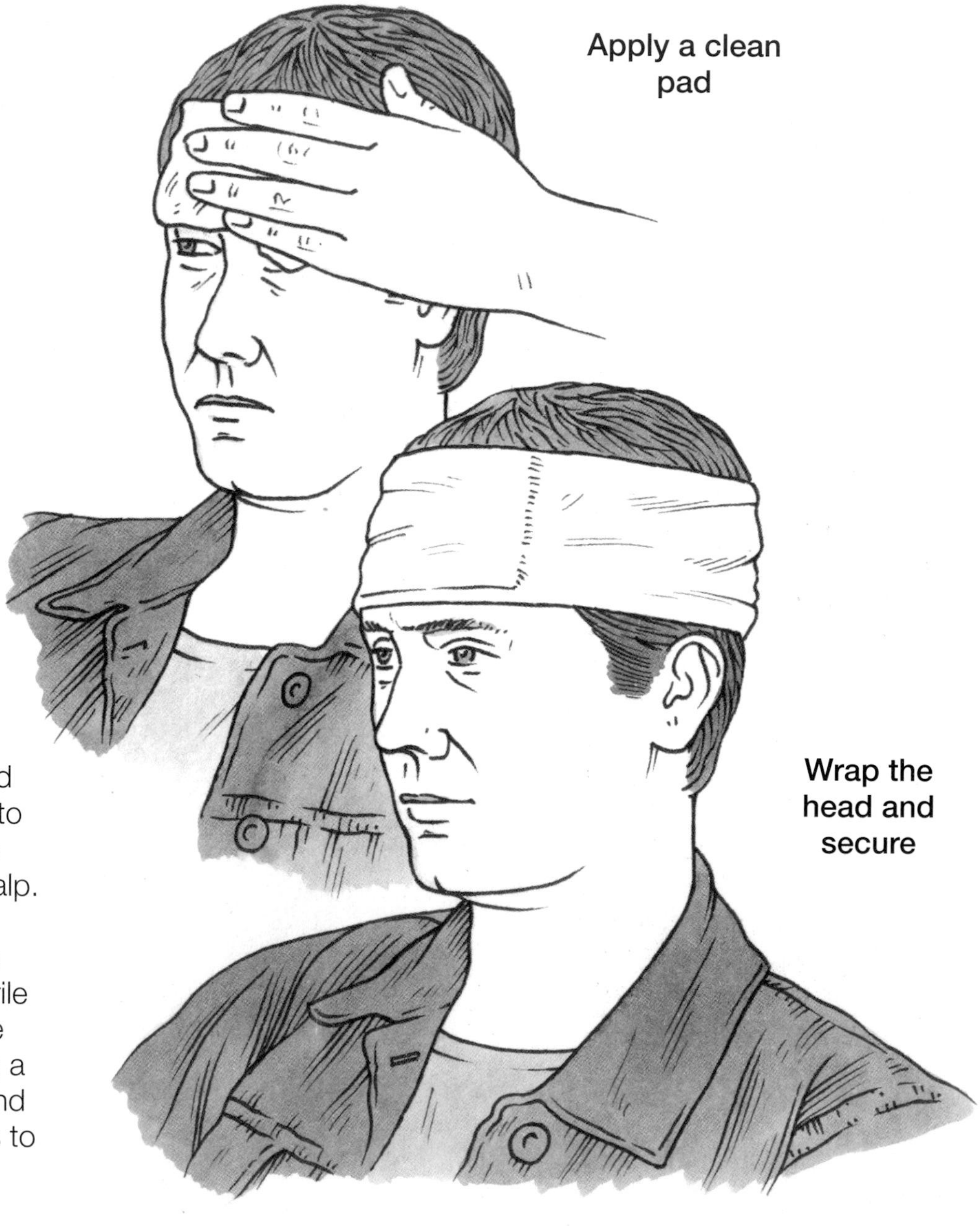

Apply a clean pad

Applying a head bandage

Any type of wound to the head can bleed dramatically owing to the many blood vessels which run through the skin of the scalp. You might need to trim away hair to clean and bandage the wound effectively. Place a sterile dressing over the wound once it has been cleaned, wrapping a roller bandage over the pad and around the head several times to keep it securely in place.

Wrap the head and secure

Skull fracture

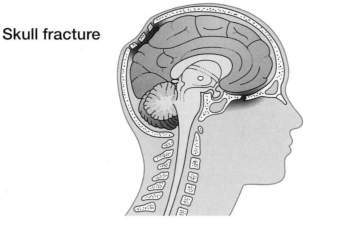

Concussion

Blow to head

Compression caused by bleeding

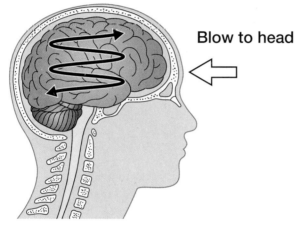

Types of brain injury

With a skull fracture, there are most likely outward signs of injury and the casualty may frequently be unconscious or steadily becoming that way. Other symptoms of brain injury include fluid or blood leaking from the ear, blood leaking into the white of the eye, asymmetry in the position of the face or body, seizures or convulsions, paralysis or weakness down one side, respiratory difficulty or a slow pulse.

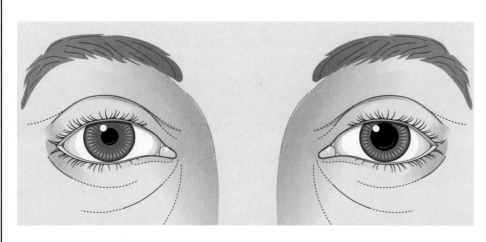

Pupil size

Unequal pupil size, or dilated pupils, can be a sign of cerebral compression. This is a serious impairment of consciousness caused by increased pressure in the brain. If you spot unequal pupils on anyone with a head injury, monitor them carefully until you can rule this out.

Burns and scalds

Serious burns can be among the most traumatic wounds a first aider may have to deal with. Whatever their cause, burns inflict great pain and potentially lasting damage on the human body.

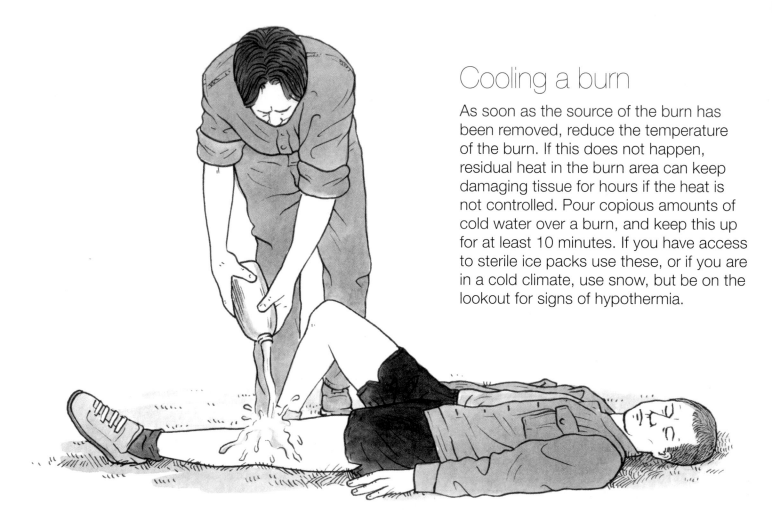

Cooling a burn

As soon as the source of the burn has been removed, reduce the temperature of the burn. If this does not happen, residual heat in the burn area can keep damaging tissue for hours if the heat is not controlled. Pour copious amounts of cold water over a burn, and keep this up for at least 10 minutes. If you have access to sterile ice packs use these, or if you are in a cold climate, use snow, but be on the lookout for signs of hypothermia.

Protecting a burnt hand in a bag

Once the burn is thoroughly cooled, dressings can be applied. A useful survival tip is to protect burnt hands with a bag. This allows the wound to be protected from bacteria, while keeping any fabric away from the burn. Do not apply anything to the burn itself and never burst blisters.

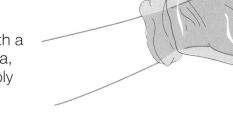

Sunburn Electrical burn Fire Chemical burn Friction burn

Sources of burns

Burns have many different and diverse causes, all resulting in injury when destructive levels of heat come into contact with a point on the human body.

The main types of burns in an outdoor survival situation are shown above. It is important to note that different burns require different treatments.

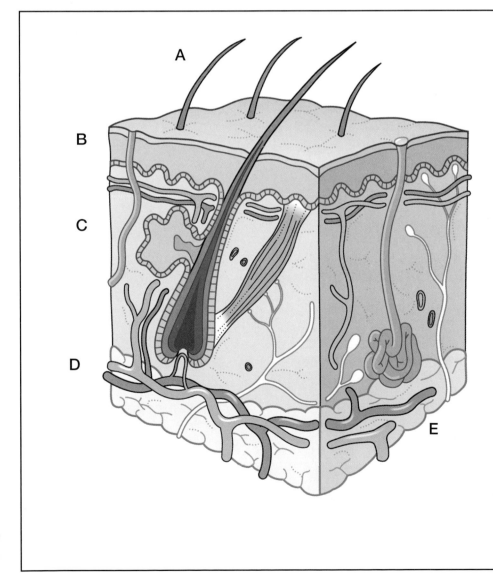

Human skin

Human skin is composed of two layers. The outermost layer is called the epidermis and acts as a protective waterproof layer. Beneath this is the dermis, the major part of the human skin. The dermis contains nerves, muscles, sweat glands and the roots of the hair folicles, which terminate in or through the epidermis. Finally, there is a layer of fat tissue beneath and separate to the dermis. This layer supplies the skin with vital nutrients.

A. Hair
B. Epidermis
C. Dermis
D. Hair follicle
E. Fat tissue

Large-area body burns

If you are outdoors, try to keep the burn area from direct contact with the ground. If clothing can be safely removed, take it off, but if any clothing is sticking, pour water directly onto the material and keep it soaked and cold. Monitor the casualty for signs of shock and replace as much lost fluid as possible. Also monitor the core temperature of the patient, being mindful of causing hypothermia.

General principles for forest fire safety

- Pick your escape route based on travelling into the wind – the wind direction will usually indicate the direction of the fire's travel.
- Even if it gets very hot indeed keep your clothing on as it will protect from burns caused by heated air.
- Stay away from high ground as forest fires burn more quickly when travelling uphill.

- If you have to run through flames, cover as much skin as possible and dampen clothing with water. Hold your breath while passing through the flames, run as fast as possible, and use a piece of damp cloth to cover your nose and mouth.

Treating a chemical burn

The treatment for a chemical burn is essentially the same as that for a thermal burn – remove affected clothing, wash with water, monitor respiration and airway closely for signs of shock. However, you should wash the area for longer; a minimum of 20 minutes is recommended.

Eye burns

If a chemical substance has come in contact with the eye, you will notice symptoms such as the swelling and watering of the eye, an inability to open the eye, and a report of sever eye pain. Keep the casualty's hands, and your own, away from the eye, but irrigate it under cold water for about 10 minutes, gently opening the eyelid to ensure a thorough washing. Make sure that the eye you are washing is lower than the other to prevent cross contamination from the water, and do not let any water flow across the casualty's mouth. Once this is completed, cover the eye with a pad, dressing or patch.

Breaks/dislocations

Although the human skeleton gives us strength, form and movement, it is also vulnerable to injury from outside forces. Damage to any of its parts is extremely debilitating and painful.

Musculoskeletal system

Bones are formed from a composition of collagen and calcium phosphate. They form a skeleton which is linked from head to toe to provide the shape and form of the human body. They also provide a protective cage around the vital internal organs of the torso. Linking the bones together are the joints which allow the skeleton to achieve a range of different movements throughout the body. Fractures occur when too much force is exerted on a bone, a common survivalist injury.

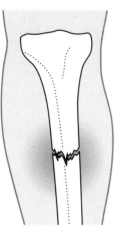

Simple fracture

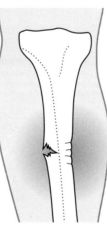

Greenstick fracture

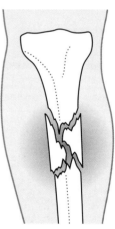

Comminuted fracture

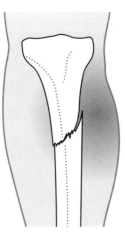

Closed fracture

Open fracture

Shoulder dislocation

A dislocated shoulder occurs when the joint of the arm bone and shoulder socket become displaced. Lying the casualty on the ground, gently pull the injured arm up to an angle of about 90° from their body, bend at the elbow and rotate the arm upwards and forwards. The joint should slip back into place.

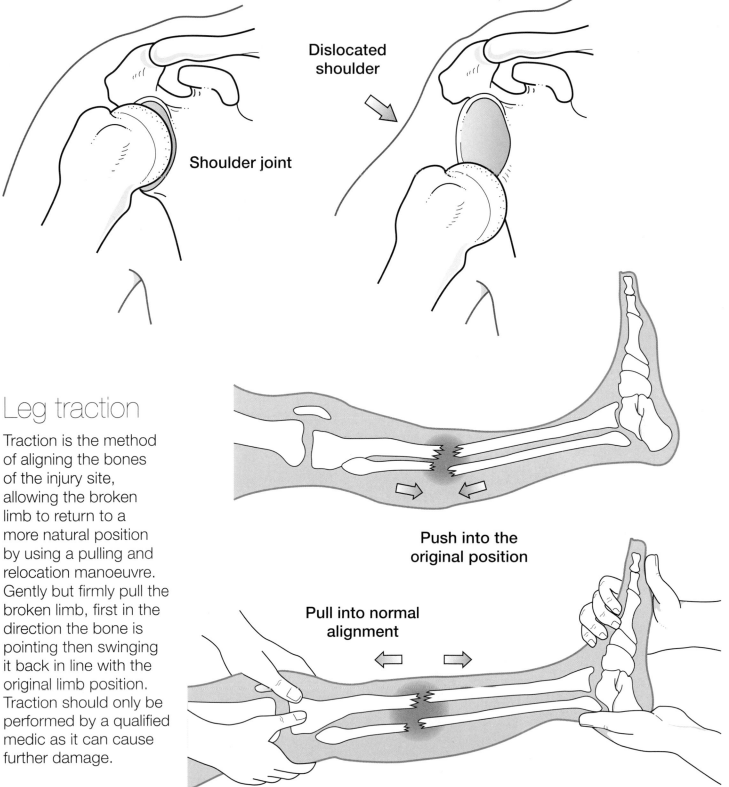

Dislocated shoulder

Shoulder joint

Push into the original position

Pull into normal alignment

Leg traction

Traction is the method of aligning the bones of the injury site, allowing the broken limb to return to a more natural position by using a pulling and relocation manoeuvre. Gently but firmly pull the broken limb, first in the direction the bone is pointing then swinging it back in line with the original limb position. Traction should only be performed by a qualified medic as it can cause further damage.

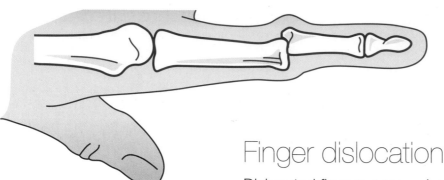

Finger dislocation

Dislocated fingers occur when the force of something striking or pulling on the fingers lifts one or several of the fingers out of joint. These often happen during falls when the hand is used to break the impact. Apply firm traction in the direction the finger is pointing before moving it back into a natural line and slipping it into position. Next, splint the finger in the mid-range position for support.

Spinal injuries

Spinal injuries are critical, threatening death or permanent paralysis. The following can be signs of spinal injury:

- Chronic pain in the back regardless of movement
- A noticeably deformed spinal column
- Chronic bruising or other injury over the spinal area
- Extreme tenderness over the spine
- Loss of bladder control; in men, the penis may be persistently erect
- A tingling or numb sensation in the limbs
- Paralysis, or a lack of response to stimulus (try scratching the palms of the hands or the soles of the feet, and ask if the casualty can feel it)

A spinal injury casualty must be transferred to professional help immediately. The person administering first aid, meanwhile, should concentrate on stabilizing the injured spine so there is no further damage caused through movement. To treat the casualty:

1. Do not let him move at all.
2. Stabilize his neck by improvising a collar out of something such as a towel or magazine. Bend it around the neck. Do not move the head while doing this, nor restrict the casualty's throat. Or, if the casualty is on his back, place a rolled-up blanket or piece of clothing underneath and around the neck to stop sideways movement.
3. Monitor the casualty's vital signs constantly, especially if they are unconscious.

Should you have to move the casualty – something that is not recommended – get a group of people, ideally five in number, to position themselves along the length of the casualty's body and slowly lift or roll him or her onto a rigid litter or board. One person should have the dedicated job of keeping the head facing forwards and naturally aligned with the shoulders. If the head is not in this position before movement, place your hands firmly over the casualty's ears and turn the head very slowly to the front without any jerking movements.

Signs of a broken limb

An open fracture means that the broken bone has pushed through the skin and the break is visible. In this case, you are not only treating the broken bone, but a potentially severe wound. A closed fracture is indicated by swelling and pain. If the casualty is unconscious, run your hands gently over the limbs to check for fractures when they are safely in the recovery position.

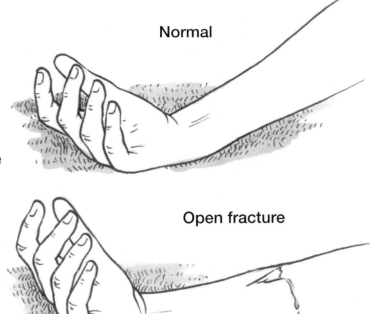

Normal

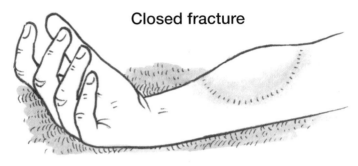

Closed fracture

Open fracture

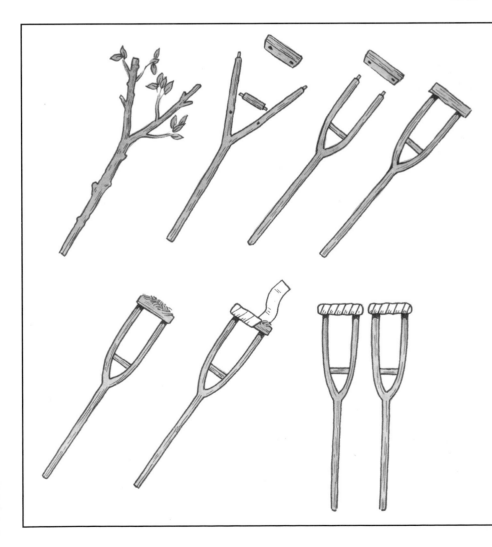

Improvised crutches

In a survival situation, fashion a crutch or pair of crutches from sturdy, straight branches. Look for branch with forks, which can be tailored to provide extra support for the casualty. Add a branch across the top of the fork to take the weight. This can be made more comfortable by wrapping spare bandages or other materials around the support. Improvised crutches can be extremely useful, allowing the injured party to be able to move quite freely once their injuries have been treated. Ensure that the crutches are tested thoroughly, as they could lead to further injury if they break or bend suddenly.

Stabilizing fractures

Once you have checked the casualty's vital signs, ascertained the injury and any complications, then given initial treatment, you need to know how to dress any fractures or dislocations.

Arm injuries

The arm can be fractured in several locations. For fractures to the main arm bones and wrists, treat them as for any fracture. Splint if the injury is an unstable one, but if it appears to be a stable injury, a simple arm sling will suffice to keep it in place and secure. An injury to the elbow is more complicated. If the elbow is in the bent position, then put in a standard sling or splint in the 90° bend (above). If it is in the stretched-out position, then simply put padding between the arm and torso, and tie the arm to the torso (wrapping the bandages right around the body) at about three different points to support the entire arm's length.

Splints

Once any dislocation or fracture is realigned, your priority is to stabilize the injured area through bandaging or splinting. Professional splinting materials can be purchased, but workable splints can be manufactured on the spot if necessary.

Splinting a limb

The technique for splinting generally follows the same principle for each situation. You will need a rigid stabilizer such as a straight branch, binding materials, such as bandages and duct tape, and padding material for comfort. Bind the stabilizers to both sides of the broken limb to immobilize it. Ensure that the joints either side of the break are also stabilized and check that circulation is not restricted.

Stabilizing the neck

Neck and spine injuries can be very dangerous, even life-threatening. Ask the casualty to inform you of any pains in the neck or back if they are able to. Look and feel along the spine for any signs of irregularity, swelling or misalignment if possible. If you remain unsure, stabilize the neck to minimize movement. Place a rolled up blanket (or piece of clothing) under the neck itself, while walking boots can be arranged to stop sideways movement.

Making a bad situation better

Knee injuries

Injuries to the knee can occur in many different ways owing to the complexity of the physical structure. Most vulnerable are the patella, or kneecap, and the ligaments which connect the femur, tibia and fibula bones, and any violent twisting motion, a blow to the knee or imposing too much pressure on the knee can displace the kneecap or strain the ligaments. With dislocations, straighten the leg gently to encourage the kneecap to pop back into place, but do not force it. For other knee injuries, place the knee in the least painful position before stabilizing it with padding around the joint. Wrap a roller bandage around the knee itself (A) before steadily widening the width of the bandage (B and C) and pinning the bandage in place below the joint (D).

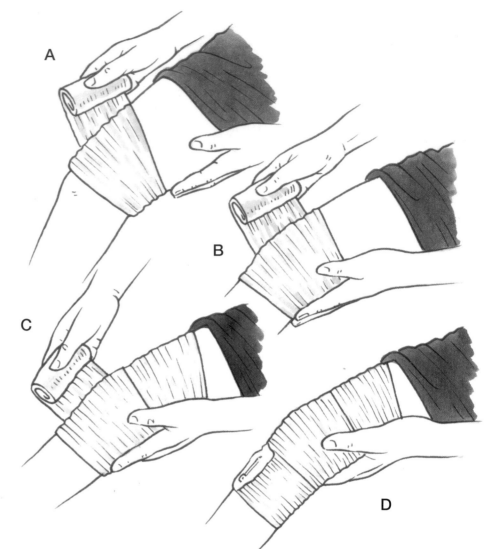

Bandaging a closed fracture

Fractures to hip bones are rare because of the strength of the bones and the muscles surrounding them. However, these, and other injuries to legs, can occur in survival situations. Once you have applied traction, bind the injured leg to the uninjured leg above and below the fracture. When two legs are bound together, always remember to tie the knots over the uninjured leg.

Splinting a wrist

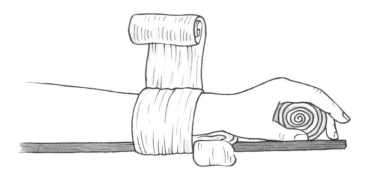

The wrist contains many delicate bones and injuries can be both common and complex. Splint the wrist securely, wrapping the area with bandages and immobilizing as much of the hand and lower arm as possible. Note that the hand is clutching a roller bandage to help keep it fixed in its natural position.

RICE procedure

Sprains, strains and bruises can be extremely debilitating injuries in a survival situation and, if the injuries are incurred in an unforgiving environment, there is the possibility that they will become dangerous. The procedure for treatment is simple to carry out and can alleviate pain. It is commonly known as the RICE procedure:

- Rest the injured part;
- Ice the injured part – chill the wound with an ice pack or cold compress;
- Compress the injury;
- Elevate the injured part.

This four-stage procedure can dramatically reduce the swelling which commonly accompanies these types of injuries. It is shown here for a sprained ankle, but could be used for any limb or bruised area of the body.

Poisoning

Poisons come in a multitude of different guises and can enter the body in a number of ways. They can be localized, systemic or both, and can be extremely debilitating in a survival situation.

Snake-bite patterns

If a person has been bitten by a snake, examine the bite marks as they can inform you whether the snake was poisonous or not. If there are one or two larger puncture wounds at the front of the bite, distinct from the rest, the chances are it was poisonous. However, this does not mean that venom has been injected, but the bite should be monitored closely.

Non-poisonous

Poisonous

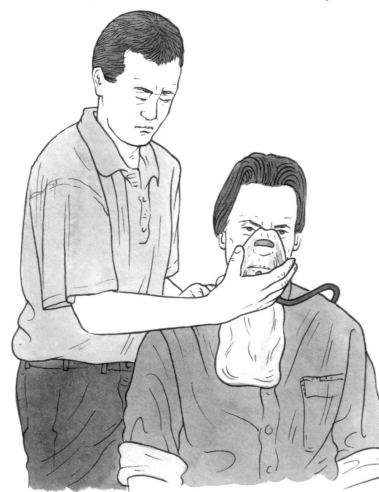

Respiratory poisoning

In the case of respiratory poisoning, including inhalation of smoke, carbon monoxide and solvents or fuels, toxins can enter the body which can be very dangerous. In the first instance, the casualty should be removed from the source into fresh air. If possible, supply the casualty with oxygen. If this is not possible, at least cover the mouth and nose with a light material. Then follow the standard procedures for checking breathing, consciousness and circulation.

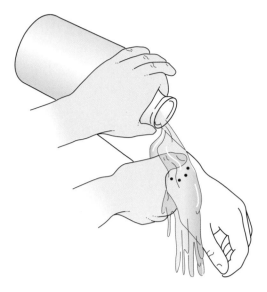

Cleaning a bite

If you have been bitten, there is little you can do to negate the effect of the venom, so focus on basic life support and on slowing the circulation of the poison around the system. Try to calm the victim as much as possible to slow their heartbeat. Wash the wound site with soap and water to remove any poison which might remain. Then tie a restricting bandage (never a tourniquet) around the bitten limb above the bite site. The effect is to restrict the infusion of the venom through the lymphatic system. However, monitor to ensure that circulation is not cut off. Never try to suck out the poison.

Poisonous plants

Most poisoning from flora sources is through ingestion. Do not eat plants (or fungi) unless you are absolutely sure what they are. If plants are ingested, monitor the casualty's vital signs as soon as possible. If you are in a wilderness setting and cannot seek medical help, induce vomiting and thus evacuate the stomach of its poisonous contents. Do this immediately upon ingestion and up to several hours afterwards. Once the stomach contents have been vomited, you should attempt to remove remaining poisonous content by absorption methods. To do this, give the patient a mixture of tea, charcoal, and milk of magnesia mixed in equal parts, or just activated charcoal (about 25–50gm [1–2oz]) mixed with water.

A. Baneberry
B. Buttercups
C. Death Canvas
D. Monk's Hood
E. Larkspur
F. Lupins
G. Water Hemlock
H. Nightshade berries
I. Water Hemlock rootstalk

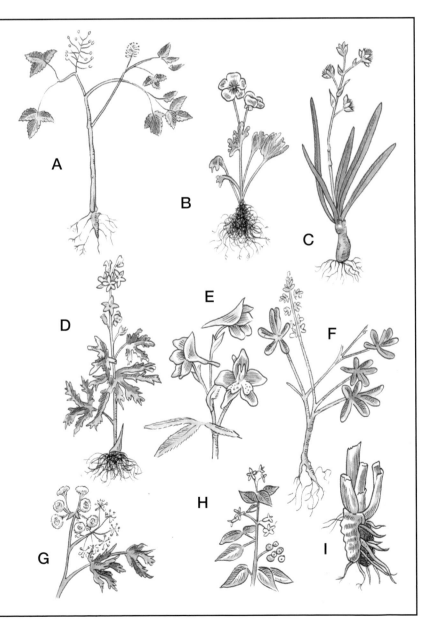

Other ailments

In a wilderness situation, there are many other ailments that can crop up unexpectedly. While you can never be ready for every eventuality, being prepared can make survival experiences easier.

Cleaning the eye

Any object in the eye is an excruciating and disorientating injury, especially in a potentially dangerous survival setting. Prevent the casualty from rubbing the eye. Inspect the eye to check that the object is not embedded. If it is not, simply try to wash it out. Alternatively, try to remove the object by using the edge of a moistened piece of soft, clean cloth. Treat with antibiotic eye ointment and monitor for signs of infection.

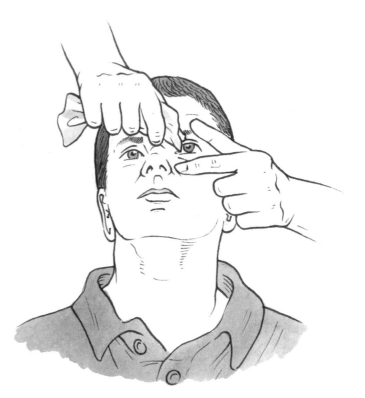

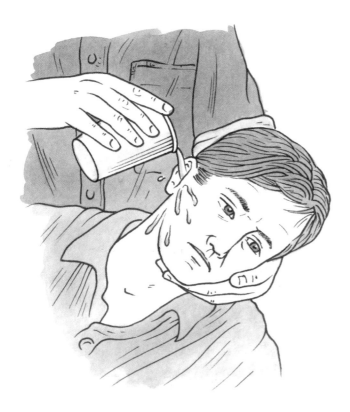

Cleaning the ears

In a wilderness situation, the foreign bodies most likely to invade the ear are insects. If a person complains of strange thumping and scratching noises inside their ear, accompanied by woolly hearing and earache, insect intrusion is a possibility. The casualty should present the problem ear flat and uppermost. Pour a steady stream of warm water into the ear, which will hopefully flush the insect out. If it does not work, seek medical help quickly as, if the insect dies, the result could be a serious inflammatory infection.

Strokes

One in five of us will die of a stroke and they can happen at any age. Strokes are also sudden and can be very debilitating. They occur when the blood supply to a specific area of the brain is disrupted or impaired. Ensure that airways are kept clear and that the casualty is breathing. If unconscious, place him/her in the recovery position. If conscious, lie him down with his head slightly higher than the feet. Turn the head to one side to allow any saliva to flow out of the mouth. Keep him warm and reassured.

Seizures

Convulsions and seizures can be some of the most alarming ailments a first aider has to treat. The cause is a disruption of the electrical patterns of activity in the brain. They tend to pass by themselves, but the main priority is to prevent the casualty from harming themselves, as well as making them as comfortable as possible until you can ascertain the cause of the seizure.

Foreign bodies

Foreign bodies such as pieces of grit or splinters in wounds can be commonplace in a outdoors survival context. To prevent infection, they must not be left in wounds. Using the sterile tweezers from your survival kit, try to grasp the grit or splinter very close to the skin, drawing it out slowly and against the direction in which it went in. Then, squeeze the wound to draw out a little blood and dress it.

Remove splinters slowly to prevent parts breaking off and remaining in the wound

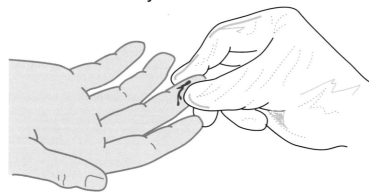

Squeeze to allow blood to flow and wash out any bacteria

Pull in the same direction the object entered the skin

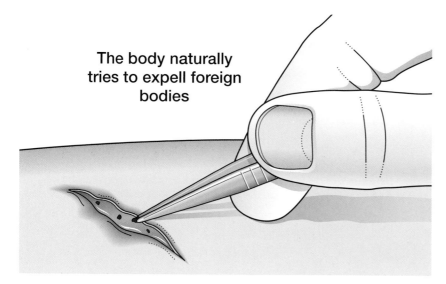

The body naturally tries to expell foreign bodies

Grit and splinters

If you cannot remove the items, bandage the wound (without closing it up over the foreign body) but check it daily to see whether or not the splinter or piece of grit has presented itself for removal. Depending on your situation and the availability of medical attention, remember that certain objects are best left temporarily in place, especially if their removal is likely to cause extreme pain, shock or blood loss.

Impaled objects

The correct procedure when dealing with impaled objects is to leave the object in place, using pressure techniques to stop the bleeding. Removing impaled objects often results in further tissue damage, so it is best to bandage around the object until it is firmly held in place, using supports as needed (shown right). Medical help should be sought as soon as possible. If there is no possibility of medical help, remove the object yourself. Work the object loose slowly, stemming bleeding (which might be profuse) as you go.

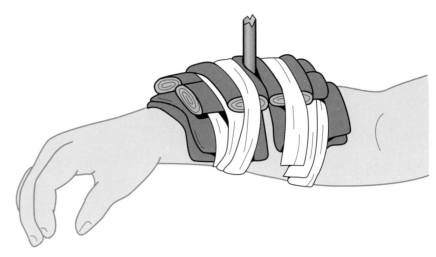

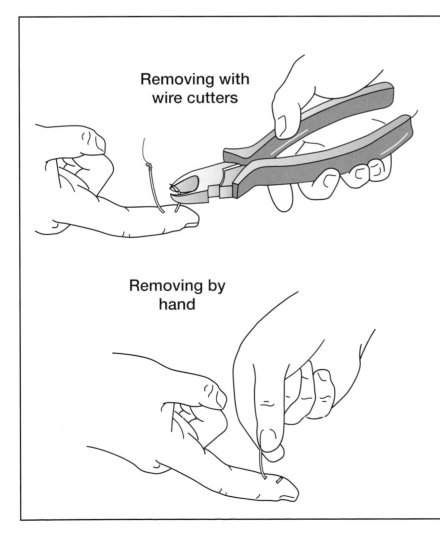

Removing with wire cutters

Removing by hand

Removing a fish hook from flesh

Fish hooks, by their very purpose, present a more difficult challenge for extraction than grit or splinters. If you have to remove a fish hook, cut away the line and, if you have wire cutters, also the barb.

Once the barb is removed, hold the eye of the hook and withdraw it, following the shape of the hook. If you do not have wire cutters, or the barb is embedded in the skin, then you will have to push the barb forward and through the skin; then take hold of it with a cloth or other protective material and withdraw it, with the eye coming through last of all.

Treat and stem any blood loss and dress the wound, checking regularly for signs of infection.

Hygiene and disease control

Hygiene quickly becomes the frontline of staying well in a disaster situation. Suddenly, systems we take for granted are gone. Issues like clean water and waste disposal become vital for survival.

Swine flu symptoms

A flu or viral pandemic, especially in close quarters, can quickly become a huge survival issue. Take every care to reduce your risk of exposure, but ensure that you can recognize the symptoms. Swine flu is a particularly nasty form of the flu virus, although the mortality rate remains below 10 per cent. Symptoms include:

A. Runny nose, sore throat
B. Muscle pains
C. Respiratory problems (coughing)
D. Joint pains
E. Intestinal problems

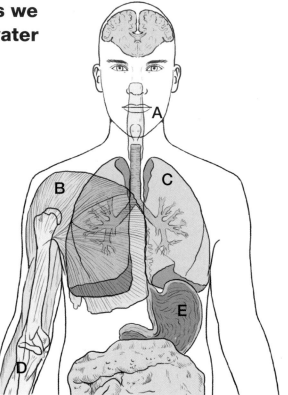

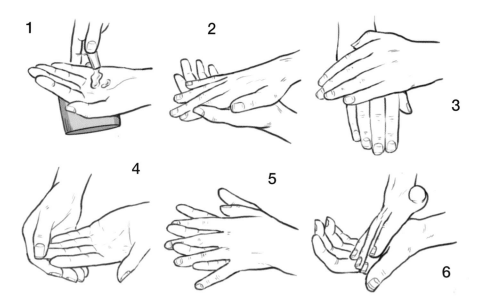

Hand sanitizer method

Hand sanitizer can be a cheap life-saver in a pandemic, and hand-to-mouth or hand-to-eyes actions are primary modes of disease transmission. Follow the sanitizer method outlined here, which treats every part of the hand, and ensure that children are taught to use this method. Also follow it when washing your hands with soap and water.

Decontamination shower

During chemical and atmospheric emergencies, take regular decontamination showers. If your clothes are severly contaminated, dispose of them in tightly sealed plastic bags following the approved methods of waste disposal.

Health and hygiene

a. Stay clean (daily regimen).
1. Minimize infection by washing. (Use white ashes, sand or loamy soil as soap substitutes.)
2. Comb and clean debris from hair.
3. Cleanse mouth and brush teeth.
   i. Use hardwood twig as toothbrush (fray it by chewing on one end then use as brush).
   ii. Use single strand of an inner core string from parachute cord for dental floss.
   iii. Use clean finger to stimulate gum tissues by rubbing.
   iv. Gargle with salt water to help prevent sore throat and aid in cleaning teeth and gums.
4. Clean and protect feet.

   i. Change and wash socks
   ii. Wash, dry, and massage.
   iii. Check frequently for blisters and red areas.
   iv. Use adhesive tape/mole skin to prevent damage.

b. Exercise daily.

c. Prevent and control parasites.
1. Check body for lice, fleas, ticks, etc.
   i. Check body regularly.
   ii. Pick off insects and eggs (DO NOT crush).
2. Wash clothing and use repellents.
3. Use smoke to fumigate clothing and equipment.

– US Army, *Survival, Escape, and Evasion* (1999)

Reducing risk

In an emergency, authorities will try to limit the spread of communicable disease as much as possible, but there are things you can and should do to reduce the risk of becoming ill.

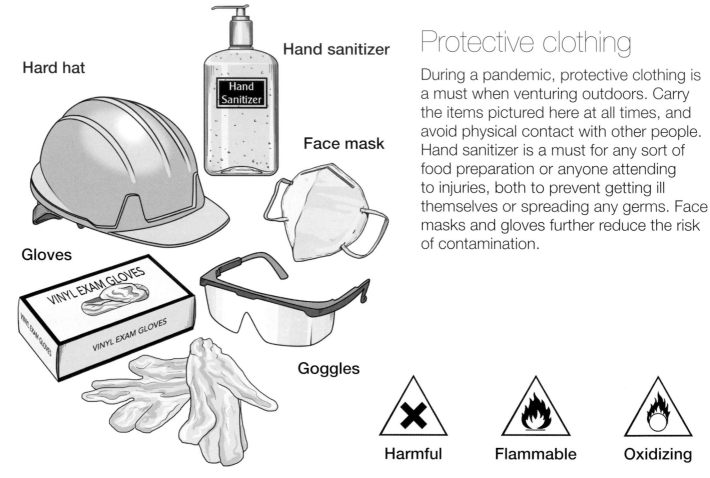

Hard hat

Hand sanitizer

Hand Sanitizer

Face mask

Gloves

VINYL EXAM GLOVES

Goggles

Protective clothing

During a pandemic, protective clothing is a must when venturing outdoors. Carry the items pictured here at all times, and avoid physical contact with other people. Hand sanitizer is a must for any sort of food preparation or anyone attending to injuries, both to prevent getting ill themselves or spreading any germs. Face masks and gloves further reduce the risk of contamination.

Harmful

Flammable

Oxidizing

Corrosive

Radioactive

Biohazard

Chemical hazard signs

Learn to identify these and any other hazard signs used, and take appropriate action when a danger is identified (which usually means putting distance between you and the threat). If you are taking care of children, make sure that they stay in pairs or groups, ideally with at least one person able to identify the signs and avoid the situation.

Explosive

Toxic

Dangerous

Temporary latrines

If you are unable to stay in your home or have to set up a semi-permanent camp, make setting up a latrine an absolute priority, to prevent the spread of disease. Site the latrine at least 50m (164ft) from your living quarters and ensure it is downwind of your camp's position.

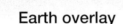

Foot boards

Earth overlay

Self-closing lid

Trench and burn-out latrines

A burn out latrine (right) can be as simple as an empty oil can with a lid. While this is simple to make, it does require the contents to be regularly incinerated. Alternatively, build a trench latrine (above), where a deep pit is dug and used as a latrine. The excavated earth is used to cover waste every time someone uses the latrine. Take care that toilet paper is disposed of carefully and sanitize your hands thoroughly after use.

How to tell if someone is dead

- Listen and look for breathing – the chest may still rise as muscles contract.
- Check for a pulse at neck and wrist.
- Check pupils for reaction to sudden light; they should contract.
- Elicit involuntary blinking by carefully touching the eye.
- Elicit a reflex by scratching the bottom of the victim's foot and watching for the toes to curl.

- There is no response to any stimulus by voice or touch.
- *Pallor mortis* – paleness or bluish tinge to the skin, which occurs 15–20 minutes after death; check lips, eyes and feet first.
- Body temperature drops.
- Sphincter muscles (the muscles that hold organs closed) relax, and bladder or bowel contents may be expelled.

Basic precautions

While it is easy to believe that only members of the armed forces or police ever come into contact with warring factions, events around the world prove that civilians can be caught in the crossfire.

Threat levels

In a survival evacuation, anyone moving into potentially hostile areas must maintain constant awareness of potential and actual threats. In this scenario, the absence of women and children on the street should give cause for concern, as should the figure in the background, watching over the wall. Civilians should aim to avoid any potential threats and move quickly on.

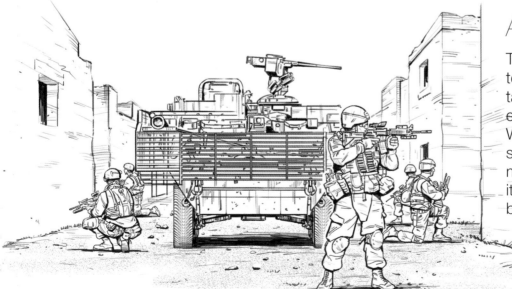

Awareness

The military are trained in teamwork, with every soldier taking responsibility for guarding each other and their vehicle. When moving in the presence of such teams, don't make sudden movements, and avoid carrying items that, at a distance, could be confused with weapons.

Authority figures

If you have to approach military units, try to make contact with people in authority. If you cannot see rank insignia, those carrying sophisticated navigation devices, radios or binoculars are likely to be at least NCO rank.

Kidnapping of soldiers

For small military units conducting patrols, manning checkpoints or outposts, mounting raids and performing general peacekeeping, there are common ingredients in many kidnap situations:

- Small units become lost within urban or remote rural areas, primarily through navigational errors or having to follow detours because of unexpected obstructions or troublesome terrain.
- Soldiers manning outposts or checkpoints are too few in number to make a convincing defence, and are often isolated from reinforcements.
- Units have to travel regularly along particularly dangerous routes, in areas where the rule of law is weak and insurgent groups dominate the local population.
- Kidnappings can sometimes involve local people known to the prisoners; certain individuals can feign friendship, while at the same time leading soldiers into compromising situations.

- Getting caught in an ambush – many kidnappings happen opportunistically, when a soldier or small unit is isolated during an ambush or improvised explosive device (IED) attack.
- A vehicle is disabled, either through an ambush or because of mechanical failure, leaving those aboard stranded in a single, vulnerable location while they wait for assistance.
- Special forces soldiers, through their common repurposing as VIP bodyguards, are all too aware of these factors, and so have developed a rigorous set of tactical behaviours that dramatically lessen the chances of being kidnapped in the first place. We will look at some of these rules in this chapter, before turning to explore in detail the fundamental techniques of evasion on the ground.

Making a bad situation better

Damaged vehicles placed by the sides of roads

Indications of road or building repair in otherwise dilapidated areas

Strangely positioned piles of earth, wood or refuse

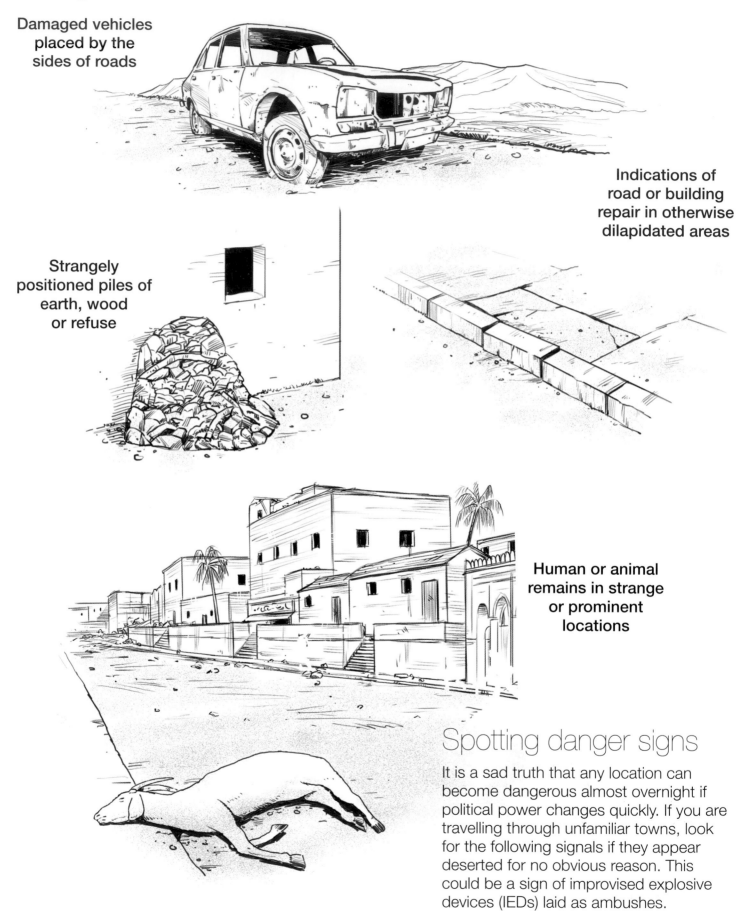

Human or animal remains in strange or prominent locations

Spotting danger signs

It is a sad truth that any location can become dangerous almost overnight if political power changes quickly. If you are travelling through unfamiliar towns, look for the following signals if they appear deserted for no obvious reason. This could be a sign of improvised explosive devices (IEDs) laid as ambushes.

Move carefully, keep moving

Ambushes and kidnapping attempts tend to be launched in predictable locations. These include:

- Places where a road narrows between natural or urban features.
- Around sharp bends (the bend limits visibility around the corner, where a roadblock or improvised obstacle could be set up).
- Isolated outposts.
- Footpaths and trails that channel a patrol along a predictable route.

- Difficult terrain, such as mountains or woodland, which can disperse a patrol.
- Any urban zone, which provides insurgents with familiar attack and escape routes, and which limits vehicular manoeuvres in response.
- Bridges, fords and any other controlled crossing points. In hostile areas, streets such as these should be avoided at all costs. The vehicles act as rough roadblocks, channelling patrols into ambush zones.

Varying routes and times

Insurgents and terrorist groups thrive on predictability. Observational intelligence can be used to plan and coordinate efficient attacks on military peace keeping personnel. If you end up stuck in a contested area, vary your times and routes of travel on a daily basis to avoid forming any regular patterns of movement of which the enemy can take advantage.

Deciding to move

Moving through dangerous terrain can throw up many dangers. However, staying put is sometimes simply not an option. If so, move with purpose, using as much natural coverage as possible.

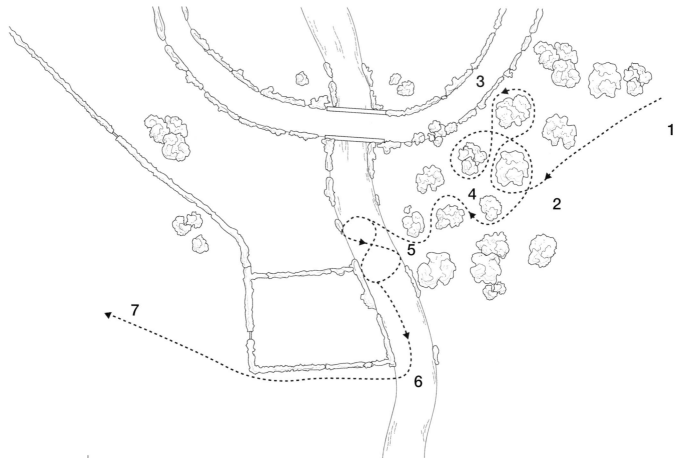

Dog evasion

Tracker dogs work best when following a single, unbroken line of scent. By winding your route around obstacles and by crossing water, you can either make the dog turn back on itself, or lose your track entirely. When you are sure you have managed this, you can hole up for a while before moving on to shelter or safety.

1. Straight line
2. Enter foliage
3. Cross trail
4. Retrace steps
5. Cross water
6. Walk in water
7. Continue journey

Using natural terrain

Whether it be soldiers or civilians, anyone moving while conducting evasion should use every scrap of cover they can find. Look for terrain that will stand directly between you and a line-of-sight observer. Remember that any cover that conceals your silhouette should be used to the greatest advantage. If you are wearing conspicuous clothing, consider muting the colours with mud or soil.

Use natural dips such as riverbanks

Walk around hills rather than over the top

Use natural cover such as trees or foliage

Making a bad situation better

Hiding places

This culvert could provide an ideal escape route from enemy search parties or any dangers a civilian might become caught up in. Following it through could lead to a secure egress point in the dense wooded area beyond, while crossing the water will make the job of the tracker dog much harder in terms of following your scent.

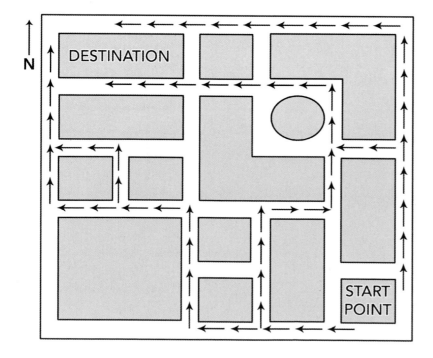

Varied routes

For those moving regularly between fixed destinations in hostile territory, it is imperative to vary the journey frequently and inventively, to prevent the enemy identifying a predictable route along which they can set up an ambush. Find out as much as you can about varied routes to your destination, noting any places where an ambush is more likely to occur.

Avoiding an ambush

A professional ambush will hit a military column at several points simultaneously, destroying lead and rear vehicles and trapping forces between these points. The same applies to any civilian groups moving in convoy. Try to avoid narrow routes flanked on both sides by high ground. You might be safer travelling alone, but that has its own dangers.

Be prepared to fight

While your aim is to cross dangerous territory without being detected, the precautions described here can limit, but not remove, your chances of being discovered and taken prisoner. The fact remains that in survival emergencies such as civil war zones, danger is generally unavoidable. based on recent experiences in Iraq and Afghanistan, the need to stay out of the kidnappers' hands is paramount, so if you are discovered or attacked, you will need to fight back – and hard.

The standard military response to attack is to find cover and return instant and heavy firepower. Kidnappers will have to get close to take someone hostage, and if the price for doing so becomes too high, there is a strong likelihood that they will back off. Civilians are unlikely to be wielding firepower, but as this book describes, many weapons can be improvised from a variety of indoor and outdoor materials.

Use any resource to its best advantage and respond to attacks with equal force. If no guns are involved on either side and you are not too outnumbered, your best chance of survival by far comes from not letting yourself be captured. Target any hostile individuals who seem to be giving orders, to 'behead' the attackers' command. However, if you number but a few against many, or are under threat of gunfire, surrender might be your best option.

Staying out of sight

In many civilian survival situations you might want to increase your visibility and be found quickly. However, in an evasion situation you can learn from the military experts.

Parallel crossing

When crossing horizontal features such as fences, keep the body parallel to the ground at all times, to reduce your silhouette to a viewer in the distance. Throw bulky equipment such as backpacks over before crossing yourself.

Horizon silhouette

When moving through a landscape, avoid silhouetting your body on the horizon. The soldier here has stopped on the crest of a hill, making himself stand out against the sky and presenting an ideal target for an enemy sniper or rifleman.

Light silhouette and shadow

Strong light sources create silhouette and shadow, both of which can betray your presence. Remember that the lower the light source to the horizon or the floor, the longer the shadow appears on the floor, making you more conspicuous to both ground observers and to those in the air. Shadows are both your friend and enemy in an evasion situation. On the positive side, you can use shadows to reduce your silhouette and shine. Negatively, shadows can expand your visible 'footprint' significantly, as shown here.

US Army tip: Critical factors in evasion

Guidelines for successful evasion include:

1. Keeping a positive attitude.
2. Using established procedures.
3. Following your evasion plan of action.
4. Being patient.
5. Drinking water (DO NOT eat food without water).
6. Conserving strength for critical periods.
7. Resting and sleeping as much as possible.
8. Staying out of sight.

– US Army, *Survival, Evasion, and Recovery* (1999)

Making a bad situation better

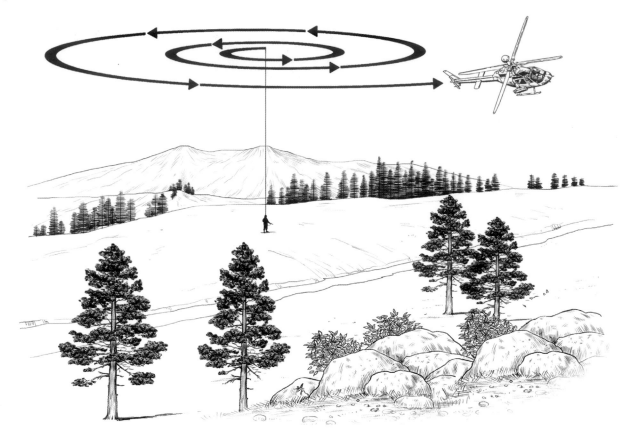

Helicopter search

A classic search pattern adopted by a helicopter crew is to start from the evader's last-known position, then fly outwards in a series of ever-increasing circles. Technologies such as forward-looking infrared (FLIR) cameras ensure that the search helicopter is one of an evader's most dangerous opponents.

Search teams

If search tems land in your vicinity, they will begin searching for you in a methodical way. Try to put yourself in their shoes – imagine the landscape features to which they will be drawn, and the places which they will naturally search.

Blending in

To stay hidden, the fundamentals of camouflage and concealment come into play. The 'Seven S's' are an useful mnemonic to remember the rules by. They are:

1. Shape
2. Shine
3. Silhouette
4. Shadow
5. Sound
6. Speed
7. Surroundings

Each of the 'Seven S's' are important. The seventh makes use of every natural advantage to blend in to the background, whatever it might be. For example, In a wilderness setting, you need to make every aspect of your body and equipment blend in with the surroundings. If you are evading danger, check yourself for the 'Seven S's'. Remove shiny objects, disguise your shape to blend in to those around you, stick to the shadows and stay as inconspicuous as you can.

Tracker dogs

Tracker dogs are an age-old threat to anyone trying to evade capture. Trained to pick up and track scents undetectable to the human nose, they dramatically improve the accuracy and tracking speed of the search party (a good tracker dog can trail at a speed of up to 16 km/h (10 mph). Although a dog's vision is poorer than humans, its sense of smell is roughly 900 times better, and its hearing 40 times more acute. However, dogs can struggle to accurately follow scent across or through water, snow and shifting sands – or if you traverse an area with many other competing smells, such as urban terrain or fertilized fields.

Camouflage and concealment

If you find yourself in a situation where concealment is necessary, use every natural form of cover available to you, both to take shelter in and to disguise your person.

Using concealment

Dense vegetation is ideal for providing concealment from view. Be aware, however, that concealment is not the same as cover – vegetation will provide no protection from small-arms fire. Note that camouflage clothing and face camouflage break up the body even further.

Using shadow

When crossing a road in sunlight, the shadows thrown by trees can create good routes to cross from one side to another. Stay low and move fast, and try to keep noise to a minimum. Remember that you can be noticed by noise as well as sight.

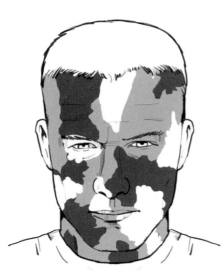

'Blotch' pattern

'Slash' pattern

Face camouflage

Camouflage can be amended to suit temperate, desert or barren landscapes ('blotch' patten), or for jungle or grassy areas ('slash' pattern). It breaks up blocks of unnatural colour.

Helmet camouflage

By attaching vegetation to his helmet, this soldier breaks up his head silhouette. The key to such camouflage is to keep it fresh and to ensure that it matches precisely the terrain through which you are moving. If you find yourself moving through different terrains, adapt your camouflage to blend in to your new surroundings. For the soldier shown here, if the vegetation had not been applied, his shape and silhouette would be different from anything found in nature and would therefore stand out.

Another method of camouflage is to create an improvised ghillie suit (like those worn for hunting and by military snipers). Attach short strips of naturally coloured material or vegetation all over your clothes, fragmenting both the outline and colour. The options for making one while on the run are limited, but help from sympathetic locals might make this possible.

Staying ahead

Any methods of making life especially difficult for your pursuers will make it easier for you to stay ahead. As well as movement and camouflage, avoid leaving tracks that can be followed.

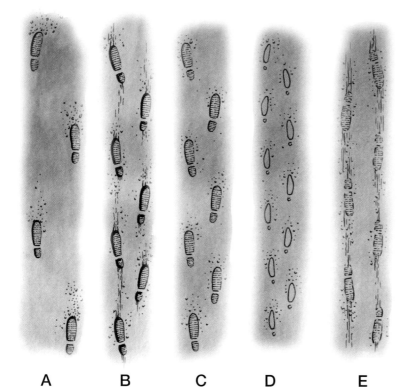

A   B   C   D   E

Types of footprints

Being able to read footprints can give you important clues about pursuers or local civilians. These footprints indicate, from top to bottom:

A. Someone running (long stride)
B. Someone carrying a heavy load (feet drag between steps)
C. A person wearing military-style boots
D. A woman in stilettoes
E. Someone walking backwards

Foot traffic

To ascertain how many people have passed a single spot, imagine a box 91cm (36in) square over a series of footprints. Count the number of footprints in the square, and then divide by two to give an idea of the number of people who have passed.

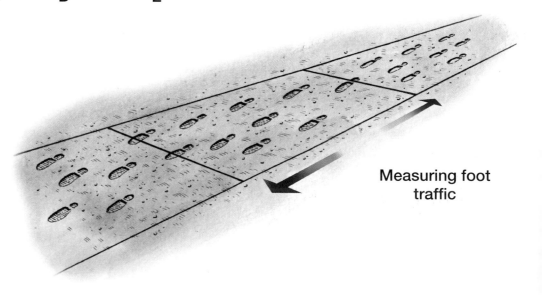

Measuring foot traffic

Masking tracks

Mask unavoidable tracks in soft footing by:

- Placing tracks in the shadows of vegetation, downed logs and snowdrifts.
- Moving before and during precipitation allows tracks to fill in.
- Travelling during windy periods.
- Taking advantage of solid surfaces (logs, rocks, etc.) leaving less evidence of travel.
- Patting out tracks lightly to speed their breakdown or make them look old.

– US Army, *Survival, Evasion, and Recovery* (1999)

Staying low

When moving through high-risk areas with the enemy nearby, adopt a low crawl, working your way forwards using your elbows and knees. If behind vegetation, maintain observation by looking through the leaves and branches, not at them. Never raise your position to look over the branches that cover you and move slowly to make as little noise as possible.

Betraying your presence

The illustrations here show ways in which you can give your position away to enemy searchers. An evader has to be aware of sound, light and smell in all their forms, and also of leaving any evidence of his presence behind in the wilderness, such as litter or footprints. Both the sight and smell of cigarette smoke is a giveaway. Other odours to avoid are scented soaps or shampoos, after-shave lotion, insect repellent and gum or candy. As with your appearance, the more your scent mirrors that of your environment, the more you will blend in. Be aware that anyone pursuing you may have training in tracking, so it is especially important to remove any evidence of your presence.

Capture

Extreme situations, such as becoming a hostage or prisoner of war, are very rare, but they do occur. It is in such situations where every element of your survival training and preparation comes into play.

First moments

The first moments of captivity are the most dangerous, as the captors will often be nervous with their new prisoner. Comply fully with any orders given, and don't make any sudden movements. If you feel there is no other option other than surrendering, keep your arms high and make sure that you are carrying no weapon.

Prisons

On your arrival at a POW camp, evaluate every aspect of the security as you pass through. Here we have a double fence arrangement, topped with razor wire and electrified cables.

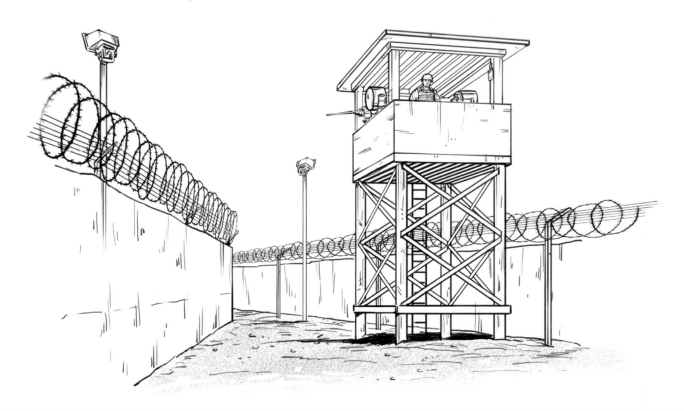

Rough treatment

In many conflicts, POWs have been paraded by their captors in front of crowds of hostile civilians. In these situations, keep your face down and shoulders hunched to protect you from blows to the head, and don't become separated from your captors – they are unlikely to want you to be killed, and are probably your best chance of protection.

Surviving guards and inmates

Prison camp survival can depend on relationships with the guards and other inmates. These may consist of very different attitudes. The key is to be aware when you should back down from conflict.

Trade

POW camps often have a lively trade in basic goods, particularly chocolate and cigarettes, and also anything that can relieve boredom, such as books. Playing a controlling part in such trade can help you survive the camp by making yourself necessary to other inmates.

Improvised weapons

In most POW camps, you will be supplied with basic equipment for cleanliness. The simplest of materials can often be turned into weapons with a bit of ingenuity, to provide you with some protection. Utilize razor blades or glass, or look for objects such as nails to turn into sharp, dangerous implements.

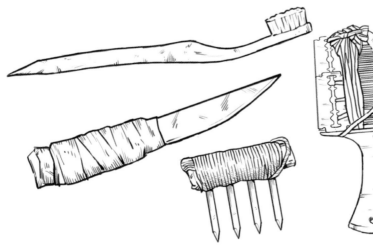

Knife threats

If attacked by another prisoner with a knife, try to grab the wrist of the knife hand in a strong double-handed grip and swing it across your body, throwing your opponent to the floor. Attack his eyes, throat or other vulnerable point to bring the attack to an end.

Dealing with your captors

The US Department of Homeland Security offers this advice for handling your captors:

- Do not aggravate them.
- Do not get into political or ideological discussions.
- Comply with instructions, but always maintain your dignity. Obedience to orders or commands need not be swift, cheerful or overtly enthusiastic, but it should be sufficient to maintain a balanced relationship.
- Talk in a normal voice. Avoid whispering when talking to other hostages, or raising your voice when talking to a terrorist.
- Attempt to develop a positive relationship with them. Identify those captors with whom you can communicate and attempt to establish a relationship.
- Be proud of your heritage, government and military association, but use discretion.

Relationships with the guards

Maintain good relations with the guards, always being respectful but implicitly treating them as human beings (even if they don't deserve such treatment). Try to find common ground, such as concerns over family and money. Avoid any sensitive topics such as politics or religion.

Interrogation and torture

Interrogation involves physically coercive techniques to extract information. When you add torture to the mix the potential for physical and mental suffering is vast.

Mental interrogation

Interrogation is not always a brutal affair. Sometime interrogators might use reason and argument to try to 'turn' a soldier to renounce his army's cause, often via distorted history lessons and biased social analysis. It can even be that this reasonable approach is more effective than threats or force.

Sensory deprivation

Hostages are often placed in conditions of sensory deprivation, to disorient them and make them more dependent on their captors. This prisoner is kept hooded and with his hearing obscured by ear defenders. With his arms tethered, he is incapable even of movement.

Signs of lying

During interrogation, be aware of your body language at all times, in case it betrays that you are lying. Nervous rubbing of the face is often an indicator of a lie, and one that interrogators will be trained to look for. Clasping your hands together in your lap can prevent unconscious touching of your face.

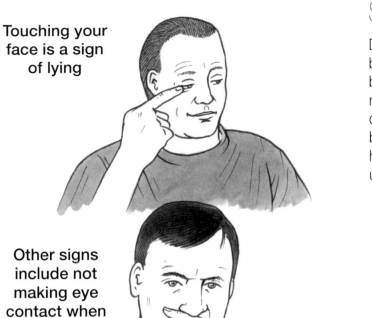

Touching your face is a sign of lying

Other signs include not making eye contact when answering

Intimidation

Intimidation can take many forms. A prisoner may be threatened or attempts might be made to bully or browbeat him. An extreme example of intimidation is a 'fake' shooting. This involves telling prisoners they are to be executed, taking them to a place of execution, then shooting them using blanks instead of live rounds.

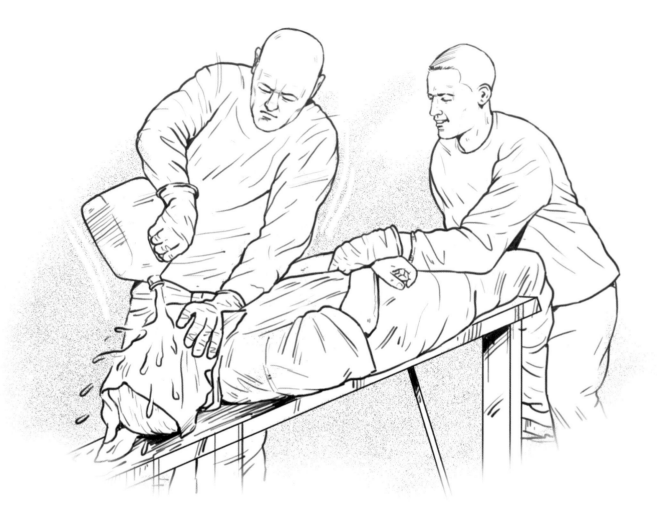

Battle of wills

Historically, detainers have attempted to engage military captives in what may be called a 'battle of wits' about seemingly innocent and useless topics, as well as provocative issues. To engage any detainer in such useless, if not dangerous, dialogue only enables a captor to spend more time with the detainee. The detainee should consider dealings with his or her captors as a 'battle of wills'; the will to restrict discussion to those items that relate to the detainee's treatment and release, against the detainer's will to discuss dangerous topics.

– CJCS, *Antiterrorism Personal Protection Guide: A Self-Help Guide to Terrorism* (2002)

Waterboarding

Although waterboarding has hit the headlines for its use in the so-called War on Terror, it is an ancient form of torture. It induces the sensation of drowning as the soaked cloth tightens over the victim's face. Note that good interrogators wil not rely on a single technique, but will mix them up in the hope for finding a weak point or catching a prisoner out with one particular approach. Platitudes and prescriptions about dealing with torture are, however, inappropriate to make by those who haven't experienced it. Unfortunately, no training can fully prepare you for it.

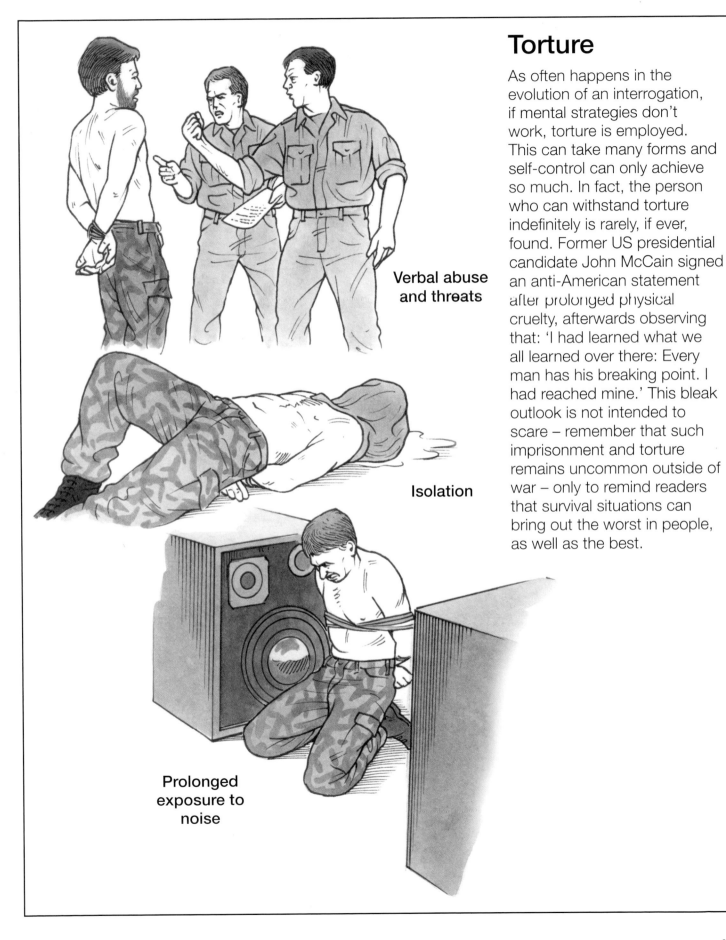

Verbal abuse and threats

Isolation

Prolonged exposure to noise

Torture

As often happens in the evolution of an interrogation, if mental strategies don't work, torture is employed. This can take many forms and self-control can only achieve so much. In fact, the person who can withstand torture indefinitely is rarely, if ever, found. Former US presidential candidate John McCain signed an anti-American statement after prolonged physical cruelty, afterwards observing that: 'I had learned what we all learned over there: Every man has his breaking point. I had reached mine.' This bleak outlook is not intended to scare – remember that such imprisonment and torture remains uncommon outside of war – only to remind readers that survival situations can bring out the worst in people, as well as the best.

Surviving mentally and physically

Under such extreme conditions, being at your mental and physical peak gives you an instant advantage. It is remaining at this peak while under such stress that is a challenge.

Capture by terrorists

In recent years, the world has been treated to a grim litany of hostage-taking stories emanating from the war zones of Iraq and Afghanistan. The tactics and outcomes of such incidents are not new to these conflicts, but they have raised awareness of the terrible dangers implicit in being taken hostage by an ideologically angry enemy.

Surviving deprivation

Deprivation (above) is a method by which captors establish dominance over their prisoners, weakening both body and mind. Keep an internal dignity in these circumstances, using a humorous and defiant inner voice to defy your captors. Boredom (left) is another difficult element of prolonged captivity. It can develop into severe depression, which in turn often leads to inactivity and a surrender to fate.

Mental life

In cases where a prisoner is isolated from others, he has to find interest within his own mind. Creating imaginary worlds, mentally writing books and solving logical or practical problems are all good coping strategies. Having a grounding in meditation or visualization techniques can also prove useful to staying calm and positive in traumatic circumstances.

Mental preparation

Most accounts of captivity from ex-POWs emphasize the fear, tension and mind-numbing boredom of captivity. Entire weeks of complete uneventfulness can be abruptly punctuated by sudden violence or mental torture. Try to establish some sense of routine, such as physical training, so as to give yourself a sense of control and purpose.

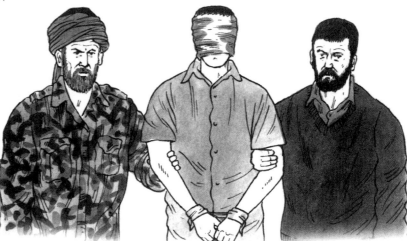

Human trophy

Hostages have a value for their captors, either commercially or for propaganda. The most dangerous scenario is one in which the prisoner is seen in ideological terms only, making him more liable to execution. A prisoner should therefore seek to increase empathy between him and his captors.

Making a bad situation better

Staying fit

Staying physically fit is a great way of fighting off both depression and boredom. It also gives the prisoner a sense of control over his own destiny. Calisthenics and core strengthening exercises can be performed in confined spaces. However, exercise should not be excessive, particularly if the POW is suffering from poor health or inadequate nutrition.

Stomach crunches

Lie on your back with your hands behind your head. Bring both knees up together, at the same time raising your head to meet them over the torso. Hold and repeat, building up the repetitions.

Twisting crunches

Lie on the floor with your hands behind your head. This time, as you raise your legs and upper body, twist your torso so that your left elbow touches your right knee. Repeat, alternating left and right elbows to touch right and left knees. Keep your knees raised and stationary for as long as possible.

Push-ups

Place the palms of your hands flat on the floor, one shoulder-width apart. Keep the legs straight, and pivot on your toes, with torso held firm and straight. Bend the arms and lower the body until it just brushes the floor. Now, straighten the arms and raise the body back to the start position. Do not bend the torso.

Setting challenges

Setting yourself physical challenges can keep your mind and body occupied, as well as giving you mental highs when you meet these challenges. Increase the intensity by adding a clap on the upward push or putting your hands together to form a diamond.

Building a rapport

Hostages may discuss nonsubstantive topics to convey their human qualities and build rapport through:
- Introducing commonalities such as family, clothes, sports, hygiene, food, etc.
- Active listening. Allowing captors to discuss their cause or boast, but not to praise, pander, participate or debate with them.
- Addressing captors by name.
- Being careful about whining or begging, as it may increase abuse.

- Introducing benign topics at critical times (impasses, demands) to reduce tensions.
- Avoiding emotionally charged topics of religion, economics and politics.
- Avoiding being singled out by being argumentative or combative.
- Avoiding escalating tensions with language such as 'gun, kill, punish,' etc.

CJCS, *Antiterrorism Personal Protection Guide: A Self-Help Guide to Terrorism* (2002)

Early escape

Escape from a POW camp or terrorist holding cell should be the priority of any captive. It can be a matter of seizing a sudden opportunity, or of meticulous planning over a long period of time.

Early escape

The first hours of captivity actually provide the best chances for escape. Taking advantage of the first opportunity to escape can work to your advantage in such a distracted situation, but should only be attempted if the full attention of the guards is diverted elsewhere.

Break for freedom

If a soldier is captured on the battlefield, distraction can provide the best opportunity for escape. Here a prisoner makes a break for freedom while his captors are thoroughly absorbed in watching the effects of an air strike just metres from their position.

Guard attack

Using surprise and swift movements, it might be possible to disarm a guard by pulling his rifle barrel up or down (away from you) and wrenching it out of his hands. Alternatively, attack a vital part of his body (bottom image) such as the throat with a spade or other tool, keeping the rifle barrel pushed to one side. Any attack on an armed guard is very risky, so do not attempt such an action unless you are reasonably confident of success. Try to gauge whether the guard is inexperienced and unused to handling weapons.

Swiftly move in to grab the rifle barrel

Pull it away from you and make your attack

Attack vulnerable areas with force

Planning

All escape planning begins with intense observation. Essentially, the captive is looking for any weak links in security, plus any navigational information that might help him outside the wire.

Security

This POW camp presents several challenges to an escapee. The gap between the barracks and the outer wire is well covered by observation towers and there is only one main gate. The outer wire is high and is topped with an overhanging configuration. However, if someone could get under the wire it is only a short distance to visual cover.

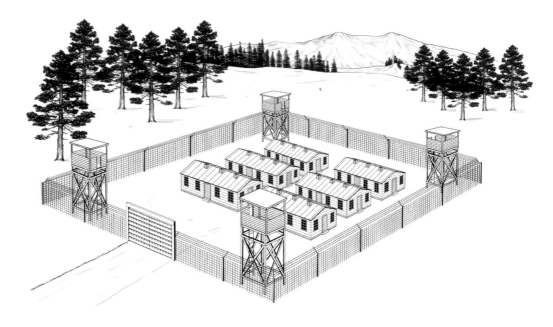

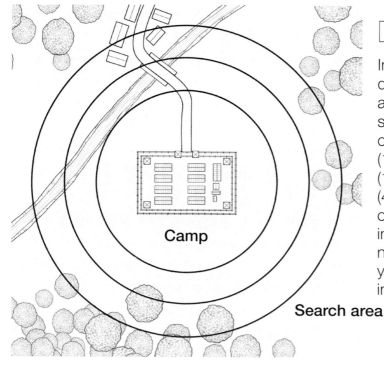

Camp

Search area

Distance and area

Im the event of escape, every metre distance you can put between yourself and the camp means that the area to be searched grows exponentially. A distance of 1km (0.6 miles) gives an area of 3km² (1.6 square miles), but a distance of 2km (1.2 miles) gives an area of 12.5km² (4.8 square miles). Look out for any signs of cover, such as the wooded area in this image. Give serious consideration to your next move prior to escape, especially if you know little or nothing about the area in which you were held.

Lock-picking

Lock-picking needs practice and some basic tools to perform with confidence, but it is a skill with an obvious utility for escape purposes. The necessary tools can to some extent be improvised in the field if you are familiar with how they look and how they work. Look for anything resembling the shape and size of the wrenches to the right, including broken or worn-out tools that are unlikely to be missed.

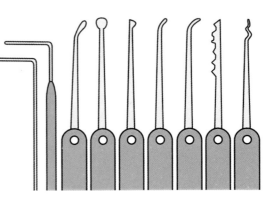

Yale-type locks

To pick a 'Yale' type cylinder lock, you need two items: a slim, flat piece of steel to insert as a torsion wrench, and a hooked piece of strong wire which will act as a lock pick.

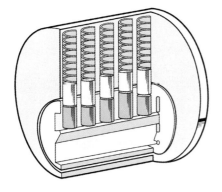

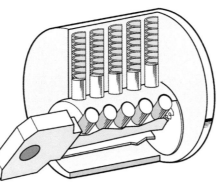

Picking locks

First, insert the torsion wrench into the base of the lock and apply pressure in the direction in which the lock unlocks. Now slide the pick in above the wrench. Yale locks work via a sequence of spring-loaded two-section pins that drop down into a cylinder. You need to align all of the upper section pins for the lock to open.

Other useful tools

Tools such as pliers, hacksaw blades and files have an obvious utility for an escapee, although they will need to be hidden with absolute diligence in case of barracks inspections by the guards. Prison guards are also all too aware of the value of tools to inmates, so will likely take careful inventories of what has gone in and out of the stores. Also look for pieces of stiff wire or scraps of clothing, which can be used to form lengths of rope or a disguise.

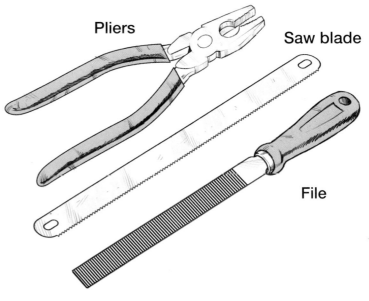

Pliers

Saw blade

File

The escape attempt

Every escape attempt is unique, and trying to lay down hard and fast rules to cover every eventuality is not possible. The basis of what any captive needs is forward-thinking and opportunity.

Tunnel to freedom

This graphic representation of the tunnel dug from Stalag Luft III during the famous 'Great Escape' of Allied POWs from a German camp in March 1944 shows how ambitious an escape attempt can become. The tunnel entrance is under the stove in a hut on the right, and it drops down to a workshop chamber below. Wooden carts were used to transport excavated soil back to the start of the tunnel. Incredibly, 76 men eventually escaped in a single night. However, only three escapees made it safely home.

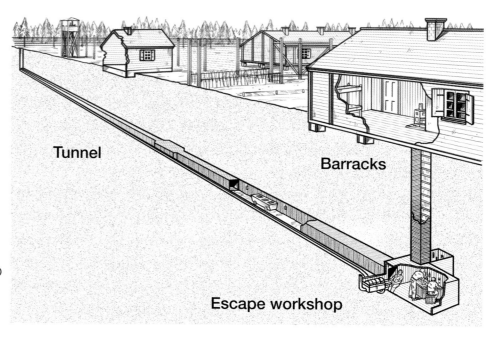

Tunnel

Barracks

Escape workshop

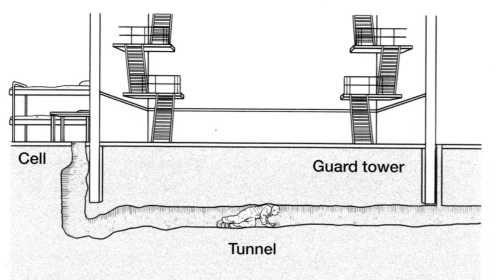

Cell

Guard tower

Tunnel

One-man tunnel

This prisoner is escaping via a crude, unsupported tunnel dug out from his cell. Such tunnels require firm, clay-like soil to hold up without artificial supports, and shouldn't be dug too deep – the deeper you go, the greater the weight of soil pressing down on the tunnel roof. Single and group escape attempts both have their pros and cons. If you do decide to share your plans, make sure whoever you tell can be trusted.

Improvised hook

While the captive should be on the look out for acquiring tools whenever possible, escape equipment can be manufactured from the most basic of materials. Here a length of old nylon cord has been tied to a bent piece of iron to form a rudimentary grappling hook, suitable for escape over wire or for lowering yourself down from a window or rooftop.

Improvised rope

Multiple strands of fabric twisted and knotted together can form a basic improvised rope for an escape attempt. Make sure that you test such a rope (or the hook shown above) for breaking strength before using it in earnest. Remember that activities such as shimmying down ropes should also be practised before the escape attempt.

Inventory of items used in digging the 'Great Escape' tunnels

- 4000 bed boards
- 635 mattresses
- 192 bed covers
- 161 pillow cases
- 52 20-man tables
- 10 single tables
- 34 chairs
- 76 benches
- 1212 bed bolsters
- 1370 bedding battens
- 1219 knives
- 478 spoons
- 582 forks
- 69 lamps
- 246 water cans
- 30 shovels
- 328m (1000ft) electric wire
- 180m (590ft) rope
- 3424 towels
- 1700 blankets
- 1400 powdered milk cans

Areas of weakness in POW camp security

- Poorly maintained perimeter fences, including holes and rust-weakened sections.
- Low morale amongst the guards, resulting in a lack of vigilance during certain hours.
- Guards who are susceptible to bribes.
- External civilian workers (especially groups whose composition changes frequently) making regular visits to the camp.
- Lack of rigorous roll-call procedures.

- Poor-quality lighting at night, or blackout because of enemy aerial activity.
- Exposed electrical junction boxes, raising the potential for cutting power at opportune moments.
- Poorly guarded store areas containing potentially useful tools.
- Slipping out of the camp in refuse trucks or other vehicles.

Making a bad situation better

Tackling a guard (1)

If you manage to make it out of your barracks or the prison camp grounds, you will need all your wits and strength to deal with any guards patrolling the perimeter. Here the escaping POW creeps up behind a guard. At the right moment, he leaps forward onto the guard's back, using momentum to knock the guard to the floor.

Tackling a guard (2)

As the guard falls forward, he will usually release his grip on his weapon to stop himself slamming into the ground. Once he is on the floor, the POW can render him unconscious with a stranglehold. While risky, this technique means the POW is now armed and able to defend himself.

Consequences

While you can render the guard silent and unconscious, it may be that the only way to ensure that he will not quickly regain consciousness and send for a search party is to kill him. Never forget that however desperate you are to escape, what you do will stay with you forever. The consequences if you are apprehended are also more severe.

Creeping

The creeping technique used by this POW is not dissimilar to the stalking movement used when hunting. You need to practice creeping slowly and as silently as possible, remembering that you may well have to cross gravel or grassy areas with hidden twigs or leaves that will crunch underfoot.

Escape networks

The value of having an escape support network is demonstrated by the following escape account, again from a German held in the United States in World War II. Tilman Kiwe, a major in the Afrika Korps, escaped on multiple occasions from US POW camps. Here he describes his third attempt:

It was not complicated to escape. The organization [escape committee] of the camp first obtained an American uniform for me that the guards must have traded for our military decorations or pretty wood sculptures. A tailor in the camp fashioned a very smart civilian raincoat. The problem was that it was grey-green, but we were not short of chemists in the camp. With boiled onions they obtained a marvellous shade of orange-yellow, and with tea they darkened it a bit to a perfect, inconspicuous color.

Before leaving this time I worked to perfect myself in English, especially in American slang. There was a prisoner in the camp who had spent 23 years in America; he was an interpreter and he took me well in hand. I could soon pass absolutely for an American … Preparations were making progress. The organization had furnished me with the necessary money – about a hundred dollars … The day was set for the escape … I slid

under a barrack. They were all on blocks; though there wasn't much room, I changed clothes, and stepped out in the uniform of an American Lieutenant. I waited until around 10:30 and went to the guard post. The sentinel must have thought I was taking a walk. I gave him a little sign with my hand, said 'Hello', threw him a vague salute, and hop! I was outside!

– Quoted in Arnold Krammer, *Prisoners of War: A Reference Handbook* (Westport, CT, Praeger, 2008)

Although captured two days later and returned to camp, Kiwe is to be admired for the sheer bravado of the escape attempt. Escape via disguise is an unpredictable business, and requires a huge amount of confidence and not a little good fortune to pull off convincingly. Kiwe's method of dressing as US military personnel was particularly high risk, as he could have been shot as a spy on recapture. Yet note how the various skill sets of the people around him contributed to his initially successful escape. Finding such broad talents is not always as easy in modern regular armies, in which many POWs will have few skills outside their military specialty, but enterprising individuals will typically find a way to achieve their goals.

Rescue

One option for escape from a POW or hostage situation does not involve any effort on the part of the prisoner at all – the rescue mission.

Danger from rescuers

If you are the beneficiary of a special forces rescue, stay down when the troops make their assault – don't stand up and wave any weapons you have acquired, as the rescuers might see a threat and shoot you.

Rescue teams

A special forces hostage-rescue team will move at speed through a building, having to make the snap shoot-don't shoot decisions. If the team is there to rescue you, be prepared for the detonation of stun and smoke grenades and for the use of heavy automatic firepower.

Rescue harness

As a rescue helicopter hovers overhead, stay in a kneeling position to stabilize yourself against downdraft. Position the harness over your head and under your arms, crossing the arms together in front of your body to lock the harness in place.

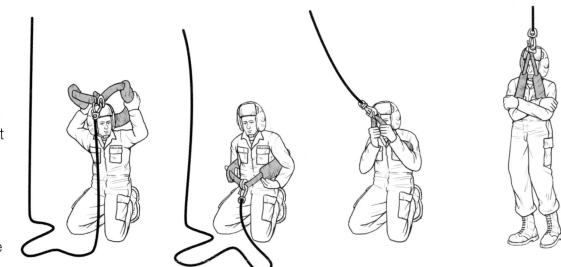

Clearing a building

During a hostage-rescue action, a special forces team will work through each room methodically, often using stun grenades to soften up any opposition before entry. As they approach your room, drop any weapons and annouce your position verbally, but stay in one place and allow them to come to you, unless doing so increases your danger. Note the team's movements in the image below, where they sweep and clear each room before moving on the the next.

Fight or flight?

Actual escape from detention is just the beginning of a dangerous journey, with threats ranging from disease and injury to a vengeful and pursuing enemy. Be prepared to fight for your freedom.

Blending in

Sometimes an evasion plan will actually take you right into a foreign civilian society. Observe every aspect of your surroundings – clothing, mannerisms, employment, etc – and model your behaviour so that you blend in. Even if guards should come across the area, they will be looking for someone who stands out and is moving away from them. Sometimes, staying put and blending in when it is assumed you will run can work to your advantage.

Taking cover

As an evader gets closer to his own lines, he may well be threatened by his 'friendly' artillery and air strikes. As he will have learnt in basic training, the important point to survival in these situations is to get low behind substantial cover. Remember that shrapnel retains lethality hundreds of metres from the explosion.

Tackling from the rear

Disposing of a sentry needs to be done quickly and ruthlessly for escape to be successful. As you are unarmed, anything that can be fashioned into a weapon will work to your advantage, such as a rock, club or sharp stabbing implement.

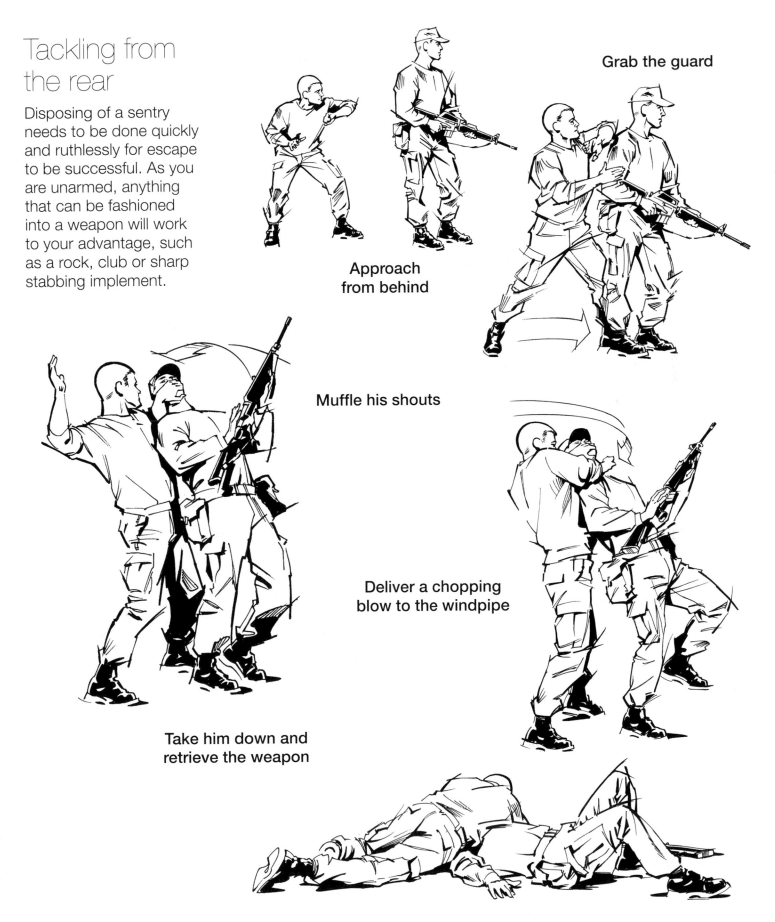

Approach from behind

Grab the guard

Muffle his shouts

Deliver a chopping blow to the windpipe

Take him down and retrieve the weapon

Glossary

bearing – the compass direction from your position to a landmark or destination.

bola – a weapon consisting of multiple weights bound together by rope and thrown to bring down prey.

calorie – the amount of heat required to raise the temperature of 1 gram of water by 1° Celsius.

carbohydrate – an organic compound of carbon, hydrogen and oxygen found in many foods. When ingested, carbohydrates are broken down to provide energy.

chart – a map used for navigation at sea or in an aircraft.

chlorine – a chemical element that may be added to water as a purifying agent.

collecting feature – a linear feature in the landscape that allows you to maintain your direction of travel without reference to the compass.

coniferous – denotes an evergreen tree with cones and needlelike leaves.

contour – a line on a map joining points of equal elevation.

coordinates – a pair of numbers and/or letters that describe a unique position.

course – the route of path between two points.

cyclone – a large-scale, atmospheric wind-and-pressure system characterized by low pressure at its centre and by circular wind motion, counterclockwise in the Northern Hemisphere, clockwise in the Southern Hemisphere.

datum – a reference point used by cartographers, from which all elevations or positions on a map or chart are measured.

dead reckoning – this is approximate navigation, using estimates of speed and direction over a period of time to gauge current position based on a known starting position.

deadfall trap – a trap designed to kill an animal by dropping a heavy weight on it.

declination – the difference in degrees between true north and magnetic north in any given place.

degree (or °) – the unit of measurement of an angle. A full circle is divided into 360°; each degree is divided into 60 minutes, and each minute into 60 seconds.

dehydration – in a person, a significant loss of body fluids that are not replaced by fluid intake.

dysentery – a chronic diarrheal illness that can lead to severe dehydration and, ultimately, death.

elevation – height above mean sea level.

fats – natural oily substances which, in humans, are derived from food and deposited in subcutaneous layers and around some major organs.

GPS - Global Positioning System – the GPS unit triangulates its position from satellites and is accurate to within 30 metres (100ft).

grid – the horizontal and vertical lines on a map that enable you to describe position.

grid reference – a position defined in relation to a cartographic grid.

hyperthermia – a condition in which the body temperature rises to a dangerously high level. Also known as heatstroke.

hypothermia – a condition in which the body temperature falls to a dangerously low level. Also known as exposure.

iodine – a chemical element that has a use in water purification.

kindling – small pieces of dry material, usually thin twigs, added to ignited tinder to develop a fire.

latitude – a measure of distance north or south of the equator.

longitude – a measure of distance east or west of the prime meridian.

lure – anything used in fishing or hunting that tempts prey into a trap or particular location.

magnetic north – the direction of the magnetic North Pole.

mammals – warm-blooded vertebrates that usually give birth to live young.

meridian – an imaginary line joining points of equal longitude, running from pole to pole on the Earth's surface.

minerals – inorganic substances that the human body requires to maintain health.

monsoon – a period of intense rainfall and wind in India and Southeast Asiathat occurs annually between May and September.

nautical mile – the standard measurement of distance used by marine navigators. It is equal to one minute of longitude, or 1.852km or 1.151 imperial miles.

peripheral nervous system – is the part of the nervous system that consists of the nerves outside of the brain and spinal cord.

position line – a line along which you know your position must lie; for example a compass bearing of a landmark, or a transit.

potassium permanganate – a chemical that can be used to sterilize water.

proteins – organic compounds that form an essential part of living organisms. Among other things, they are integral to the function of body tissue, muscle and antibodies.

quarry – in tracking, the animal or human that is being hunted or pursued.

resection – the method of fixing your position by taking two or more compass bearings of landmarks and plotting the point on the map where they intersect.

satellite geometry – the arrangement of satellites in the sky above a GPS receiver as it tries to compute its position.

savannah – grassy plains of tropical and subtropical regions with flat terrain and very few trees.

sign – any physical indication of the passage of an animal or human quarry. A footprint is the most obvious example of sign.

somatic nervous system – is the part of the peripheral nervous system associated with the voluntary control of body movements via the skeletal muscles.

stalking – in tracking, the art of moving silently and stealthily so as not to alert the quarry to your presence.

temperate – any climate characterized by mild temperatures.

tinder – small pieces of light and dry material that are very easily ignited and are used to initiate a fire.

track – a line of sign that indicates the route of an animal or human quarry through an environment.

tracking – the pursuit of an animal or human quarry by observing and following the sign they have left behind. See also **sign**.

trailing – another word for tracking.

transit – an imaginary line extended through two landmarks and used as a position line.

tropical – denotes the latitudes 23° 26' north or south of the equator.

true north – the direction of the geographic North Pole.

vitamins – a group of organic compounds that are an essential part of human nutrition, though they are required in only very small doses.

waypoint – a particular, user-specified location along a route. GPS receivers follow a winding course by navigating from one waypoint to the next.

Index

Index